Black Womanist Leadership

Black Womanist Leadership

tracing the motherline

edited by TONI C. KING and S. ALEASE FERGUSON

SUNY PRESS

COVER ART: *Secrets from My Mother* by Gary Williams, created for this text in May 2010.

Published by
STATE UNIVERSITY OF NEW YORK PRESS, ALBANY

© 2011 State University of New York

All rights reserved

Printed in the United States of America

No part of this book may be used or reproduced in any manner whatsoever without written permission. No part of this book may be stored in a retrieval system or transmitted in any form or by any means including electronic, electrostatic, magnetic tape, mechanical, photocopying, recording, or otherwise without the prior permission in writing of the publisher.

For information, contact State University of New York Press, Albany, NY
www.sunypress.edu

Production, Laurie Searl
Marketing, Anne M. Valentine

Library of Congress Cataloging in Publication Data

Black womanist leadership : tracing the motherline / edited by Toni C. King and S. Alease Ferguson.
    p. cm.
  Includes bibliographical references and index.
  ISBN 978-1-4384-3601-2 (hardcover : alk. paper)
  ISBN 978-1-4384-3602-9 (pbk. : alk. paper) 1. Womanism. 2. African American mothers. 3. Leadership. I. King, Toni C., 1953– II. Ferguson, S. Alease.
  HQ1197.B56 2011
  306.874'308996073—dc22

2010032056

To our Mothers, Otissey and Thelma, . . . who made us be

Contents

Preface: Writing African American Women's Leadership — ix
Acknowledgments — xix
Introduction: Looking to the Motherline — 1

PART I
THE MOTHERLINE: ROOTS AND SIGNIFICANCE — 23

1. Legacies from Our Mothers
   Frances K. Trotman — 27
2. Sisterlocking Power: Or How Is Leadership Supposed to Look?
   Valerie Lee — 45
3. Braiding My Place: Developing a Foundational Selfhood through Cross-Racial Mothering
   Nancy Gibson — 57

PART II
THE FOUNDATIONS OF MOTHER-DAUGHTER TUTELAGE — 67

4. Ìdílé: The Power of Mother in the Leadership Tradition
   Oare' Dozier-Henry — 71
5. Hard to Define
   Ceara Flake — 85
6. "Don't Waste Your Breath": The Dialectics of Communal Leadership Development
   Toni C. King — 87

Part III
Visions of the Motherline: Templates for Daughters — 109

7. "I Earns My Struttin' Shoes": Blues Women and Leadership
   Judy Massey-Dozier — 113

8. Thelma's Self-Sufficiency Paradigm: Every Tub Must Stand on Its Own Bottom
   S. Alease Ferguson — 123

9. I Remember Mama: The Legacy of a *Drylongso* and *Ajabu* Leader
   Rhunette C. Diggs — 143

10. "A Little Lower Than the Angels": A Partial Legacy from My Mother and Mom-Mom Ione
    Simona J. Hill — 163

Part IV
Tensions along the Motherline: Translating Mother Templates to Daughter Actions — 175

11. Mother's Transformative Medicine: An Inoculation against Intergenerational Stagnancy
    Sonya M. Turner — 179

12. "Contending Forces" or Contrariant Strains in the Mother-Daughter Leadership Dynamic
    Sandra Y. Govan — 193

13. "Like Mother, Like Daughter": Prophetic Principles from the Motherline—A Sermon
    Leah C. K. Lewis — 207

14. Othermothers, Amazons, and Strategies for Leadership in the Public and Private Spheres
    Lakesia D. Johnson — 217

Conclusions: Becoming the Motherline—Leadership for a New Generation — 231

Contributors — 249

Index — 255

Preface

Writing African American Women's Leadership

> When you educate a woman, you educate a nation.
> —African Proverb

BEFORE WE EVER STUDIED LEADERSHIP in its formal and organizational terms we both knew that our mothers were leaders. We also knew they had imbued us with the power to be leaders. At their hands we were taught that leading was a natural phenomenon that sprang directly from and in proportion to one's clarity, conviction, and caring about what happened in the world. While we grew up in two different regions of the country—Oklahoma and Ohio—we were each steeped in the lived traditions of leadership we saw around us in the black church women, sorority and club women, neighborhood women, and working women we had known. We were exposed to nurses, teachers, social workers, child care providers, domestic laborers, shopkeepers, and business owners. They were straight and lesbian, single, married, separated, divorced, abandoned, and widowed. We saw women work two and three jobs to sustain their lives and the lives of loved ones; we saw them leave violent homes, taking their children with them with no assurance of employment or livelihood; and we watched them give sanctuary to other women and girls who were for whatever reasons also going through a time of being on their own without financial or emotional support.[1] These lives we witnessed were our first teachers in the cultural laws of leadership from our mothers and women of our communities.

Although much of what we learned we absorbed by what we saw women do, there was also the spoken tradition. Initially we learned by overhearing women talk with each other in a soul-to-soul sharing of their lives, dreams, and goals. As girls not yet invited to the table where "grown folk's business" took place, we hovered as close to this power and mystery as we were permitted. This way we could feel for ourselves the exhilarating energy of women as they deconstructed the lives of other folks, or problem solved, made plans, and delineated visions. But as we came of age, these kitchen-table-talking women intentionally included us. Our incremental acceptance was the rite of passage that culminated in a seat at the table.

We watched as they not only crafted their visions but in "due time" carried them out. In our watching tutelage, we saw glimpses of the struggles that accompanied bringing a vision to fruition. Admittedly, we were invested in "knowing more than was good for us"[2]; and, through our "womanish"[3] interest, we learned something of the costs of asserting one's self in the world. Our tutelage began to reveal that the price for this self-assertion was heightened by the fact of race, further complicated by the presence of gender and exacerbated by the conditions of poverty or socioeconomic class "status" that gave or denied social skills and entre.

All around us we learned of the consequences to women who took a stand to create self-actualized lives. We knew of neighborhood women who fought bloody emotional or physical battles with husbands or boyfriends to stop abuses to themselves and their children or to assert their right to further their educations. We knew of women who pushed against the dictates of society, by working outside the home in settings disapproved of by their own families; by risking their employment for refusing to perform certain kinds of tasks; or by accepting a job heretofore unheard of for a black woman to take on. We knew of women who defied expectations about who they should or should not "take-up with" or marry, about how they should express their sexuality or sexual identities, or about how they would fashion lives of dignity for themselves and for their families, in spite of being single mothers. We began to discover that each of these hard-won battles, no matter how dramatic or seemingly mundane, was in reality a monumental assertion of black women's humanity in the face of a society that questioned that humanity. And as we watched, we learned that we too could step up to such tests of our "belief in self greater than anyone's disbelief."[4]

While we were enamored of the range of victorious stances women around us took to lay claim to their own liberation, not every contest resulted in victory. Yet among the broken or silenced women, among the depressed or despairing women, among the substance abusing or suicidal women, among the self-sabotaging or self-deceiving women, and among the women felled by physical or mental illness were "sheroic" examples of reversals of these downward spirals. We beheld our own Tina Turners, Oprah Winfreys, Maya Angelous, Iyanla Vanzants, Natalie Coles, Whitney Houstons,[5] who, just when the village murmurings prophesied defeat, would find their way back and lay claim to their right to live a healed and whole life. And—more important for our leadership tutelage—these women would ultimately bring their newly acquired wisdom and hope into our communities, showing others that they too could find a way through.

Our early exposure to women who broke through conditions of oppression also occurred through what we were taught about the epic tales of our foremothers. Our upbringing and education varied, yet each of us was exposed to learning about some of the legendary black women leaders who preceded us: Harriet Tubman, "Moses" of the Underground Railroad, leading more than two hundred slaves to freedom, and reconnaissance spy for the Union Army; Sojourner Truth, itinerant preacher, abolitionist, and human rights activist; Ida B. Wells Barnett, journalist, activist, leader of the antilynching campaign of the 1890s; Althea Gibson, volleying a serve as the first black woman to play in the U.S. Open; Wilma Rudolph, who overcame polio to win an Olympic gold medal; and Phyllis Wheatley, America's first woman poet and first published black poet. As coauthors, our exposure to these vital women figures in the cultural memory of African Americans became a part of how we saw leadership.

We cut our teeth on stories of these legendary foremothers as well as on those of women in our own blood lineage who had shown extraordinary efforts toward "uplifting the race," "making a way out of no way," "taking up one's burden in the heat of the day," or "staying on the battlefield." Through them we imbibed will, gumption, courage, bravery, intestinal fortitude, striving, and an attitude of "overcoming." Although we had internalized these leadership lessons of our female forebears, our expression of these recollections was kept close to our hearts. Typically, such cultural knowledge was shared only in the company of intimates and trusted colleagues. To share this knowledge openly exposed us to a negation of the very culture in which our spirits were rooted and from which we continued to draw nourishment.

We had each earned our doctorates in the era of the late eighties and early nineties. During these decades, *leadership studies* was the hot new organizational term. However, the private sector's dictate of what constituted leadership knowledge was only beginning to include women's leadership as a topic of serious study. These studies often compared women's "styles" and approaches to those of men, but little querying of women's leadership on its own terms occurred. During the 1980s and nineties, the language, values, vision, and strategies passed on to us from mothers and allomothers served to aid us in deciphering the new codes of modern racism.[6] Allomothers are those women who helped mother us by developing our characters, providing us with emotional support, or mentoring us to leadership. In short, they are women who played a role in our mothering. These women within the cultural communities of our youth and young adult years transmitted gender-specific cultural insider knowledge to us that could not be recognized or understood in the context of then current paradigms of leadership. Such paradigms, on the cusp of recognizing women's leadership, were not prepared to recognize and understand the cultural context and assumptions key to the meaning of black women's leadership. Black women's leadership remained, as Mary Belenky and colleagues would later describe, "a tradition that has no name" (Belenky, Bond, and Weinstock, 1997, pp. 11–12; Omolade, 1994).

We knew that our contribution to the various organizations and individuals we were working with as academics and organizational consultants was an *integration* of two paradigms. Our own praxis portrayed *both* the mainstream theoretical perspectives of leadership *and* some finely honed theoretical perspectives molded by our experiences and cultural worldviews as African American women. So, for over two decades as academics and professional consultants, we dispensed leadership development knowledge to a range of organizations and groups. We did this work for the purpose of advancing leadership skills linked to professionalism, team building, performance and production, goal attainment, leadership succession planning.

In addition, through our work with groups of young, mid-, and late career professionals in the corporate and nonprofit sectors, we gained a wealth of knowledge concerning what is construed as leading behavior and leadership in the most mainstream, traditional sense. And during this period of assimilating and dispensing knowledge, we joined the paradigms of what was passed on to us from our mothers and othermothers to what we had learned in our formal education and in our organizational work. Yet we also knew that this culturally resonant body of knowledge from our lives as African American women, "trained up to lead," needed to be articulated before it could be recognized and acknowledged. Finally, we knew that to articulate this race-gender specific body of knowledge and its relevance to leadership theory would require going to its source. We view the source of this knowing and practicing leadership as emanating from our mothers and allomothers.

Hence, we turned to the mother-daughter relationship as the crux of our analysis. This relationship is the beginning of our own leadership knowledge. It becomes for us the "unit of analysis" for understanding the cultural traditions and methods of socialization through which African American girls are prepared to cultivate their own leadership identities. To observe the transmission of leadership via the lens of the African American mother-daughter dyad reveals the interpersonal and intergenerational dynamics of leadership. In particular it offers for scrutiny such provocative questions as the following: (1) How do mothers exorcize the trauma of racism, classism, and sexism as well as any negative personal or social histories to assist daughters in working through trauma and growing in healthy ways that prevent hegemony from winning out? (2) How do black mothers gain conscious access to both their gifts and frailties as a preliminary step in becoming leadership mentors and preceptors for their daughters? And (3) How do mothers serve as guides and leadership role models themselves who are capable of imparting leadership knowledge and skills useful to their daughters' lives?

Mother-daughter leadership transmission is certainly not the only mode of leadership development that is available. We acknowledge the leadership development that occurs from fathers and community father figures to daughters as well as the leadership development that occurs among mothers, othermothers, and sons. All of these methods of cultural reproduction and preservation are worthy of scholarly attention. Although we need to bring attention to this form of leadership development in black communities, we are also conscious of the fact that mother-daughter leadership transmission has historically been a well-guarded body of knowledge that has been passed on from women to women as insider knowledge to protect its power and vitality as a form of resistance to oppression. We now see a need to make this knowledge available on the world stage, while still protecting its integrity.

The text that follows is a montage of our exploration of these questions over time. Together and apart, we have looked at our own mothers' guidance. We have also looked at how we applied their tutelage to our communal contributions and our career advancements. Conversely we have looked at how we applied their teachings to ensure that we learned from not only our professional coups, but to our foibles, as well as to our development into adulthood. And although we grew up separately, both of us have found that our interest in the topic of black women's leadership flourished under our exposure to these streams of women's history, women's ways, and women's talk. Beyond our mothers and allomothers this interest has been further enriched by discussions with our African American female mentees, workshop and training participants, and professional women clients.

Joining our voices are the voices of twelve other African American womanist scholars in this anthology. They represent the disciplines of African American studies, education, English, communications, cultural studies, law, organizational behavior, psychology, social work, theology, and women's studies. They, in turn, chart their recollections of their own mothers' teachings that aided in the promotions of their identities as leaders. Many of our contributors came of age during these eras, and others have exercised most of their leadership in the time period following the 1964 civil rights act and the age of affirmative action, and still others were born after 1964 and have launched into leadership during the post–civil rights era and age of affirmative action backlash. Six of the fourteen contributors (including the pieces by the coeditors) to this work were a part of a writing group at Denison University, the Third Shift Writers' Collective, that Toni King, coeditor of this volume, formed and led for two years.[7] Two of the fourteen contributions to this anthology were written by biological sisters, S. Alease Ferguson and Leah C. K. Lewis. They show us how we each experience mother-daughter dynamics distinctly even when we share a mother. All of the contributors, by reaching for their remembrance of the Motherline teaching process, and casting their experiences in terms of leadership, help us to claim the leadership dimensions of Motherline presence and tutelage in all our lives.

We selected the literary tradition of memoir as a useful tool for excavating and defining the functional artifacts of matrilineal leadership. The oral tradition and storytelling are paramount within black cultures throughout the diaspora, so we urge that further exploration of leadership transmission honor the storytelling process prior to applying other methods of analysis and prior to situating the knowledge within or in relationship to disciplinary frameworks. Sharing our stories in this anthology recreates the space of the "kitchen table" that women of color use as a metaphor for women's conversation in daily life. It is at the kitchen table that much of the socialization and cultural rites of passage occur. The kitchen table, seen as insignificant domestic space, is actually a place of power, utilized by women to give and receive support, problem solve, plan, and create. At this table we gain access to intimate remembrance and meaning. Barbara Kingsolver tells us, "Memory is a complicated thing, a relative to truth, but not its twin."[8] The writers here bring us their remembered experience and the translation of that experience into how they lead.

This anthology is our gathering at the table to discuss "grown women's business" via promoting, preserving, and passing on what Andrea O'Reilly calls the "funk and ancient properties" of Motherline knowledge (2004, p. 19). This excavation of intergenerational Motherline influences celebrates the triumphant legacy that is African American female leadership and is a response to the current crises in African American womanist and communal leadership development. This is our gathering. The women of whom we speak are the source points of our own learning.

With this writing we invite you to the table.

NOTES

1. This is not to exclude the care black women and families extend to children, youth, and young adults of both genders, by providing for or adopting them and raising them as their own.

2. Alice Walker's "Definition of a Womanist," from *In Search of Our Mother's Gardens*, refers to the desire to question, understand, and take action in the world around them that is typical of girls who show an early propensity for feminist and Afrocentric leadership, which she frames as "womanist" (pp. xi–xii).

3. Alice Walker's "Definition of a Womanist" uses the term *womanish* from black folk vernacular to describe the behavior of black girls as referenced in the previous footnote (pp. xi–xii).

4. This is an African American adage, commonly used by community mothers, and othermothers to motivate and develop self-esteem in black girls. See T. Robinson and J. V. Ward, (1991), *A Belief in Self Far Greater Than Anyone's Disbelief: Cultivating Resistance among African-American Female Adolescents*, in C. Gilligan, A. G. Rogers, and D. L. Tolman (Eds.), *Women, Girls, and Psychotherapy: Reframing Resistance* (pp. 89–91), (Binghamton, NY: Hawthorn).

5. Each of the women has revealed experiencing a range of personal tragedies including social and relational violations. Each has also engaged in in-depth recovery strategies.

6. We use the term *allomothers* interchangeably with the more widely used term *othermothers*.

7. In 1999, Toni King formed the Third Shift Writers Collective, which lasted for two years, and supported the African American women academics and administrators at Denison University in writing about their leadership in higher education. This group coauthored "Andrea's Third Shift: The Invisible Work of African-American Women in Higher Education," by Toni King and others, in Gloria Anzaldua and Analouise Keating, *This Bridge We Call Home: Radical Visions for Transformation,* 2002.

8. From the novel *Animal Dreams*, p. 48.

REFERENCES

Belenky, M. F., Bond, L. A., & Weinstock, J. S. (1997). Introduction: Otherness and silence. In *A tradition that has no name: Nurturing the development of people, families, and communities* (pp. 3–18). New York: Basic.

King, T. C., Barnes-Wright, L., Gibson, N. E., Johnson, L. D., Lee, V., Lovelace, B. M., Turner, S., and Wheeler, W. I. (2002). Andrea's third shift: The invisible work of African American women in higher education. In G. Anzaldua and A. Keating, *This bridge we call home: Radical visions for transformation* (403–15). New York: Routledge.

Kingsolver, B. (1990). *Animal Dreams*. New York: HarperCollins.

Omolade, B. 1994. *The rising song of African American women*. New York: Routledge.

O'Reilly, A. 2004. A Politics of the heart: Toni Morrison's theory of motherhood as a site of power and motherwork as concerned with the empowerment of children. In *Toni Morrison and motherhood: A politics of the heart* (pp. 1–46). Albany: State University of New York Press.

Robinson, T., & Ward, J. V. (1991). A belief in self far greater than anyone's disbelief: Cultivating resistance among African American female adolescents. In C. Gilligan, A. G. Rogers, and D. L. Tolman (Eds.), *Women, girls, and psychotherapy: Reframing resistance* (pp. 89–91). Binghamton, New York: Hawthorn.

Walker, A. (1983). Definition of a womanist. In *In search of our mothers' gardens: Womanist prose* (pp. xi–xii). San Diego: Harcourt Brace Jovanovich.

Acknowledgments

WE ARE OVERJOYED to offer this anthology on black women's leadership development. Thank you to each and all who helped usher this text through to fruition whether by editing, reading, or listening to segments, offering us technical support, advice, assistance, encouragement, and your unwavering belief that we could and should write this book. Special thanks to Larin McLaughlin for sheparding the vision of this book, to Andrew Kenyon for support seen and unseen, and to Laurie Searl for expert steering of the production process. Overall, sincerest appreciation to State University of New York Press for the opportunity to speak in print.

I, Toni, express appreciation to my Denison University circle of support. I thank Marlene Tromp for your sister friendship and way showing. Your guidance at critical junctures and deep affirmation of me as a scholar continue to rejuvenate and restore. John Jackson, thank you for your wise counsel, particularly during the time that I was chairing black studies. Your collegiality and friendship kept me sane enough to thrive in the academy while writing this book. To my women students of such amazing courage and passion for social justice—you have all shown me what leadership looks like in this new millennium and what women of the current generation need from the Motherline. To the gifted Susan Richardson whose editing gave me a renewed appreciation for the elegance of simplicity in the written word; to Sandy Spence whose professional attention to detail polished our final product; and to Jane Dougan without whose administrative support the world would stop—I thank you all. Thanks too, to those mighty five who came whenever to do whatever and indexed the book like pros: Mary (Molly) Anderson, Stephanie Chan, Alexcia Davis, LaKeesha Leonard, and Jasmine McGhee—you were and are awesome! To Betty Lovelace, your early support of this project and our "third-shift" work with so many students at Denison taught me how to support students without giving away my own dreams. To Carol Jones and Carole Duncan—and all of my sister circle near and far—thank you for being there and for your lives of integrity and leadership grace. To my othermothers, Wynona Bush, Virginia Schoats, Audrey Ward, Mary Wynn, Mozelle Stewart—you have filled my "medicine bag" with wisdom that I draw upon daily. To Thomas King, you have been a most generous husband who keeps the outer world at bay, in order, and functioning smoothly so that I can find the inner world from which to write. More than that you have been the believing constant, and I am deeply grateful. And to my coauthor and partner—S. Alease Ferguson—joining you on this quest to write the Motherline has been a joyful labor. We are still the *ibejii*—soul twins who work together as if we are one spirit.

I, Sheila Alease, express my thanks as follows. Coauthorship of this book has provided me with a multitude of gifts and epiphanies. Most enjoyable was the added time and interaction with Toni C. King, my writing and scholarly research partner of almost twenty years. Our exploration into the theme of Motherline leadership transmission sparked off many reflections about being a daughter, sister, mother and grandmother, othermother and woman who works to help other women mother better. To Ken Ferguson, thank you for handling both the everyday and surprise life details. To my sisters, Sharon and Leah Lewis, and cousin, Judy B. Knight, thanks for your love and encouragement. Thanks to dearest friends Pamela Bradford, Mary Bazie, Elaine Gohlstin, Ira Bragg-Grant, Rosemary Hill, Sharon Szabo, Gloria Ferguson, Debi Green, Reesa Ellerbee, and Aunties Mary, Corrie, and Cleo—your collective excitement about the book helped to keep the medicine wisdom of Thelma, Corrie, Pearl, and Lucretia close at hand. To my sister-friend Cynthia Lampkin, thank you for being Nicky's loving othermother. You have enriched both of our lives. To Nicholas, you are Grammy's inspiration and proof that the Motherline will always reign triumphant. Thanks for the daily "I love you/s" and the chance to play. You've got me convinced that I really can jump higher, fly, and dunk just like LeBron. To Jessica B. Horne—Cleveland UMADAOP's founding boss woman, revolutionary sister-friend, raconteur, and communal mother—thanks for recognizing my personhood and creativity. Your kindness affords me the latitude to serve as a scholar at large and be a leading Motherline change facilitator. Last, to Tahirah Mujahid, Nicole LaVan, Darlene Mayes, Marian Howard, and Cathey Moore, you are each divine mothers in your own right. Together our workaday efforts exemplify how it is that the building of a communal Motherline has the tremendous power to heal, repair, and restore. Glory to the Motherline.

From both of us to each of our contributors, we are grateful beyond words. You have remained faithful throughout the long journey of publishing this book. You have outlasted our major career advancements, setbacks, interruptions, and transitions. Ultimately, you stood by as we worked through, worked out, and just made it work in terms of our life span needs and those of our families and extended families. Through it all your contributions were the pearls of rare price. We hope we are returning your pearls as well strung and resplendent links to matrilineal leadership wisdom.

Finally, we thank our mothers, Otissey and Thelma, wise Motherline women, whose teachings have guided us from birth to this day. We translate those teachings for use in this new millennium. Through our narratives and those of each contributor we trace the source points of our leadership.

Introduction

Looking to the Motherline

> A nation is not conquered until the hearts of its women are on the ground.
> —Lakota proverb, Mary Crow Dog, *Lakota Woman*

THE VALUE OF THE MOTHERLINE and its wisdom are inestimable. According to Edelman (1994) and Lowinsky (1992), "without knowledge of her own experiences and their relationship to her mothers," a daughter is snipped from the female cord that connects the generations of women in her family, the feminine line of descent known as the "Motherline." A woman achieves her psychic connection to generations of feminine wisdom through hearing her mother's and her grandmother's narratives about women's physical, psychological, and historical changes—bleeding, birthing, suckling, aging, and dying. According to Lowinsky: "When a woman today comes to understand her life story as a story from the Motherline, she gains female authority in a number of ways that help her . . . [reclaim] her female perspective, from which to consider how men are similar and how they are different" (Lowinsky, 1992, p. 13).

Lowinsky theorizes the ways women gain "female authority" when they understand their life stories in the context of the Motherline: the reclamation of our carnal body knowledge, particularly its "blood mysteries and their power"; the attainment of a life cycle perspective that creates a compassionate gaze at our current situation and the discovery of our female roots and their parallel struggles; and development into connection with the archetypal mother and the accompanying ancient world view and its wisdom. From this world view, a woman learns that the body and soul are unified, that all of life is interrelated, and from this way of knowing women soften into the perspective that life changes, babies grow, people age and die, there is a cycle to all of life. Finally, Lowinsky tells us that the Motherline gives women grounding as they come to terms with the new options now open to us as women.

In other words, Motherline stories ground women in a gender, a family, and a feminine history. By centering this investigation on the transmission of leadership knowledge through the Motherline, we help to define the contours of black womanist knowledge. In this way we counter the dominant culture's pattern of imprinting its values, experiences, and interpretations of maternal strivings on the symbiosis of the African American mother-daughter dyad. Our efforts support the naming of our own reality(ies) and refute external sources of labeling and constructing what constitutes leadership for us. In naming our own ways of passing on leadership we engage in the African American tradition of resistance, empowerment, and what Parker (2005, pp. 130–32) describes as transformation that dislodges, disrupts, and diverges from societal conceptions of "female only" leadership.

STEPPING UP TO THE COUNTERNARRATIVE: LOOSENING THE UNTOLD STORY

> There is no agony like bearing an untold story inside you.
> —Zora Neale Hurston

The value of story in women's lives is a cultural anchor.[1] Scholars such as Johnetta Betsch Cole and Beverly Guy-Sheftall (2003) suggest that the stories women tell bring us into the deep structure of the culture and the texture and quality of daily life. They also widen the circle of knowledge, spur change, and aid other women in reframing the contours and rough edges of their lives. In this anthology, we choose to have black women tell us stories about the Motherline as a means of

INTRODUCTION

entering this cultural realm. Bettina Aptheker's explanation of the central role of story in women's lives helps us see why story as the medium for learning about women's lives is so crucial. She writes: "Women use stories in their everyday lives, and especially as a way of doing emotional work ... [S]ome have been stitched into quilts or planted in gardens or painted or sculpted or written in letters and journals ... [W]omen's stories evoke distinct meanings, distinct special and temporal arrangements. They have been crafted out of the artifacts of daily life, beckoning us to see" (Aptheker, 1989, pp. 44–45).

In the case of this book, the importance of stories is contradictory. On the one hand, there is a need to hear women speak in their own voices so that we are invited into the ways women use language and experience to shape meanings on their own terms. On the other hand, particularly when one looks at two vast subjects such as motherwork and leadership, there is the risk of revealing a system of knowledge designed to preserve black women's lives and role in liberating the race. For this reason, such a tradition was intentionally kept "close to the vest" and behind the veil of black women's double consciousness. Double consciousness, first conceptualized by W. E. B. DuBois in *The Souls of Black Folks* is the ability of marginalized groups to sustain a consciousness of both how they perceive themselves and how the dominant group perceives them. For black women, it was imperative that they know and understand the dominant white cultural group, rather than "be known" by dominant others. Just as it behooves the oppressed to cultivate stratagems unknown to the power elite, open access to black women's leadership knowledge would undermine their capabilities for maintaining inviolable boundaries of spirit and pragmatic boundaries of action so necessary to personal and social uplift.

We advocate a selective relinquishing of our former vigilance in favor of a deliberate unveiling in our own time and space, with our own methods, and in our own voice.

> Black women need to articulate and claim this knowledge to create a strong imprint of the collective knowledge that structures our cultural context. We need to be able to name, legitimize and hold up our own paradigms of cultural meaning in the light of day. Perhaps this is why Patricia Bell Scott (1994)

says that Black women write "about" and "for" their lives . . . and says that "personal writing is/has always been a dangerous activity because it: "Allows us the freedom to defy culturally imposed negative identities . . . and has offered avenues for resistance and recreation." (pp. 17–18)

In addition, there is much historical precedent for black women intellectuals—particularly those we now frame as black feminist intellectuals—to give voice to social issues, particularly those pertinent to black life and culture, and to the isms arising from the social hierarchies of power (Cole and Guy-Sheftall, 2003; Guy-Sheftall, 1995). Black women intellectuals from the 1800s to the present gave voice to some of the most highly contested issues of their time and used the power of the pen, including personal narrative, to take on and engage in psychosocial resistance and to effect change. Given the geophysical dispersion we are now subject to in the aftermath of urban migration, integration, urban renewal, gentrification, and the many other sources and forms of displacement we have been subjected to (e.g., Hurricane Katrina, mass corporate lay-offs, predatory lending), we now need to create sites for telling the stories that keep the fabric of African American culture whole.

In the case of mother-daughter leadership transmission, black women need to reconnect to the Motherline and seek the stories of leadership and then tell these stories to clarify and empower ourselves with common knowledge of our own leadership narrative and how knowledge of leadership was handed down to us. To affirm this knowledge dismantles the limits that patriarchy would place on us. To not have these stories consciously available to us structures a subtle form of subjugation that leaves us no tools for our own defense or for our own redefinition. We need the shared knowledge that we have participated in the human project of leadership. We need the language for structuring the meaning of our own leadership capacities, skills, and approaches. We need the imagination of the sheroes that have gone before us, including both those epic historical figures and those close to home in the bodies of our own mothers and othermothers. This work seeks to recast the privileged notion of leadership (Komives and Wagner et al., 2009, McKenzie, 2001) as one that resides in our own lived experience and as one that emanates from our own Motherline herstories.

Ain't I a Leader? Barriers to Laying Claim to Leadership

In constantly meeting the demands for survival and fending off the noxious stimuli of discrimination it is altogether possible for black women to not be cognizant of their own performance as leaders.[2] As a case in point, many of the women writers who submitted works to be considered for this anthology, including those whose works were selected—did not see themselves as leaders. Many of the women called us by phone, some more than once, to share their ideas for the paper they would like to write. Following the majority of these phone calls or queries was the refrain: "So is my idea related to leadership?"

After we reassured potential contributors that their ideas were exactly the kind of narrative we hoped to receive, we found that there was still another level of uncertainty to address. Many of the women would then share with us their doubts about the terminology of leadership itself. Commonly we heard them say things such as: "I know I've achieved a number of things in my life, and I know that my othermothers prepared me well to achieve those things, but I never actually think of myself as a leader." When we explored this conundrum further with them by pointing to some of the things they currently were doing or had done and asking whether they felt this was leadership, they would laughingly affirm that indeed it was! Some would even discover the incongruence between their willingness to use the labels of *leader* and *leadership* when speaking of their mothers and othermothers or their colleagues—but not themselves.

Answers to why black women pull back from owning their influence and accomplishments as leadership can be directly tied to early patterns of socialization and the large looming social forces. We have observed the following barriers to black women laying claim to their own leadership identities:

> Gendered Projections. Women leaders are commonly perceived as harsh, masculine, seemingly alienated from and possibly

compromised in the appropriate performance of their gender roles. Society also views women leaders as puppets easily coopted by male power, as sexual objects susceptible to various "casting couch" dynamics, or conversely wielding power as women in ways that are officious or narcissistic. Summarily there is a belief that both women and black women leaders will be rendered impotent because of the systemic forces of racism (Wilson, 2007).

Cultural and Racial Projections. To the extent that systemic racism has created an imbalance in the male-female relational dyad causing females to assume leadership in the areas of family care taking, child discipline, and economic support, stepping up to the leadership challenge places black women at risk for being perceived as usurping black male power and fulfilling the stereotypical "matriarch" function in which men of the race are prevented from taking a leadership role in family, community, and nation.

Negative Perceptions of Leadership. To lead with unabashed passion, spoken clarity of one's leadership and its raison d'etre in response to needed change or the building of equity imperils the actor with labels of *militant* or conversely of *bleeding heart liberal*. In addition, there are numerous negative projections reserved for women who are perceived as "uppity," and out of "their place."

Socialization to Deny or Downplay One's Contribution. As a matter of home training and tutelage in humility, black women modestly accept thanks and praise or shrink at acknowledgment of our leadership accomplishments. Earnest self appreciation of one's leadership capacity is often mired in a conflictual state of emotions about whether we are deserving of the leadership role. Moreover, our communal upbringing teaches us that everyone's contribution is necessary to the success of a venture; thus it is unfair to emphasize the organizer to the exclusion of the group, village, community, or team. Consequently, black women readily demonstrate leadership abilities behind the scenes, without becoming the public face of leadership (Smooth and Tucker, 1999; Gilkes, 2001).

Contradictions between Terminology and Action. Such contradictions can include verified daily leadership that is seldom acknowledged or described as such. We call our works "helping," "serving," "nurturing," "ministering to," "stepping up," or "assuming duty and responsibility." In the most immediate sense, *leaders* and *leadership* are white male and institutionally inscribed terms referring to an individual or body of supreme power. The actual term of 'leader' is typically reserved for those in authority, the president of the company, upper management, team captains, or one's superior.

Vocalization of the words *I am a leader* eludes a good many African American women in particular and women in general. In order for black women to lay claim to leadership in its most generic terms, there are a series of questions they must ask of themselves. These questions guide personal reflections about what constitutes leadership and how to craft a personal style of leading that integrates cultural and bicultural orientations. In this anthology, each writer had to confront and explore questions of personal and cultural relevance such as the following:

1. What is leadership? How do I know when I am leading, and what are the many ways to be a leader?
2. Where can I find the keys to understanding my own distinct leadership potential, and how can I identify what my particular leadership style consists of?
3. How do I resolve the dilemmas of bringing something different to the mainstream in terms of how I lead versus conforming to mainstream leadership methods?
4. How do I take what I know to be culturally validated styles of leadership and parlay them into a mainstream leadership role of value and worth, or how do I take my skills validated in the mainstream and utilize them to support and develop my own community?

The exploration into matrilineal leadership is itself a key inroad into the morass of laying claim to one's self as leader. Typically this is a process that can only deepen after sufficient experience with the perception of one's self as leadership contender results in some bittersweet encounters with victories and defeats that culminate in gazing inward and raising compelling questions about the consequences and outcomes of one's leadership. Ultimately, the laws of diminishing returns force a reckoning with self and a desire to understand those factors that most influence the ability to lead without compromising what is core to one's identity. While leadership experiences can result in achievement and even accolades, the need to feel comfortable about the leadership process, its effects on others, and the authenticity of self one brings to leadership performance commonly grows in importance. Conversely, experiences of failure, inadequacy, self-compromise, or self-other alienation may also raise questions that return a woman's attention to earlier experiences of culturally based leadership development and its cultural wisdom.

Regardless of whether the external stimulus is one of relative success or failure, women find themselves returning to unlock the wisdom of the Motherline by reflecting on questions of interpersonal (and particularly matrilineal) relevance such as the following:

1. Who were my leadership role models?
2. What tools did they give me to make my ascent as a leader?
3. How am I similar to and how am I different from my leadership role model(s)?
4. What did they teach me that seemed to be strategically aimed to combat patriarchal oppression?

For black women the teaching and demonstration of leadership begins in one's family and society of origin and is part and parcel of the socialization process. According to scholars who have examined black women's lives in the context of African cultural mores that survived the middle passage, enslavement, the Jim Crow era, and the morphing of these forms of institutionalized oppression into the modern day versions of the interlocking oppressions of race, class, and gender, black women are the recipients of a very particular and acute socialization process. Overall, leadership is a complex and prismatic issue for African American women. Therefore, it is not always easy to know how to view black women's leadership or where to look for this fine-tuned integration of dual socialization and its application.

THE MOTHERLINE AND THE VALUE OF OUR EPIC STORIES

In *Africana,* Kwame Anthony Appiah and Henry Louis Gates (1997; 2003) suggest that the traditions of African and African American female leadership are Janus-faced. They at once "look forward to the women's new goals and backward to the status and roles that women leaders have played in the past" (p. 738). Culturally, the expression of African American female leadership and that of the women of the African Diaspora are called "black feminism" and "Womanism" (Walker, 1983). In the Americas, the template for black feminism emerged from the lived experiences of the free traditional African woman and the enslaved black woman. Scholar Patricia Hill Collins (in *Africana,* pp. 742–45) portends that "black feminism is a means of human empowerment rather than an end in and of itself. It encompasses a comprehensive, anti-sexist, anti-racist and anti-elitist perspective of social change."

Historically, black feminism has progressed across three distinct phases. The first phase was laying the foundation 1800–1920. This phase was characterized by a conceptualization of liberty, freedom, dignity, and voice. The second phase, working for change 1920–1960, was exemplified by communalism and the development of collective movements, voice, and self-help organizations. The third and current phase is contemporary black feminism, 1960 to the present. This latter phase reflects the diversification of the African American female and her communal experiences, life styles, issues, and concerns. Notably the evolutionary path of black feminism intersects with what Bogardus (1981) calls the seven epochs of racism: captivity and slavery; miscegenation; liberation and independence; Reconstruction, Jim Crow; civil rights and modern racism. At each juncture, the substance of black feminism has been strategically framed to respond to the expressions of racial injustice, social trends, and key challenges to survival.

Since its inception in the nineteenth century, black feminism/womanism has held a consistency in its themes and philosophical outlook. Structurally, black feminism and black female leadership are undergirded by four basic pillars: (1) the legacy of struggle; (2) the search for voice and the refusal to be silenced; (3) the impossibility of separating intellectual inquiry from political activism; and (4) the direct application of empowerment to everyday life. Resting on these four pillars are common experiences of race, gender, and economic discrimination that force attention to the necessities of forging and sustaining various forms of leadership and resistance.

The legacy of struggle is the core impetus for black female leadership and feminism. This energetic struggle has been aimed at eliminating and transcending racial and social oppression by transforming societal relations and controls. Voice is a tool aimed at striking down the mythology of demeaning stereotypes and reinventing black women through acts of individual and collective self-expression. Historically, black women have been subject to such objectifying labels as *breeders, wet nurse mammies, aunties, conjurers,* and *jezebels*. These depictions provide the most common symbols of our objectification and commodification and have been put in place as mechanisms of social control, domination, and justification of the negative. Black women challenge the dominant authorities and their accompanying projections by asserting the power to speak and name themselves. Moreover, this reclamation of identity on our own terms delimits the authority system's efforts to quash visibility. As black women's lives require complex negotiations and the mediation of contradictions, the capacity for leadership has been shown in our ability to create strategies for survival and advancement that include self-authentication, through unending self-invention and reinvention.

In the black feminist/womanist posture, African American women of all strata strive for a measure of self-acceptance and appreciation such as that articulated by Alice Walker when she described womanists as intentional leaders, who love "[the] self. *Regardless*" (p. xii).[3] Known for self-expressiveness, they have scripted their own ways of "being in the world" in both their public and private personas. For example, Madame C. J. Walker's founding of a national corporation that grew into a multi-billion-dollar international industry fueled primarily by a consumer base of black women illustrates the strength of black women's beauty ethic. The formation of this self-styled beauty ethic is indicative of self-regard, psychological uplift, and a supportive, pro-black community—despite the context of oppression and neocolonization. In writing their own script, black women have built a lattice of self-identification and unity that casts off the shackles of internalized oppression, self-hatred, and self-sabotage (Bundles, 2001). In either refusing to look or act like the oppressor or in claiming self-authentication even when appearing to conform to mainstream standards of beauty, black women consciously choose resistance over patriarchal authority.

Having reckoned with the concrete experience of oppression black women have devised effective strategies for action out of their struggle for personal and collective liberation. In this book, we define leadership as *the desire, ability and efforts to influence the world around us, based upon an ethic of care for self and other and fueled by a vision that one sustains over time.* The actions of black women historically demonstrate leadership as we have just defined it. This leadership is characterized by the assertion of free will choices to empower ourselves across a range of oppressive situations. History records countless ordinary and historic black women who have seized the reins of leadership. Their works have been integral to the creation of adages that transmit core values and that apply these values to daily life. Some of the most commonly heard and inspiring "old folks'" sayings to this effect include "each one teach one" or "each one reach one"; "every tub must stand on its own bottom"; "making a way out of no way;" "lift as we climb"; "service is the rent we pay for being on this earth"; and, "speaking life into it (it being our own or another's reality or experience)." These adages prescribe ways to lead and to empower self and the communal network.

Although feminism can be used to frame black women's proclivity to empower self and others and to "uplift" people, families, and communities, black women as a group have perceived the doctrines of feminism as lacking in breadth. Accepting actions that liberate only on the basis of gender when an entire community ails is tantamount to sacrilege in the Africentric world view. Thus, whether black women have rejected feminism outright or worked to redefine its parameters, they have challenged and critiqued it for placing conditions on liberation or for failing to reach across the lines of race and class to include the presence, voice, and influence of poor women or people of color (hooks, 2000; Jones Royster, 2000).

Characterizing this view is one of the earliest black feminists, Sojourner Truth, who challenged the tendency for feminists of her day to act in moderation even on their own behalf. Of this she says: "Sisters, I aren't clear what you be after. If women want any rights more than they got, why don't they just take them and not be talking about it?" (Ortiz, 1974, p. 81). History provides ample evidence of the ongoing urging by black feminists to their white sisters to expand the inclusiveness of feminism and to confront woman-to-woman racism and classism within the movement itself (Hine, 1994). To bridge the chasm in worldviews, black womanists have opted to widen the movement and make it more accessible to more women by promoting social and economic equality for all.[4]

The merits and voracity of black womanism and leadership are without question. They are transgenerational phenomena and a survivor's legacy, despite the mainstream societal insistence on black female invisibility and subjugation. To counter stereotypes, the voices of black women leaders tell true, heal, sing, decree, lament, testify, admonish, scream, and thunder as an expression of power, presence, and connection. At no time since coming to the North American continent have women of the African Diaspora been effectively and permanently silenced. Our legacy of leadership stems through time to the "Great Black Mother" and the culture of allomothers. Some out of many mother figures include the great queens of Africa such as Nzingha, Nefertiti, Sheba, Hatshepsut, Cleopatra, and the Kandake queens of Meroe; Abla Pokou, founder of the Baule nation in West Africa; Kahia la Kahina and Karsifa, warrior queens who resisted Arab conquest, Ashanti matrilineage queens; and the women of the West African marketplace. We can also name women farmers, business women, weavers, artisans, and musicians; women's Mystery School leaders (Neale Hurston, 1938);[5] and the survivors of the middle passage. On the American shores, the legacy is carried on by such women as Harriet Tubman, Sojourner Truth, Ida B. Wells, Angelina Weld Grimke, Charlotte Forten Grimke, Maggie Lena Walker, Margaret Murray Washington, Mary Church Terrell, Fannie Burroughs, Anna Julia Cooper. Even more recent figures include Zora Neale Hurston, Amy Jacques Garvey, Mary McLeod Bethune, Florynce Kennedy, Rosa Parks, Fannie Lou

Hammer, Ella J. Baker, Septima Clark, and Dorothy Height to name a few of those who have garnered some degree of public recognition.

Some of the exemplars of the contemporary black feminist movement include Pauli Murray, Alice Walker, Toni Morrison, June Jordan, Audre Lorde, Sonia Sanchez, Ntozake Shange, Angela Davis, bell hooks, Barbara Smith, Michelle Wallace, Deborah King, Shirley Chisolm, Eleanor Holmes Norton, Barbara Jordan, Kelley Brown Douglas, Beverly Guy-Sheftall, Bonnie Thornton Dill, Cheryl Townsend Gilkes, Delores Williams, Patricia Williams, Patricia Hill Collins, and countless more both known and unknown.

Further recessed from public consciousness are the "different other voices" of black women scholar-leaders who bring the leadership contributions and concerns of black women to the foreground. The works these scholars produced include Gloria T. Hull and Patricia Bell Scott, *All the Women Are White, All the Blacks Are Men, But Some of Us Brave: Black Women's Studies* (1982); Nellie McKay, *Colored Woman in a White World (African-American Women Writers, 1910–1940)* (with Mary Church Terrell (1996); Darlene Clark Hine, *Hine Sight: Black Women and the Re-Construction of American History* (1994); Paula Giddings, *When and Where I Enter* (1984); Dorothy Sterling, *We Are Your Sisters* (1984), Nell Irvin Painter *Sojourner Truth: A Life, a Symbol* (1996); Beverly Guy-Sheftall, *Words of Fire: An Anthology of African-American Feminist Thought* (1995); Jacqueline Jones Royster, *Traces of a Stream: Literacy and Social Change among African American Women* (2000); Valerie Lee, *Granny Midwives and Black Women Writers* (1996), Cheryl Townsend Gilkes, *If It Wasn't for the Women: Black Women's Experience and Womanist Culture in Church and Community* (2001); Trudier Harris, *Saints, Sinners, Saviors: Strong Black Women in African American Literature* (2001); *Beverly Guy Sheftall, African American Women: The Legacy of Black Feminism* (2003); Kristin Waters and Carol Conway, *Black Women's Intellectual Traditions: Speaking Their Minds* (2007); and Dutchess Harris, *Black Feminist Politics: From Kennedy to Clinton* (2009).

Yet the voices of black women scholars from the behavioral and organizational sciences sectors were also needed to reflect the psychosocial, organizational and systemic pressures arrayed against black women who engage in leadership assertion. Recent examples include Ella Bell and Stella Nkomo, *Our Separate Ways: Black and White Women and the Struggle for Professional Identity* (2001), Trevy McDonald and T. Ford-Ahmed, *Nature of a Sistuh: Black Women's Lived Experiences in Contemporary Culture* (1999); Kimberly Springer, *Still Lifting Still Climbing: Contemporary African American Women's Activism* (1999); Cydney Shields and Leslie Shields, *Work Sister, Work* (1993); Patricia Reid-Merritt, *Sister Power* (1996); Belinda Robnett *How Long? How Long? African-American Women and the Struggle for Civil Rights* (1997); Leslie Jackson and Beverly Greene, *Psychotherapy with African American Women* (2000); Charisse Jones and Kumea Shorter-Gooden, *Shifting: The Double Lives of Black Women in America* (2003); Reverend Vashti M. McKenzie, *Not without a Struggle: Leadership Development for African American Women in Ministry* (1996); Syenia Rose, *Rise Up: A Call to Leadership* (2004); and Patricia Parker, *Race, Gender, and Leadership: Re-Envisioning Organizational Leadership from the Perspectives of African American Women Executives* (2005). Each of these books offers insights into the leadership dilemmas of black women in organizational settings or helps us to see the great psychospiritual challenges that black female leaders face in their lives and in society.

With this panoply of divergent voices, it is eminently possible to bring forward a comprehensive exploration of human leadership across differences. However, to arrive at an appreciation of the intergenerational nature of black women's leadership, we need to honor the matrilineage process. Sensitizing readers to the viability of black women's leadership as a service and a gift prompts myriad questions about the genesis, conception, mode of operation, and relational intricacies involved in the apprenticing of women to traditions of empowerment and social change.

The next three sections illustrate the vast scope and dimension of matrilineal transmission of leadership. The section titles are part 1. "Motherline Roots and Significance"; part 2. "The Foundations of Mother-Daughter Tutelage"; part 3. "Visions of the Motherline: Templates for Daughters"; part 4. "Tensions along the Motherline: Translating Mother Templates to Daughter Actions." We end with a chapter entitled "Conclusions: Becoming the Motherline."

These mother-daughter narratives are written on the insides of trees.[6] They claim a place at the core of leadership knowledge. Through their daughters, the elders' intentional ideas about leadership are realized. The role of the daughters in the following chapters is to show us this space of powerful motherwork.[7] Daughters write motherpower in the pages of their reflections. Through them we learn not only how their mothers pushed the edges toward a more just world, but how their mothers influenced the daughters' life chances and prepared daughters to step into the struggle of dismantling systems of oppression.

The writings here by scholarly black women stoke our understanding of what black leadership means. Their writings burn an imprint across the twentieth century, a time in world history rife with totalitarianism and aggression. The authors are notable scholars, practitioners, and educators. Their collective voices combine a grand diversity of storyline time, place, and setting with a common focus along the continuum of black matrilineal leadership.

In studying this legacy of leadership, it became apparent to us that African American mothers of the late nineteenth and twentieth centuries moved with a clear awareness of the objectification of black womankind. And knowing this, they intentionally fed their daughters the tactical nourishment necessary to outwit oppressive forces. This Brer' Rabbit ingenuity grown out of the soil of U.S. oppression, passed from hand to hand in subtle yet explicit teachings, was designed to preserve life. At the same time, the mothers also gave their daughters permission to step beyond guile if need be. These mothers ignored the rules of the master's house that linked proper womanhood with submission. Instead they taught that all humans have access to a force that defies internal defeat of the spirit. The ultimate resistance to being "broken" is seen time and again in women's refusal to accept the status quo, in the forced breaking of exclusionary barriers, and in the continuance of their will to live. Rather than whistling in the wind, hoping for deliverance, black women have created and passed on their own brand of activism, charged with the fires of hope and "belief in self greater than anyone's disbelief." For this book, these scholars show us how they were taught, what they were taught, and how they now leave their leadership imprint on the world.

The common theme among the writings is that of resistance to social, race, class, and gender oppression. They show us that resistance is a mechanism for refusing the social death served up by oppression. Social death occurs when oppression from without takes root within the psyche and erodes the capacity to relate, care, or believe that one's actions contribute to the humanity of self and other. Resisting, however, consists of countless ways for women to summon presence, clarify voice, and discern a path of action to restore human vitality. Within this anthology, the theme of resistance is carved deep by the rendering of daughter-scholars' expressions of the mothering they received. They show us "a line of cutting women"[8] who bring a creative tension through tenderness. They confirm their daughters' strengths while urging daughters' self critique. They provide the safe spaces of communal connection at the same time that they prepare daughters for the tough trials of isolation. And they model woman-bonding in a way that rejects the sacrifice of one's own selfhood as the price of having sister-friends. The contributors to this book show us mothers who commune, encircle, challenge, and correct. They confirm that a wide swath of experiences comprises what it means to mother someone to leadership. But in the wake of their tellings, we see a collective mural of mothers who have envisioned human solidarity in the cultivation of whole daughters, emotionally well and able to join the venture of world making.

The substance of these writings is intergenerational and arises from the residue of imperialism and conquest that has positioned American black women within a story of subjugation and the struggle for liberation. As such, their reflections honor a broad-loomed leadership tapestry woven by American women of African descent. They write about how they were taught to become leading women in their own lives, in their communities, and in the wider world.

We believe African American women, and all women, must examine their own capacity for leadership and acknowledge the tools passed on to them by their Motherline. There is power in women remembering, memorializing, chronicling, and archiving the leadership continuum that is at once Motherline heritage and future contribution. Historically these contributions span the realms of work, family, church, and community life as well as the specialized fields of entrepreneurship, management, business administration, education, law, agriculture and animal husbandry, the sciences, sports, and literature and the arts. As daughters who wrote the contributions to this anthology, we know our own allomothers personally. However, we also know the larger stream of our Motherline legacy from across the pages of history and the airwaves.

Thus, our own mothers and allomothers join the long line of wise women folk, cultural sheroes, way showers, beacons, pillars, and legends. They are all our pioneers; trail blazers, innovators, divas, high priestesses, queens, pop culture icons, and sometimes fabulous firsts. We acknowledge the distinguished legacy of black woman leaders and their contributions of faith, talent, hard work, commitment, follow-through, and a brand of determination that "ain't gone let nobody turn [them] around."

NOTES

1. From the *Encarta Book of Quotes,* ed.Bill Swainson (2000) p. 457, which cites Zora Neale Hurston's *Dust Tracks in the Road* (1942). The phrase "Ain't I a Woman" invokes the famous speech that Sojourner Truth (1797–1883) delivered in 1851 at the Women's Convention (1851, Akron, Ohio), in which she calls into question the larger culture's denial of black women's feminine identity. We similarly call into question the framing of leadership in ways that keep black women from seeing themselves as having a viable leadership identity. See "Ain't I a Woman," *Feminist Frontiers* (p. 20), Laurel Richardson, Verta Taylor, Nancy Whittier (Eds.) (Boston: McGraw-Hill).

2. "Definition of a Womanist," in *In Search of Our Mother's Gardens* (1983).

3. Our overall argument does not negate the in-group tensions and struggles among black women in the quest for social change. These intragroup issues include classism, heterosexism, internalized oppression, and differences in political perspective and strategies for change. To read more on this subject we recommend Darlene Clark Hine (1994) and Paula Giddings (1984).

4. The Women's Mystery School leaders are those women of preliterate and tribal societies who possessed knowledge of the sacred feminine and who used ritual as a means to access this font of spiritual power. These leaders or priestesses were consulted for the purposes of helping women through cycles of birth, the passage from childhood to womanhood, marriage and maturity, aging and death. They carried with them advanced knowledge concerning the cycles of the moon, ritual manifestation, animal husbandry, herbalism, reincarnation, and healing. Through the ages and across cultures (Eastern, Western, American Indian, Caribbean) these women leaders have preserved a sense of communality, tradition, health, wholeness, and connection to the numinous and divine.

5. Gloria Anzaldúa speaks of the need to write as spilling [herself] "on the insides of trees." *Borderlands/La Frontera: The New Mestiza.* 2nd ed. (San Francisco: Aunt Lute Press, 1999), p. 93.

6. Hill Collins uses the term *motherwork* to refer to the ways that women in the community provided developmental, emotional, and practical support. These mothering activities were intentional and geared to ensure physical, cultural, and social survival of the community and particularly its youth and those in need. In this sense the mothering activities were political acts in themselves and also developed a political consciousness in others. See Patricia Hill Collins, *Black Feminist Thought,* ch. 9, "Black Women's Activism." New York: Routledge, 2000.

7. "A Line of Cutting Women" is the title of a book edited by Beverly McFarland, Margarita Donnelly, Micki Reaman, Teri Mae Rutledge, et al., Corvallis, Oregon, 1998.

REFERENCES

Anzaldúa, G. (1997). *Borderlands/La Frontera: The new Mestiza.* 2nd ed. San Francisco: Aunt Lute.

Appiah, K., & Gates, H. L. (1997). Africana: *The encyclopedia of the African and African American experience.* New York: Oxford University Press.

Aptheker, B. (1989). *Tapestries of life: Women's work, women's consciousness, and the meaning of daily experience.* Amherst: The University of Massachusetts Press.

Beauboeuf-Lafontant, T.(2005). Keeping up appearances, getting fed up: The embodiment of strength among African American women. *Meridians: Feminism, Race, Transnationalism, 5*(2), 104–123.

Bell, E. L., Edmondson, J. & Nkomo, S. M. (2001). *Our separate ways: Black and white women and the struggle for professional identity.* Boston: Harvard Business School Press.

Bell-Scott P. (1994). Black women writing lives: An introduction. *Life notes: Personal writings by contemporary Black women* (pp. 17–26). New York: Norton.

Bogardus, E. (1967). *A forty year racial distance study.* Los Angeles: University of Southern California Press.

Braun-Williams, C. (2000). African American women, Afrocentricity and feminism. *Women in therapy, 22*(4), 1–6.

Bundles, A. (2001). On her own ground: The life and times of Madame C. J. Walker. New York: Scribners.

Cole, J. B., Guy-Sheftall, B. (2003). *Gender talk: The struggle for women's equality in African American communities.* New York: Ballantine.

Collins, P. H. (1997). In Appiah, K., & Gates, H. L. (Eds.) *Africana: The encyclopedia of the African and African American experience.* New York: Oxford University Press.

Collins, P. H. (2000). Rethinking Black women's activism. In *Black feminist thought: Knowledge, consciousness, and the politics of empowerment* (2nd ed.) (pp. 201–25). New York: Routledge.

Crow Dog, M. (1990). *Lakota woman.* New York: Harper Perennial.

Edelman, H. (1994). *Motherless daughters: The legacy of loss.* New York: Delta.

Estes, C. P. (1992). Self-preservation: Identifying leg traps, cages, and poisoned bait. In *Women who run with the wolves: Myths and stories of the wild woman archetype* (pp. 214–55). New York: Ballantine Books.

Giddings, P. (1984). *When and where I enter: The impact of Black women on race and sex in America.* New York: Bantam Books.

Gilkes, C. T. (2001). *If it wasn't for the women: Black women's experience and womanist culture in church and community.* Maryknoll, NY: Orbis Books.

Greene, B. (1997). Psychotherapy with African American women: Integrating feminist and psycho-dynamic models. *Smith College Studies in Social Work. 67,* 299–322.

Guy-Sheftall, B. (1995). *Words of fire: An Anthology of African-American Feminist Thought.* New York: New Press.

Guy-Sheftall, B. (2003). *African American women: The legacy of Black feminism.* New York: Washington Square Press.

Harris, D. (2009). *Black Feminist Politics: From Kennedy to Clinton.* New York: McMillan.

Harris, T. (2001). *Saints, sinners, saviors: Strong Black women in African American literature.* New York: Palgrave.

Hine, D. C. (1994). *Hine sight: Black women and the re-construction of American history.* Bloomington: Indiana University Press.

hooks, b. (2000). *Feminism is for everybody: Passionate politics.* Cambridge, MA: South End.

Hull, G. T., Smith, B., & Scott, P. B. (1982). *All the women are white, all the Blacks are men, but some of us are brave: Black women's studies.* Old Westbury, NY: Feminist.

Jackson, L. C. & Greene, B. (Eds.). (2000). *Psychotherapy with African American women: Innovations in psychodynamic perspectives and practice.* New York: Guildford.

Komives, S. R., Wagner, W., and Associates. (2009). *Leadership for a better world: Understanding the social change model of leadership development.* San Francisco: Jossey-Bass, Wiley Imprint.

Lee, V. (1996). *Granny midwives and Black women writers: Double-dutch readings.* New York: Routledge.

Lowinsky, N. R. (1992). *Stories from the Motherline: Reclaiming the mother-daughter bond, finding our females souls.* Los Angeles: Tarcher.

McDonald, T., and Ford-Ahmed, T. (Eds.). (1999). *Nature of a sistuh: Black women's lived experiences in contemporary culture.* Durham, NC: Carolina Academic.

McFarland, B., Donnelly, M., Reaman, M., Rutledge, T. M., et al. (1998). *A line of cutting women.* Corvalis, OR: Calyx Books.

McKay, N. (1996). *Colored woman in a white world (African American women writers, 1910–1940)* with Mary Church Terrell. London: MacMillan.

McKenzie, V. M. (1996). *Not without a struggle: Leadership development for African American women.* Cleveland, OH: Limited Church.

McKenzie, V. M. (2001). *Strength in the struggle: Leadership development for women.* Cleveland: Pilgrim.

Ortiz, V. (1974). *Sojourner Truth: A self-made woman.* Philadelphia: Lippincott Williams and Wilkins.

Painter, N. I. (1996). *Sojourner Truth: A life, a symbol.* New York: Norton.

Parker, P. S. (2005). *Race, gender and leadership: Re-envisioning organizational leadership from the perspectives of African American women executives* (Lea's communication series). Mahwah, NJ: Erlbaum.

Porter, J. L. (1999). There's always a line of separation. In T. McDonald & T. Ford-Ahmed (Eds.). *The figuring of race, gender, and class in the construction of corporate identities* (pp. 133–42). Durham, NC: Carolina Academic.

Reid-Merritt, P. (1996). *Sister power: How phenomenal black women are rising to the top.* New York: Wiley and Sons.

Robnett, B. (1997). *How long? how long? African-American women and the struggle for civil rights.* New York: Oxford University Press.

Rose, S. (2004). *Rise up: A call to leadership for African American women.* Intervarsity.

Royster, J. J. (2000). *Traces of a stream: Literacy and social change among African American women.* Pittsburgh: University of Pittsburgh Press.

Shields, C., & Shields, L. C. (1993). *Work sister work: How Black women can get ahead in today's business environment.* New York: Fireside.

Shorter-Gooden, K. & Jones, C. (2003). *Shifting: The Double lives of Black women in America.* New York: HarperCollins.

Smooth, W. G., & Tucker, T. (1999). Behind but not fortotten: Women and the behind-the-scenes organizing of the Million Man March. In K. Springer, *Still lifting still climbing: Contemporary African American women's activism.* New York: New York University Press.

Springer, K. (1999). *Still lifting still climbing: Contemporary African American women's activism.* New York: New York University Press.

Sterling, D. (Ed.). (1984). *We are your sisters: Black women in the nineteenth century.* New York: Norton.

Truth, S. (2004). "Ain't I a Woman." In Laurel Richardson, Verta Taylor, Nancy Whittier (Eds.). *Feminist Frontiers,* 6th edition. (p. 20). Boston: McGraw-Hill.

Wade-Gayles, G. (1993). *Pushed back to strength: A Black woman's journey home.* Boston: Beacon.

Walker, A. (1983). *In search of our mothers' gardens: Womanist prose.* San Diego: Harcourt Brace Jovanovich.

Waters, K. B., & Conway, C. (Eds.). (2007). *Black women's intellectual traditions: Speaking their minds.* Lebanon, NH: University of Vermont Press.

Wilson, M. C. (2007). *Closing the leadership gap: Add women change everything.* New York: Penguin.

PART I

The Motherline

Roots and Significance

> Every woman alive is connected to all the women before her through the roots of her particular family and culture. The Motherline is body knowledge, and birth story and family story and myth . . . Every woman who wishes to be her full, female self needs to know the stories of her Motherline.
> —Naomi Lowinsky, *Mothers and Daughters: Connection, Empowerment, and Transformation*

THIS SECTION RESPONDS to the questions: What are the roots of Motherline knowledge? Why and how is this knowledge significant for black women's leadership? These chapters show us the spectrum of the forms that the Motherline can take. Be it a grandmother, an adopting, nonbiological mother, a collective of community mothers—any woman who serves as a source of Motherline knowledge constitutes a link in this intergenerational chain. Women who pass on values of an African-centered worldview, women who help daughters learn to read the social clime, heal from dominant culture oppression, fashion a culturally grounded identity, form and carry out resistance aimed at a particular social context or institution are the Motherline.

Three writers speak of the roots and significance of this lineage: Frances K. Trotman in "Legacies from Our Mothers," Valerie Lee in "Sisterlocking Power: Or How Is Leadership Supposed to Look?" and

Nancy Gibson in "Braiding My Place: Agency and Foundational Selfhood through Cross-Racial Mothering." Each chapter testifies that Motherline knowledge will help us to find that which is divine within the self "and love her fiercely."[1] This foundational self-love is a necessary element of awareness. The ability to love one's self puts us in conscious opposition to the agenda of hegemony in which all thought serves the interests of dominant power holders. The very presence of black women is politicized by the social construction of race in which it functions as a structural prop for white supremacy. Therefore the Motherline serves the essential role of teaching black girls and women how to address this systematic politics of subjugation—through self-love, social critique, an astute opposition to oppression, and a belief in a self-determination that can transform our world.

The first writer in this section explains the functions of Motherline knowledge. As a grandmother herself and as a scholar and therapist, she shows us that this knowledge is a coat of protection against the prevailing pathologized view of black womanhood. Motherline knowledge grounds women in their cultural and historical past. Frances Trotman's chapter powerfully reflects on this contribution to mothering particularly as expressed by grandmothers. She explains that "African-American grandmothers are also the ones who have directly experienced and can place in perspective important aspects of our history.

Motherline knowledge purposefully and unequivocally aims to ensure the survival of black women, men, and children. Patricia Hill Collins (2000) and Andrea O'Reilly (2004 p. 12) suggest that black mothers have used motherhood and mother leadership as a form of social activism and have used effective nurture as resistance. Even so, Motherline knowledge is not content with survival alone but insists that we recall our ability to thrive. Trotman's contribution to this anthology points to the way in which black women's survival and ability to thrive also promote these same fortunes for the collective—for black culture in general. Further, in our view, the survival of any group contributes to the humanity of all.

In "Sisterlocking Power: Or How Is Leadership Supposed to Look?" our second writer for this section, Valerie Lee, summons the presence of her beloved grandmother Ma Bell, who taught her progeny all about the political implications of blackness, womanhood, presence, self-packaging, impressions management, and authenticity of choices as they formed their identity. Not only does Lee relay the kind of elder wisdom and mother wit so familiar within black culture, but she also connects us to exactly how her grandmother's sharp intellect and critical consciousness inform Lee's daily life—particularly the politics that surround appearance and dress. Now a department chair in one of the largest and oldest departments of a state university, she has learned from her grandmother to assess and craft the persona that has been instrumental in her leadership presence. She has learned how to dance the dance of biculturalism so that her presentation of self meets her needs for culturally defined self-expression yet also meets her needs for the professional tasks at hand.

The third writer in this section draws the Motherline beyond women of African descent. Nancy Gibson makes clear that the Motherline cannot be limited to blood ties or racial similarity alone. Gibson writes: "The fact that my early lessons in resistance came from my white mother is a testimony to how she tuned in to each of her children's particular needs based on our identities." At the same time, this tuning-in led Gibson's white mother to see the need Gibson had for an ethnic/cultural home. In this chapter, Gibson explains that for girls growing to womanhood an intractable sense of one's own personhood is necessary. Gibson shows us how her mother ensured that her daughter would find both roots and wings. In her current leadership setting as an administrator in higher education, the daughter can now take on the tasks of leadership before her with a focus and verve solidified by the bridge to a cultural/ethnic home her white mother built.

What these chapters teach, tell, reveal, delineate, deliver, and decode are the many ways women prepare women to take a position in their culture. Motherline women mother daughters to take a position of their own making that defies the position the mainstream culture would assign them. To all of them, albeit very differently, Motherline knowledge was used to ground them with a fierce love of self so that they can access clarity of vision. This grounding in self love fosters modes of influence that are ethical and just then urges: *action*—in the midst of the whirlwind of sociopolitical agendas to cocreate a world.

NOTES

1. The phrase "i found God in myself & i loved her/ fiercely" (p. 63) is found in the choreopoem, *For Colored Girls Who Have Considered Suicide When the Rainbow Is Enuf*, by Ntozake Shange. This poignant chant of psychospiritual victory signifies the inviolable dignity of black womanhood.

REFERENCES

Collins, P. H. (2000). Rethinking black women's activism. In *Black feminist thought: Knowledge, consciousness, and the politics of empowerment* (2nd ed.) (pp. 201–25). New York: Routledge.

O'Reilly, A. (2004). *From mothering to mothering: The legacy of Adrienne Rich's Of Woman Born*. Albany: State University of New York Press.

Lowinsky, N. (2000). Mothers of mothers, daughter of daughters: Reflections on the Motherline. In Andrea O'Reilly and Sharon Abbey (Eds.), *Mothers and daughters: Connection, empowerment, and transformation* (pp. 227–35). Lanham, MD: Rowman and Littlefield.

Shange, N. (1975). *For colored girls who have considered suicide when the rainbow is enuf*. New York: Scribner.

1

Legacies from Our Mothers

Frances K. Trotman

AFRICAN AMERICAN MOTHERS have borne children on these shores since before the arrival of the *Mayflower* in 1620, yet there is a dearth of knowledge, little is understood, and much has been pathologized about African American mothering. We must begin to view the domain of motherhood through the lens of African Americans who mother, rather than from the traditional ethnocentrism of the psychological community. European American psychologists have consistently failed to acknowledge experiences that differ from those with which they are personally familiar (Fox, Prilleltensky, and Austin, 2009; Bernal, et al., 2003; Altman, 1995; Andolsen, 1986; Brown, 1995; Cross, Klein, and Smith, 1982; Davis, 1989; Dill, 1983; Espin, 1995; Greene, 1995; Greene and Sanchez, 1997; hooks, 1981; Moraga and Anzaldua, 1981; Smith, 1982). However "human" and understandable such ethnocentrism may be, we cannot continue to ignore the salience of ethnicity as a dimension that transforms the experience of sexism and motherhood. The history of African American women differs from that of European American women. It is not surprising therefore that different present-day behavioral patterns of African American women and mothers have evolved out of their historical experiences. As Mays reports, "The process of slavery and its debilitating effects on the development of a self-identity imposed on the African American present a unique psychological development that is not comparable with any other group lacking such an experience" (Mays, 1985).

This article is an attempt to address deficits in the psychological literature of the dominant culture by bringing the perspective of an African American grandmother and psychotherapist to the psychology of African American mothering. I will present my historical narratives and viewpoint. Some additional thoughts on African American mothering, grandmothering, and "othermothering" (see Troester, 1984) will be followed by some famous, and some not so famous, words of and about African America's mothers and foremothers. By presenting my own words and perspective and those of other African American mothers, I hope to increase the fund of knowledge about the influences on African American women. I will present glimpses of African American mothering to enhance the understanding of the diversity of talents that girls learn from and women bring to African American motherhood. Some additional implications and applications of these "understandings" are discussed at length elsewhere (see Trotman, 2000).

AN AFRICAN AMERICAN'S PERSPECTIVE

I was born and raised in Harlem, New York. I am a light-skinned (or high yella') African American woman. The earliest recollection that I have of the pain associated with American racism took place not where I was born but at the beach when I was four years old. My Aunt Miriam (who was not really my aunt but rather my Mom's friend who had grown up with her at the Negro orphanage) watched me from a distance as I played in the sand at Orchard Beach with a newfound friend, a little girl, slightly older than I (I thought she looked like me.) Suddenly our play was interrupted as the little girl, staring at my arm, admired the darkness of my suntan. Giggling, I casually told my new playmate that I was not tan; I was Negro. I still experience pain as I recall her stunned and disgusted expression, as she quickly turned away from me and ran to her parents. Hurt, puzzled, and confused, I returned to my aunt's beach blanket to recount the incident. Hiding her own pain, my usually kind and loving aunt's response to me, a half century ago, was to reprimand and admonish me that I should never have told the girl that I was Negro. Apparently, there was something very wrong with being a Negro—and therefore with being me.

Back in my neighborhood, when "the number" came out, I wondered why when it happened to be a zero, it was referred to as a "Jackie Robinson." The term expressed both pride and shame; it was a variation of "a nigger ain't nothing." To be called "black" or "African" was the highest insult and clearly "fightin' words" in the Harlem of my youth. I looked out of the window as I rode in the bus down famous Fifth Avenue with my mother. I preferred those buildings and that way of life yet wondered why everyone there was white.

Despite, or perhaps because of, these and many other attacks on my self-esteem, the influence of my mother and my grandmothering fictive kin has prevailed, and I have gone on to complete a Ph.D. at Columbia University and become the first African American woman to be licensed as a psychologist in the state of New Jersey. Of course, I never once, in my four years as an undergraduate, raised my hand or spoke in class. I was convinced that white students were smarter and knew more than I did. I was just foolin' people, pretending to be a college student, so I thought that I had better remain quiet and unnoticeable. I did begin to express myself in writing, however. At seventeen years old, in my freshman English 1 class, I wrote an essay that contained the following sentiments:

> I am a Negro. I live in an example of "man's inhumanity to man," the horrible, filthy, hostile, gang-ridden, junkies haven—Harlem. I am what is called in Harlem a White Negro. I have been mistaken for almost everything from a Puerto Rican to a Japanese, but I can never forget that I am a Negro.
>
> I have envied, feared and despised the White man, had contempt for my friends, my family and myself because we are Negroes, watched hatred and bitterness blind an entire community. I have seen my friends, some very dear to me, blinded, maimed or killed from gang fights, hooked on heroin, or just plain existing in the frustrated, bitter, empty life of the Harlem Negro. I can walk through my neighborhood and see gatherings of Muslims or just plain haters, shouting, "Down with the White man!" or "Let's kill 'em all!" simply to somehow cover

their own feelings of inferiority and self-contempt. I can see drunken men lying in the streets or young people "stoned" and dazed, waiting for their next "fix." I say "hello" to an old classmate and her three illegitimate children. I think of all my neighbors who have ended up in the narcotics' ward, Bellevue, or the East River. I am a Negro, and this is what my country has done to its people and itself.

My parents, tired and frustrated from fighting, just exist. They go to work, come home, eat, watch television, go to bed, get up and start all over again, day after day, year after year. My father escapes with alcohol. My mother's only escape—other than an occasional fight with the landlord or the man downstairs—is her pride in me.

I remember that when I was a child I used to hate white people. I had never met any, but I hated them anyway. I can remember pretending to be asleep, but really listening to the stories coming from the living room. My uncle used to tell about life in the South—stories that never reached the newspapers—about Negro women who, married or not, were taken by the White men as bed-partners, about the knifings, shootings, and lynchings. I remember vividly the lynchings—the stories of men hanging from trees with their sex cut away from them. I wondered why the White man was so mean and savage.

. . . I had known my race, heard a few stories, memorized a few clichés, read a few editorials and I could have wasted my life, hating and attacking other human beings, making my life miserable for myself and everyone else. I finally realized that this was what many others, Black and White had been doing . . . It is that easy to be part of the destruction of humanity. I know now that I used to live this passive existence as a sort of "pawn" of my circumstances. But I still don't know—as "corny" as it may sound—who I really am. I still don't understand and can't explain my life. All of my awareness doesn't help me to accept or fully understand why men force people into horrible ghettos like Harlem, send children to wars, drop bombs on churches, hang men, kill Presidents, or drop an Atom Bomb on Nagasaki.

I wrote that essay a long time ago, as a somewhat dramatic youth. A lot has changed since then. I have marched and sat-in, been arrested and jailed for civil rights actions, sung and yelled and been carried to police vans. It was not, however, until my second masters' and a doctorate at Columbia University that I began to realize that I might have something to contribute to psychology and to people. While working on my dissertation, which refuted some of Arthur Jensen's (1970) suggestions concerning the intellectual inferiority of blacks, a well-known Columbia University professor told me that my life proved Jensen's theory. It was, in his view, my "white genes" that accounted for my achievement in the face of adversity and "disadvantage!"

In addition to African American mothering influences on me, it is my early and continuing pain about ethnic/race relations that has inspired much of my motivation, career choice, research interests, and publications. My research concentration on race, IQ, and the middle class; race, IQ, and rampant misrepresentations; psychotherapy with black women and feminist and psychodynamic psychotherapy with African-American women (Trotman, 1977, 1978, 1984, 2000; Trotman and Gallagher 1987) results from my interests, born of early pain and confusion. My light skin and eventual middle-class trappings opened doors that would have remained closed if I were more obviously black and fit more closely to white America's preconceptions and stereotypes about African Americans. I am certain that my *look* also played a part in my affinity for education and educators' affinity for me. As a child, I always knew that teachers liked me. I didn't realize then that it was possibly because mine was the face in the Harlem classroom that looked most like theirs, the European American teachers who taught us. Things may have changed somewhat. Today my grandson is the only one in *his* school with gorgeous brown skin and beautiful kinky hair, and he is doing great. In fact, he is considered to be really "cool." With the advent of Tiger Woods and the latest term *multiracial*, I wait to see what happens next. My greatest fears are for when my grandson becomes a black or "multiracial" teenager, followed by retailers and feared by taxi drivers and police.

I have been a psychotherapist for over thirty years, and now I impart what I have learned to students in my newest role as a counselor at a small, private, predominantly white university. (I am the university's first and only tenured African American faculty member.) <u>I feel the weight and responsibility of being the only African American professor to whom many of these students will ever be exposed.</u> Most of them will at some time counsel African American clients, based, possibly, on stereotypes and half-truths. I may be the best hope they have of learning something "real" about black humanity, yet many of them do not initially see me as African American. Perhaps one of the best things that I can do is to introduce them to a little cognitive dissonance about racial differences. Students, who might ordinarily either idealize or dismiss me if I were more obviously African American, have the chance to get to know and perhaps like me as a teacher and as a person before they eventually learn or realize that I am black. Those students might otherwise never truly get to know, like, or respect an African American before they encounter one as a client. I still have much to do as a psychologist and educator. I hope that sharing myself, as I am now doing, will have an impact on future psychologists, that I can inspire my students as other African American mothers and grandmothers have inspired me.

AFRICAN AMERICAN WOMEN AS MOTHERS, FOREMOTHERS, AND OTHERMOTHERS

Influenced by my Harlem upbringing, and using the lens of an African American psychotherapist and educator, I examine the roles of African American mothers and foremothers. From my perspective as an African American granddaughter, daughter, mother, grandmother, and psychologist, I share subtleties of African American life, and perhaps I can contribute my knowledge of it to the practice of psychotherapy (see Trotman, 2000). In other volumes, I point out some important differences between black and white women (Trotman, 2000; Trotman and Gallagher, 1987). I would now like to look at some of the characteristics of African American women as mothers. How do we, the daughters, mothers, and grandmothers of African America, see each others and ourselves? Some well-known African Americans have spoken of their ancestral mothers. I will share some of their voices and examine their thoughts on African American mothering. As I conduct my examination, I hope that the reader will gain knowledge and glimpse a piece of African American life with which the study and practice of psychology can be expanded and enriched.

Given the isolating and peculiar nature of enslavement, racism, discrimination, and oppression in America, many of the seventeenth-, eighteenth- and nineteenth-century West African tribal customs, values, and attitudes brought here by our ancestors have been retained and passed on by our foremothers. Williams and Trotman (1984) examined four areas that contribute to the uniqueness of the African American female experience: (1) physical characteristics; (2) historical/social/cultural dynamics; (3) emotional/intellectual characteristics; and (4) sex roles and male/female relationships (see also Trotman, 2000). As I have written: "An oral rather than a literary tradition, polyrhythmic musical influences, black English, an extended family, the central role of religion, as well as different values, priorities, and attitudes are all African and slavery influences that have been perpetuated across centuries in the United States by racism and isolation" (Trotman and Gallagher, 1987, p. 119).

Naomi Lowinsky (1990) gave a name to the generations of women who carry within them the history and biology of a family: the grandmother, daughter, granddaughter, and great-granddaughter. She calls them the "Motherline." Grandmother is not only a tie to female ancestors but symbolizes for female family members their future as women. The grandmother has the paradoxical function of joining mother to her daughter by separating them, by offering a more objective, less personalized stance than they can assume on their own, and she also offers a "transcendent function to the younger generations" (Lowinsky, 1990, pp. 87–99).

Being an African American granddaughter, daughter, mother, and grandmother, I have experienced the power of Lowinsky's "Motherline." As the grandmother of my single daughter's son and my married daughter's daughters, I reflect on my role as "the grandmother archetype which guides . . . in our development, allowing us to unfold in harmony with our feminine selves and to experience the cyclical nature of life, not as a limitation, but as a vehicle for individuation" (Lowinsky, 1990, p. 97). What do our culture and our African and slave ancestral legacies bring to our roles, places, and significance as a link to our history and future in this description? African culture honors the ancestors as a significant guiding force. Eighteenth- and nineteenth-century African tribal customs and attitudes about the interdependence of the extended family and the role of the mothering influences are consistent with Lowinsky's description of the Motherline (Cattell, 1994). "It is in the grandchildren that ancestral spirits are reborn" (Blacking, 1990, p. 120).

Indeed in the African American culture, the grandmother often plays a central role in the parenting of her grandchildren. Kennedy (1991) found that of all the groups studied, African American grandchildren were closest to their grandmothers. Many African American children are being born to single mothers, and often it is the grandmother who has the major responsibility for mothering the African American child.

African American grandmothers are also the ones who have directly experienced and can place in perspective important aspects of our history (Ruiz, 2004). Currently, African American grandmothers were alive before the 1964 civil rights law was enacted. We experienced Jim Crow and know firsthand about the humiliation, degradation, and soul-destroying oppression of America in the 1940s and 1950s. Many of us protested. We were arrested. We risked our lives, and laws were changed. We also experienced a time when, no matter how poor, the African American community really was a "village" where everyone took responsibility for raising the children. I was born and raised in Harlem before drugs, crime, and fear became rampant. We left our doors open day and night so that the infrequent summertime breeze could flow from one apartment to another, and the children could easily decide which aromas would attract them to which neighbor's dinner table that evening. There was "always room fo' one mo' child" at whichever table enticed our senses. Our community was both a symbol of and a haven against ravages of discrimination and racism.

Often my own mother's words reverberate in my mind. Many of her "sayings," though not restricted to our ethnic group, reflect the same sentiments with which many African American women were raised: "Mama may have, and papa may have, but God bless the child that's got her own";[1] "Where there's a will, there's a way"; "The Lord helps those who help themselves"; "I'd scrub Macy's lobby to provide for my daughter"; and "Anything worth doing is worth doing well."

My mother was an orphan and never knew her mother. My father's mother died when he was four years old. I never knew a biological grandmother, but I felt the love and significance of my African American friends' grandmothers and othermothers. Mama Sellers was my best friend's grandmother, and I felt her strength, love, and power. Other "community mothers" (see Troester, 1984) similarly impressed me. Now, in my role as a grandmother, I am awed by the power and responsibility of my position. In my efforts to discern how much of my experience is universal to the African American community as opposed to idiosyncratically mine, I review in the next section the thoughts and some of the maternal words of advice given to some of my African American sisters.

Understanding the roles and words of African American mothers, foremothers, and othermothers is important to the psychological understanding and treatment of African American women. The cultural history of African American mothering is indeed crucial to the interpretation of psychological theory. The belief that "the process of slavery and its . . . effects . . . on the African American, present a unique psychological development that is not comparable with any other group lacking such an experience" (p. 385) is echoed in the lives and words of African American mothers.

IN A DIFFERENT VOICE

In order to understand some common threads of black maternal influences, it is important to view how some of the daughters, mothers, and foremothers of African America see each other. Some well-known African American women have spoken of their mothers. Their voices and thoughts on African American mothering may contribute knowledge and a glimpse of African American life with which a psychological map can be detailed.

Depicting the African link in the role of motherhood, Maya Angelou reflected that "Africa is herself a mother—the mother of mankind. We Africans take motherhood as the most sacred condition that human beings can achieve" (Angelou, 1994a). The intensity of the African American mother/daughter connection was emphasized by singer Diana Ross, who reports that her mother said, "I'll be with you always, and even when you don't want me to be" (cited in Smith, 1978, p. 113), and by Audre Lorde when she exhorted, "We are African women and we know, in our blood's telling, the tenderness with which our foremothers held each other" (Lorde, 1984, p. 152).

Maya Angelou (1994b) expressed both inspiration and a sense of responsibility when she wrote the poem "And Still I Rise," which so eloquently honors "the gifts that my ancestors gave" because we "are the hope and the dream of the slave" (Angelou, 1994b, p. 165). Similarly, Rosa Parks also spoke of her inspiration and stressed the perceived strength of African American grandmothers when she admitted she has "problems just like everyone else." When encountering those problems, she writes, "I think about my grandmother and my mother. They were such strong women" (Parks and Reed, 1994, p. 57).

Our culture recognizes the regal strength of black women. Many African American women demonstrated their strength through their work. We have always worked. Indeed we were brought to this country to be workers and breeders of workers. The well-known words of an early feminist, Sojourner Truth, speak of the strength exhibited by black women throughout our history (see Linthwaite, 1987, p. 129). The myth of the black superwoman, notwithstanding (see Romero, 2000; and Thompson, 2000), the attitudes of African American women concerning employment and their role in the family, as passed down from our foremothers, present a subtle difference from that of her European American counterpart. On the African American women's view of working outside the home, Mary Harrison, associate brand manager at Revlon, said, "Our mothers always assumed we would work outside the home. There was never a choice—work was a necessity, not a privilege. We would follow in the footsteps of our grandmothers and great grandmothers, working our fingers to the bones because 'money doesn't grow on trees! Girls,' she would say to my sisters and me, 'pray as though everything depended on God, but work as though everything depends on you'" (cited in Nikuradse, 1996, p. 155).

LEGACIES FROM OUR MOTHERS

Author Zora Neal Hurston was encouraged when her "mama exhorted her children at every opportunity to 'jump at de sun.' We might not land on the sun, but at least we would get off the ground" (Hurston, 1969). Filmmaker Julie Dash believed, "In my world Black women can do anything" (cited in Johnson, 1995, p. 15), and singer Lena Horn's "mother wanted me to be a star and I worked hard for her goal" (Home and Schickel, 1965).

Feminists had to *teach* white women that they are capable, but black women have always *assumed* that they are capable and proud. Gloria Wade-Gayles' mother said to her: "Keep your eyes on the prize. Move on ... She had a way of seeing around sharp corners, over high fences, beneath thick layers of confusion and uncertainty to the very center of truth and practicality. She had a 'single eye' she would tell my sister and me. 'A single eye,' that eye was focused on my sister and me, on our wholeness, our ability to stand tall in the light of our own suns" (Wade-Gayles, 1991, p. 214).

White feminists are often surprised and confused by our attitudes and behavior, which might reflect sentiments born of having already "been there and done that." For example, we may have less resentment of full-time mothering, having rarely had the opportunity and less excitement about the prospect of working outside the home. Author Charlayne Woodard told of her grandmother's desire to rest:

> When the women's lib movement came about, we were all very anxious to hear grandmama's views on the subject. She gathered her granddaughters around her. She said, "Generations and generations of Woodard women have always had ... the opportunity ... to work like a man, at a man's job. Oh, we have all worked in the fields, chopped wood, driven trucks, and tractors, and buses. I myself worked on the railroad during the war. A woman must always be prepared to do whatever she has to do for the sake of her family and her loved ones ... But if any of you should find a nice young man ... he comes walking down the street, and this young man just happens to be offering you a pedestal, I want you to climb on it, and take a nap for me." (Woodard, 1995, p. 42)

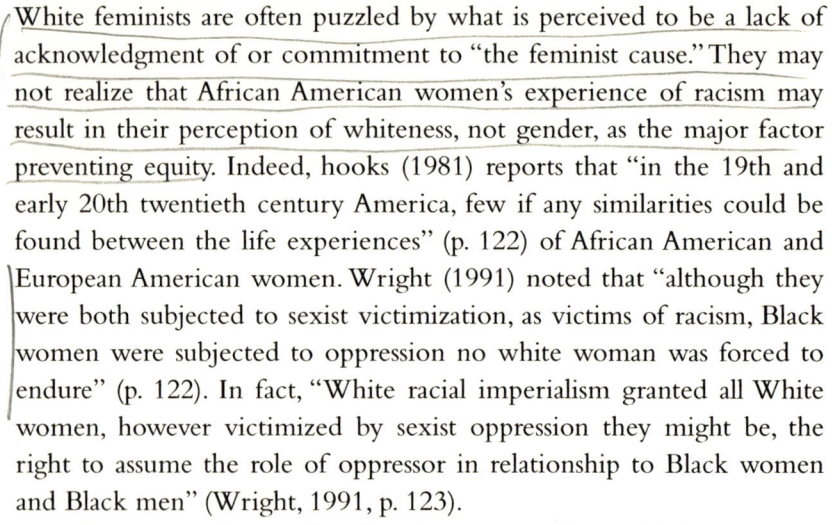

White feminists are often puzzled by what is perceived to be a lack of acknowledgment of or commitment to "the feminist cause." They may not realize that African American women's experience of racism may result in their perception of whiteness, not gender, as the major factor preventing equity. Indeed, hooks (1981) reports that "in the 19th and early 20th twentieth century America, few if any similarities could be found between the life experiences" (p. 122) of African American and European American women. Wright (1991) noted that "although they were both subjected to sexist victimization, as victims of racism, Black women were subjected to oppression no white woman was forced to endure" (p. 122). In fact, "White racial imperialism granted all White women, however victimized by sexist oppression they might be, the right to assume the role of oppressor in relationship to Black women and Black men" (Wright, 1991, p. 123).

Many West African cultural traditions, attitudes, and behaviors were preserved by our foremothers in the lives of the enslaved in the United States. Jules-Rosette (1980), for example, identified six distinctive features of West African spirituality incorporated into the religious practices of African Americans, presumably passed down by African American women who were the caretakers of spirituality (see Jules-Rosette, 1980, p. 275). Even if African American families are not actively involved in a particular church, their religious heritage will probably shape their beliefs and values. In order to make well-informed intervention decisions with African American clients, it is important that the feminist psychologist is aware that the religious background and the influence of the foremothers may shape attitudes and practices.

African American mothers have acquired and continue to need strength to fight for and protect their children, argued Johnetta B. Cole as she wrote:

> This experience is inevitable. Even if the child attends an elite preparatory school or lives in a "liberal" neighborhood, that child is going to be hurt by racism. When a child, asks "Mama what's a nigger" or says, "Mama, Joanie said her parents told her not to play with me," the pain and frustration a mother experiences is almost indescribable. What should she tell her child who is black? An enormous tribute is owed African American parents,

particularly mothers, who for years have had the responsibility of providing balm for the wounds racism inflicted upon their children and the task of counseling them on how to weave their ways through and around its horrors. (Cole, 1993, pp. 72–73)

Author Annette Jones White expressed evidence of her African American mother's influence and concern as she acknowledged that her "mother's careful rearing of me made me see how wrong, unfair, and humiliating it was to have to live [with the knowledge] that your children might come to harm for just being themselves" (White, 1991, p. 188).

Collins (1991) has observed that, "ironically, feminist theory has . . . suppressed Black women's ideas" (Altman, 1995; Andolsen, 1986; Brown, 1995; Cross et al., 1982; Dill, 1983; Espin, 1995; Greene and Sanchez, 1997; Hall, Garrett-Akinsaya, Hucles, 2007; hooks, 1981; Smith, 1982). Yet it is important to not underestimate the role of those ideas and the significance of African American mothers and grandmothers, and ancestors in the lives of African Americans. As Niara Sudarkasa observes, "The African American family structure evolved from African family structure[s], in which [the strength of African cultures] has been the flexibility and adaptability of their family organization" (Sudarkasa, 1993, pp. 81–89). Such legacies of black history and African cultural derivatives may have afforded African American women some degree of resilience that some European American women may lack (Carey, 1979; Kuppersmith, 1987; Mahmoud, 1998).

It is often difficult for those unfamiliar with African American culture to understand and not pathologize the flexible and adaptive roles of foremothers in African American families. They are often not only a source of comfort and pleasure but also of identification, strength, history, and inspiration. Psychologists and psychotherapists must understand not only the impact of specific mothers, but also the significance of African American mothering in general.

We often speak of growth through feminine relationships, and we might theoretically espouse Lowinsky's (1990) mother archetype, which reflects growth through the female ancestral relationship. Successful African American women have often used their mothers and foremothers as guides to their development, which allow them to unfold in harmony with their feminine selves and to experience the cyclical nature of life not as limitation, but as a vehicle for individuation.

In practice, particularly non-African American psychologists must be mindful not to impose their values on their African American clients' maternal struggles and life experiences. If so they may tend to see the African American adult daughter/mother symbioses as pathological. In particular, as economic forces compel more adult children to stay or return home, we might want to further investigate some of the positive aspects of African American mothering and the role of the extended family in fostering mental health and happiness.

Moreover, if we are to attempt to expand psychology, we must continue to examine the parental influences and significance of African American mothers, foremothers, and other mothers from the African American woman's point of view. The pervasiveness of psychologists' white privilege (Wildman, 1996) and their roles in racial oppression have not been sufficiently considered (see Altman, 1995). Much of adult personality, as well as problems that may arise from repressed emotions during childhood, are presumed to have their basis in conflictual relationships with significant caregivers; yet the concepts of mothers and mothering are based on white middle-class constructs and leave psychologists with "a poor understanding of child care relationships in the many diverse contexts in which contemporary mental health clinicians encounter them" (Greene, 1997). Psychologists may want to continue to examine the words and stories of African American mothers and foremothers for a clearer sense of the meaning of motherhood and mothering for African Americans.

Among the tasks of psychologists/psychotherapists is to help the student/client to discover how the past influences the present. An underlying assumption in this endeavor is that both share and at least understand the same language of nuanced experiences. Complicating this endeavor is that the same word, spelled in exactly the same way in the English language, can mean very different things as spoken by the African American as opposed to her European American sister. The result of this miscommunication can, at best, mean little discovery of how one's actual past influenced the present and, at worst, a professional pathologizing with its concomitant lowering of the African American's knowledge and self-esteem.

As psychology begins to broaden its sites to include, for examination, the full array of diversity among women, and the different shapes and effects of various types of oppression on women, perhaps psychology/psychotherapy will soon begin to have the language and understandings with which to assist African American women in uncovering and interpreting their psychological determinants and the accompanying leadership implications for black women's lives.

NOTES

1. This saying is derived from the song "God Bless the Child," written by Billie Holiday and Arthur Herzog Jr. in 1939, first recorded on May 9, 1941, under the Okeh label. http://en.wikipedia.org/wiki/God_Bless_the_Child_(Billie_Holiday_song)

REFERENCES

Altman, N. (1995). *The analyst in the inner city: Race, class, and culture through a psychoanalytic lens.* New York: Analytic.

Andolsen, B. H. (1986). *Daughters of Jefferson, daughters of bootblacks: Racism and American feminism.* Macon, GA: Mercer University Press.

Angelou, M. (1994a). *And still I rise.* New York: Random House.

Angelou, M. (1994b). *The complete collected poems of Maya Angelou.* New York: Random House.

Bernal, G., Trimble, J. E., Burlew, A. K., Leong, F. T. L. (2003). Introduction: The psychological study of racial and ethnic minority psychology. In G. Bernal, J. E. Trimble, A. K. Burley, and F. T. L. Leong (Eds.), *Handbook of racial and ethnic minority psychology* (pp. 1–12). Thousand Oaks, CA: Sage.

Blacking, J. (1990). Growing old gracefully: Physical, social, and spiritual transformations in NDA society, 1956–66. In P. H. Spencer (Ed.), *Anthropology and the riddle of the sphinx: Paradoxes of change in the life course* (pp. 112–30). New York: Routledge.

Brown, L. S. (1995). Antiracism as an ethical norm in feminist therapy practice. In J. Adleman & G. Enguidanos (Eds.), *Racism in the lives of women: Testimony, theory, and guides to antiracist practice* (pp. 137–48). New York: Haworth.

Carey, P. M. (1979). Black women: A perspective. *Tenth-Year Anniversary Commemorative Monograph Series, 1* (3). New York: New York University Institute for Afro-American Affairs.

Cattell, M. G. (1994). Nowadays it isn't easy to advise the young: Grandmothers and granddaughters among Abaluya of Kenya. *Journal of Cross-Cultural Gerontology, 9,* 157–78.

Cole, J. B. (1993). Conversations. *Monograph Series, 1* (3). New York University, Institute for Afro-American Affairs. New York: Doubleday.

Collins, P. (1991). *Black feminist thought.* New York: Routledge.

Cross, T., Klein, F., & Smith, B. (1982). Face-to-face, day-to-day, racism-CR. In G. Hull, P. B. Scott, & B. Smith (Eds.), *But some of us are brave* (pp. 52–56). Old Westbury, NY: Feminist.

Davis, A.Y. (1989). *Women, culture, and politics.* New York: Random House.

Dill, B. T. (1983). Race, class, and gender: Prospects for an all-inclusive sisterhood. *Feminist Studies 9* (1), 131–50.

Espin, O. (1995). On knowing you are the unknown: Women of color constructive psychology. In J. Adleman & G. Enguidanos (Eds.), *Racism in the lives of women: Testimony, theory, and guides to antiracist practice* (pp. 127–35). New York: Haworth.

Fox, D., Prilleltensky, I., and Austin, S. (2009). Critical psychology for social Justice: Concerns and dilemmas. In D. Fox, I. Prilleltensky, and S. Austin (Eds), *Critical psychology: An Introduction* (pp. 5–19). London: Sage.

Greene, B. (1995). An African American perspective on racism and anti-semitism within feminist organizations. In J. Adleman & G. Enguidanos (Eds.), *Racism in the lives of women: Testimony, theory, and guides to antiracist practice* (pp. 303–13). New York: Haworth.

Greene, B. (1997). Psychotherapy with African American women: Integrating feminist and psychodynamic models. *Smith College Studies in Social Work, 67,* 299–322.

Greene, B. (2000). African American lesbians and bisexual women in feminist-psychodynamic psychotherapies: Surviving and thriving between a rock and a hard place. In L. C. Jackson & B. Greene (Eds.), *Psychotherapy with African American women: Innovations in psychodynamic perspectives and clinical applications* (pp. 82–125). New York: Guilford.

Greene, B., & Sanchez, J. (1997). Diversity: Advancing an inclusive feminist psychology. In J. Worell & N. Johnson (Eds.), *New directions in education and training for feminist psychology practice* (pp. 173–202). Washington, DC: American Psychological Association Press.

Hall, R. L., Garrett-Akinsaya, B., Hucles, M. (2007). Voices of Black feminist leaders: Making spaces for ourselves. In J. L. Chin (Ed.). *Women and leadership: Transforming visions and diverse voices* (pp. 281–96). Malden, MA: Blackwell.

hooks, b. (1981). *Ain't I a woman: Black women and feminism.* Boston: South End.

Horne, L., & Schikel, R. (1965). *Lena.* New York: Doubleday.

Hurston, Z. N. (1969). *Dust Tracks on the Road.* New York: Arno.

Jensen, A. R. (1970). Can we and should we study race differences? In J. Hellmuth (Ed.), *Disadvantaged child, 3: Compensatory education: A national debate* (pp. 24–57). New York: Brunner Matzel.

Johnson, D. J. (1995). *Proud sisters.* New York: Peter Pauper.

Jules-Rosette, B. (1980). Creative spirituality from Africa to America: Cross-cultural influences in contemporary religious forms. *Western Journal of Black Studies, 4,* 273–85.

Kennedy, G. E. (1991). Grandchildren's reasons for closeness with grandparents. *Journal of Social Behavior and Personality, 6,* 697–712.

Kuppersmith, J. (1987). The double bind of personal striving: Ethnic working class women in psychotherapy. *Journal of Contemporary Psychotherapy, 17* (3), 203–16.

Linthwaite, I. (1987). *Ain't I a woman: Poems of Black and white women.* New York: Bedrock.

Lorde, A. (1984). *Sister outsider: Essays and speeches.* New York: Crossing.

Lowinsky, N. R. (1990). Mother of mothers: The power of grandmother in the female psyche. In C. Zweig (Ed.), *To be a woman: The birth of the conscious feminine* (pp. 87–99). Los Angeles: Tarcher.

Mahmoud, V. (1998). The double binds of racism. In M. McGoldrick (Ed.), *Revisioning family therapy: race, culture, and gender in clinical practice* (pp. 255–67). New York: Guilford.

Mays, V. (1985). The black American psychotherapy: The dilemma. *Psychotherapy, 22* (2), 379–88.

Moraha, C., & Anzaldua, G. (Eds.). (1981). *This bridge called my back: Writings by radical women of color.* Watertown, MA: Persephone.

Nikuradse, T. (1996). *My mother had a dream: African-American women share their words of wisdom.* New York: Penguin.

Parks, R., & Reed, G. (1994). *Quiet Strength.* Michigan: Zondervan.

Romero, R. (2000). The icon of the strong black woman: The paradox of strength. In L. C. Jackson & B. Greene (Eds.), *Psychotherapy with African American women: Innovations in psychodynamic perspectives and clinical applications* (pp. 225–38). New York: Guilford.

Ruiz, D. S. (2004). *Amazing grace: African American grandmothers as caregivers and conveyors of traditional values.* Westport, CT: Greenwood.

Smith, B. (1982). Racism and women's studies. In G. Hull, P. B. Scott, & B. Smith (Eds.), *All the women are white, all the blacks are men, but some of us are brave: Black women's studies* (pp. 52–56). Old Westbury, New York: Feminist.

Smith, L. (1978). *The mother book.* New York: Doubleday.

Sudarkasa, N. (1993). Female-headed African-American households: Some neglected dimensions. In H. P. McAdoo (Ed.). *Family ethnicity: Strength in diversity* (pp. 81–89). Newbury Park, CA: Sage.

Thompson, C. (2000). African American women and moral masochism: When there is too much of a good thing. In L. C. Jackson & B. Greene (Eds.), *Psychotherapy with African American women: Innovations in psychodynamic perspectives and clinical applications* (pp. 239–50). New York: Guilford.

Troester, R. R. (1984). Turbulence and tenderness: Mothers, daughters, and othermothers. P. Marshall, *Brown Girl Brownstones*. *Sage: A Scholarly Journal on Black Woman, 1* (2), 13–16.

Trotman, F. K. (1977). Race, IQ, and the middle class. *Journal of Educational Psychology, 69*, 266–73.

Trotman, F. K. (1978). Race, IQ, and rampant misrepresentations: A reply. *Journal of Educational Psychology, 70*, 478–81.

Trotman, F. K. (1984). Psychotherapy with black women and the dual effects of racism and sexism. In C. M. Brody (Ed.), *Women therapists working with women: New theory and process of feminist therapy*. Springer Series: Focus on women, volume 7 (pp. 96–108). New York: Springer.

Trotman, F. K. (2000). Feminist and psychodynamic psychotherapy with African American U.S. women: Some differences. In L. C. Jackson & B. Greene (Eds.), *Psychotherapy with African American women: Innovations in psychodynamic perspectives and clinical applications* (pp. 258–74). New York: Guilford.

Trotman, F. K., & Gallagher, A. H. (1987). Group therapy with black women. In C. M. Brody (Ed.), *Women's therapy groups: Paradigms of feminist treatment*. Springer Series: Focus on Women 10 (pp. 118–31). New York: Springer.

Wade-Gayles, G. (1991). Connected to mama's spirit. In P. Bell-Scott & B. Guy-Sheftall (Eds.), *Double stitch: Black women write about mothers and daughters* (pp. 214–38). Boston: Beacon.

White, A. J. (1991). Dyad/Triad. In P. Bell-Scott & B. Guy-Sheftall (Eds.), *Double stitch: Black women write about mothers and daughters* (pp. 188–95). Boston: Beacon.

Williams, B., & Trotman, F. K. (1984, April). *Black women: The original superwomen*. Paper presented at Annual Meeting, New York State Psychological Association, New York.

Wildman, S. (1996). *Privilege revealed: How invisible preference undermines America*. New York: New York University Press.

Woodard, C. (1995). *Pretty fire*. New York: Penguin.

Wright, M. (1991). African American sisterhood: The impact of the female slave population on American political movements. *Western Journal of Black Studies. 15* (1), 32–45.

2

Sisterlocking Power

Or How Is Leadership Supposed to Look?

VALERIE LEE

> What can we say then about the representation of the black female body as we begin the twenty-first century? Perhaps simply that history repeats itself given that this body remains a highly contested site of meaning both within and without the black community and that African American women still struggle with its representation, vacillating between the poles of sentimental normalization and the flaunting of eccentricity.
> —Carla L Peterson, "Eccentric Bodies"

> Without organized struggles like the ones that happened in the 1960s and early 1970s, individual black women must struggle alone to acquire the critical consciousness that would enable us to examine issues of race and beauty, our personal choices, from a political standpoint.
> —bell hooks, "Straightening Our Hair"

"WHY DO COLORED PEOPLE always have to disfigure themselves?" At the height of the civil rights movement, this is the question that my grandmother, Lydia Sardonia Morris Bell, asked her Afro-sporting, dashiki-wearing grandchildren. Lydia, or Ma Bell, as everyone in the community called her, had been a beauty in her heyday, a heyday that described beauty as light skinned with "good hair" (long, silky tresses). She was quick to say that some of her "yellow had been wasted"[1] from having married two very black men. Her recessive genes produced only one fair-skinned child and no children who carried forth the blue and green eyes of her brothers. Nevertheless, she was very proud of her three daughters and especially her seven sons. She claimed that she also had a set of twin sons who died in infancy, but no one in the family has been able to verify that tale. Her own grandmother, the last female slave in the family, had fourteen sons who were all sold from the "Carolinas to Florida," as Grandma explained it.

By the time that I came along, her first grandchild and only four years younger than her last child, my Uncle Brooke, Ma Bell was stooped-shouldered with very few years left—or so we thought. When angry, she would curse us with the threat, "These trees will see you under."[2] Having a knack for life herself, she died in 1999, one hundred years after the date she was born. She had lived long enough to watch "colored people" go through all kinds of changes. I remember the day that a distant cousin, Freddie Hawkins, corrected the terms that she was using:

"Colored people—" Freddie interrupted her tirade, "we're not colored anymore, Ma Bell."

"Colored people, Negroes, blacks, whatever y'all are calling yourselves now," Grandmother retorted.

It wasn't that Grandma worshipped white people. She didn't. In fact, she couldn't stand most of them. She had worked in the homes of too many upper-class folks from as far south as Baltimore, Maryland, to as far north as Greenwich, Connecticut, to think that race was a determinate of manners, or intelligence, or anything that really mattered. Ma Bell never doted over white children or held her lip when sassin' white employers. And she was quite protective of her race when whites criticized blacks in her presence. During Nixon's presidency, one of her employers expressed her joy that Nixon had taken crime off the streets of Washington D.C. My grandmother's swift reply was, "He took it off the streets and placed it in the White House."

A very smart woman, Ma Bell was especially protective whenever anyone hinted that her children or grandchildren were not intelligent. From the time I was very young, she was quite proud of how well I could read. Once, when I was around eight years old, I went to visit her in one of those Greenwich, Connecticut, mansions where she worked as cook, maid, nanny, whatever was needed. (Of course, this meant that her ten children were in Maryland without a mother because out of necessity she had to mammy someone else). Grandma overheard me arguing with a little white girl who was the same age as I was. We both wanted to read the story and were fighting over the opportunity to do so. In a whirlwind, Grandma raced in the room, grabbed the book from the white girl and announced, "My granddaughter can read." I felt vindicated. Slaves may not have learned how to read, but her granddaughter knew how to read and read well. And I was just as proud of my grandmother's explanation when fourteen years later at my graduation from a private college in New England, a white woman asked her to explain the foreign words (*magna cum laude*) attached to my name. Unable to read Latin, but knowing that I had studied abroad in France, Grandma used her sharp wit to quickly formulate a response: "When one has traveled, one's name must reflect all the places where one has been."

I grew up watching my grandmother assume all kinds of leadership roles. Her style was to do what was needed to get the job done. When we grandchildren got on her nerves, she would take her five-foot, one-inch frame and swing us against the walls or shake us silly. Today, she would be arrested for child abuse. Back then, she raised grandchildren, neighborhood children, and foster children, and we all loved the many birthday parties she threw for us, the freedoms she gave to us that only grandparents know how to give, and the open house that she kept. She hated going to senior citizen classes because old people bored her. Instead, she enjoyed young people, eventually embracing all of the identity changes and racial politics that we were expounding.

As with so many African American women, Ma Bell used the moments while braiding hair to dispense her wisdom. Of course the changing era of the 1960s was a time when both boys and girls, men and women were having their hair braided. As the narrator states in *Dessa Rose*, Sherley Anne Williams's neoslave narrative, "Child learn a lot of things setting between some grown person's legs, listening at grown peoples speak over they heads."[3] Ma Bell, who lived through perms, 'fros, jherri curls, hair extensions, and synthetic and human hair braids, never missed a moment using hair as a site of political struggle.

When she lost most of her hair, she refused to wear a wig, declaring that "you are what you are, and this is what I am. Besides it's not what's on your head; it's what's in it."

When Ma Bell was in her eighties and nineties, her arthritic fingers prevented her from braiding the hair of her great-grandchildren. She no longer had a captive audience to tell her tales of how she had set people and the world straight. On trips home, I tried to explain to her what I did in my new role as a departmental chair. She concluded that I wasn't teaching; rather I was running the whole university. As someone who had worked several jobs all of her life, she was not surprised by the long hours that I labored; she never expected me to stay home, even after I gave birth to twins and had four children under the age of four. She worked; my mother worked; I work. My one regret is that by the time I had moved fully into my women's studies office, she was ninety-nine years old and too weak to travel to visit me. Had she been able to visit, she would probably have made a comment about my office décor, a comment that I would translate to mean a commodification of Africanness. Nevertheless, she would approve of the Haitian and Jamaican sculpture on my bookshelves, the copper figurine of five women of color holding hands called "Feminist Five," the Varnette Honeywood paintings, the headragged woman that a friend made for me in her ceramics class, and all kinds of other odds and ends that occasioned one visitor to my office to ask, "How do you think this office will make white students feel?" No one has ever asked black students how the offices of white faculty make them feel. The offices of white faculty are seen as the norm, their decorating habits are seen as neutral, so anything different risks being judged as poor professional taste. Audiences are assumed to be white. As Toni Morrison says in her preface to *Playing in the Dark*, "until very recently, and regardless of the race of the author, the readers of virtually all of American fiction have been positioned as white."[4] I would truly learn this when years after chairing a women's studies department, I became the first woman, and of course, the first African American, to chair a very large Department of English. One day, while sitting in my office during my first year as chair of English, I was going through some decades old files and I came across a letter from a woman who had given scholarship money to the department. She specified that she did not want any of the money to go to Negro or Jewish students. Although the note trembled a little in my hand, I was not that fazed by that part of the inscription. Who does not know about restrictive housing covenants and the long history of Jim Crow? What caught my eyes, however, was her remark that preceded the inscription, "I trust the Chair will make sure that no Negro or Jewish students receive the money." "I trust the Chair," the benefactor wrote. I do not know if she ever imagined a woman chair; but she certainly did not imagine a black chair. She probably imagined a white male chair in a blue three-piece pin-stripped suit whose mission was to preserve the sanctity of a male Eurocentric canon, faculty, and student body. "I trust the Chair"—I reread the note and keep repeating, "You can't trust the chair. Don't trust the chair . . ."

★ ★ ★

A few months after Ma Bell died, I ended my first year as chair of the Department of Women's Studies. The editor of the department's newsletter asked me for the obligatory column on what I had learned about administration. What I had learned, however, had nothing to do with the fundamentals of management. My learning had its own set of Murphy's Laws: on the one morning when you decide not to read the fifty new e-mail messages, the provost, trustees, and state legislators will change the location of the 7:30 a.m. power-breakfast meeting; on the one college survey that you decide to complete the night before it is due, question 15 will ask you for information that you needed to have begun compiling ten days earlier; on the one day that your fiscal officer is on vacation, the dean will ask you a complicated question about the budget. So I was still too caught up in the minutiae of all the paperwork on my desk to write a column that aspired to heights higher than the stack of memoranda in my in-box.

As an alternative, my editor asked if I would do a typical "state-of-the-department" address. Well, my department is an excellent one, and I could have easily written this type of message. However, having recently attended my daughter's high school graduation and the graduations of eight of my friends' children, I didn't want to hear another word about "success," "dreams," or "achievement." Rather, I chose to write a column about what made me most apprehensive about assuming the position of a departmental chair: hair politics.

That's right. Hair politics. But not just any type of hair politics—African American women's hair politics. The Ma Bell arguing with her children type of hair politics. The type of hair politics that Ntozake Shange celebrates in *Nappy Edges*, that Audre Lorde questions in her article "Is Your Hair Still Political?" and bell hooks supports in "Straightening Our Hair"—the type of hair politics that Gwendolyn Brooks lauds in her poem "To Those of My Sisters Who Kept Their Naturals, Never Again to Look a Hot Comb in the Teeth," or the type that Alice Walker exposes in her essay "Oppressed Hair Puts a Ceiling on the Brain." I had spent a considerable amount of my personal time during my first year as chair thinking about the type of nappy hair that Lucille Clifton links to "tasty greens" and Toni Morrison describes in *Tar Baby* as "wild, aggressive, vicious hair that needed to be put in Jail. Uncivilized, reform-school hair. Mau, Attica, chain-gang hair." Just when I reached the point in my career when I wanted to "go natural" (because full professors can go anywhere they want), I was asked to make a rather conservative move—become a departmental chair.

In workshops for new chairs, there are sessions on tenure and promotion, on what to do when there is money in the budget and what to do when there isn't. There are workshops on how to handle difficult colleagues, write annual review letters, job appointment letters, promotion and tenure letters, thank-you-to- donor letters—everything except how to wear one's hair in the "natural" styles available to black women and still look "professional." Obviously, African American women aren't the ones running the faculty training workshops at most research intensive universities. Otherwise, gender and racial representation of leadership would be on the agendas.

As a full professor, especially one in women's studies, I could have sat in my office and balded, spiked, purpled, or done anything I wanted to my hair. Among our undergraduate and graduate students, nothing I could have done with my hair would have seemed odd. But as a *chair*, I had to go out and greet people who still think afros are radical or the new wave of black teens wearing bantu knot, cornrow, and sisterlock[5] hairstyles are too ethnic. How would I look in what sistahs call "sisterlocks," but what many outside African American communities, and even some within, call "dreadlocks"? The difference between the two words is the difference between affection and fear. Reportedly, the term "dreadlocks" came about when Europeans first encountered Africans' hair in locked styles. They saw the hair as "dreadful."

Just when I was prepared to go cold turkey with my plan (the first step in locking relaxed or processed hair is to cut off all your hair), I had to come up with an alternative that would not be as shocking. As a new department chair, I had to revert to a longer, more gradual plan of growing and cutting and braiding and unbraiding. I know that some people noticed that I had at least five major changes of hairstyle that first year and wanted to know why but were too polite to ask. Here's the answer: everything was in preparation for locking, a style thought to be more fitting for the Ziggy Marleys and Lauryn Hills of the world than those who wield academic power. Although Alice Walker and Toni Morrison proudly wear dreadlocks, they are not department chairs. The decision I most debated was which type of locks I wanted: combed twists, two-stranded twists, Nubian locks, silky locks, genie locks, extension locks, sisterlocks . . . One can check out the full photo gallery on many online sites.

In women's studies, we discuss issues relating to body politics. And certainly in black women's studies the body has always been a contested site. Whole categories of black women have been dismissed, derided, and devalued based on their bodies. When conducting research on the dwindling numbers of black lay midwives who delivered a nation of babies during the first decades of the twentieth century, I discovered that one of the ways that health officials discredited them was through their physical appearance and their bodily parts. They were told that their hands that had "caught" so many babies were too "fleshy" and unclean. When County Health Boards aggressively began to intervene in the lives of black lay midwives, they began by attacking their bodies. Many started to treat them "as if the grannies were black [Pontius] Pilates, continually trying to wash off historical prejudices which had already been inscribed on their bodies."[6] In addition to the bodies of black lay midwives, the bodies of black mothers themselves have been the subject of much critique. In *Killing the Black Body*, Dorothy Roberts addresses the government's assault on the reproductive rights of black women. Again, it is a battle that takes place on the bodies of black women: "White childbearing is generally thought to be a beneficial activity: it brings personal joy and allows the nation to flourish. Black reproduction, on the other hand, is treated as a form of *degeneracy*."[7] In "Wearing Your Race Wrong: Hair, Drama, and a Politics of Representation for African American Women at Play on a Battlefield," Noliwe Rooks refers to the black female body as a battlefield where "the meaning of certain styles on a black female body come into conflict with individual understandings held by members of an outside group invested with the power and authority to bring those bodies and styles in line with what they believe to be acceptable."[8]

Although issues of class[9] very much inform selection of hairstyles, neither vocational nor socioeconomic class have made a marked difference in the ways in which black women's bodies have been dismissed. Black women who hold professional leadership roles have not escaped society's tendency to critique black women's bodies and hair technologies.[10] In 1980, Dorothy Reed, a television news reporter, was suspended by the station for wearing cornrows to work. KGO-TV argued the hair style was not "consistent" with the station's image.[11] The editors of *Hair Story: Untangling the Roots of Black Hair in America*, in chronicling the recent backlash on black hairstyles that are read by society as too natural or too nappy, point out that "while corporate America accepts yarmulkes, turbans, and other ethnic or religious signifiers, dreadlocks and other Black hairstyles are often seen as signs of militance and anger.[12] African American women in particular, as literary and cultural critic Ann DuCille points out, "by virtue of our race and gender, ... are not only the second sex—the other, in postmodern parlance—but also the last race, the most oppressed, the most marginalized, the most deviant, the quintessential site of difference, ... function[ing] as an erotic icon in the racial and sexual ideology of western civilization.[13]

In response to my grandmother who wondered why black people would want to "disfigure themselves," the critic in me would answer that black women are always already disfigured. From the time we first appeared on auction blocks in America, stripped to the waist and deeply probed, we have been asserting our bodily rights. In her introduction to *Recovering the Black Female Body*, Carla Peterson speaks of the ways in which black women have actively responded to bodily assaults and embraced the "eccentricity"[14] "acknowledge[ing] and honor[ing] the eccentric black female body." Since the 1990s, many black women professionals are choosing natural hair styles at the risk of their careers.

Defending black women's right to wear braided hairstyles in the workplace has been the subject of legal cases.

If Ma Bell were still alive, I would want her to know that my preoccupation with hair and leadership has little to do with hair itself. Rather, it's about agency and whose standards dare announce themselves as definitive in determining the technologies and economies of administrative arenas. Who defines professionalism and how it must look? If Ma Bell were still alive, she would rub her balding head and commend me for bringing to the academy the experiences of black women, their hair, and their leadership—experiences braided and coiled in the textures of sisterlocking power.

NOTES

1. "Yellow wasted" is a folk expression referring to blacks who do not make "effective use" of their light skin. "Marrying dark" dilutes the advantage of lightness. For a discussion of the politics of this type of "colorism," see Margo Natalie Crawford's analysis of Wallace Thurman's *The Blacker the Berry* in (2008) *Dilution Anxiety and the Black Phallus*.

2. This is a folk expression alluding to the long life cycle of trees as opposed to the brevity of human lives.

3. Sherley Anne Williams, *Dessa Rose* (New York: Berkley Books, 1986), p. 257.

4. Toni Morrison, *Playing in the Dark: Whiteness and the Literary Imagination* (Cambridge: Harvard University Press, 1992), p. xii.

5. Note that there are two spellings for locks (locs) and two spellings for dreadlocks (dredlocks).

6. Valerie Lee, *Granny Midwives and Black Women Writers: Double-Dutched Readings* (New York: Routledge, 1996), p. 38.

7. Dorothy Roberts, *Killing the Black Body: Race, Reproduction, and the Meaning of Liberty* (New York: Pantheon Books, 1997), p. 9.

8. Nowlie Rooks, "Wearing Your Race Wrong: Hair, Drama, and a Politics of Representation for African American Women at Play on a Battlefield," in *Recovering the Black Female Body: Self-Representations by African American Women*, (Ed.) Michael Bennett and Vanessa D. Dickerson (New Brunswick, NJ: Rutgers University Press, 2000), p. 284. For a historical overview of the topic of African American women's hair that pays particular attention to Madame C. J. Walker and the aesthetics of African American women's culture in general see

Rooks' book, *Hair Raising: Beauty, Culture, and African American Women* (New Brunswick: Rutgers University Press, 1998).

9. Many of the hairstyles with which African American women have experimented have been associated with "low class" taste, primarily because teenagers have been the major wearers of certain styles (e.g. synthetic extension braids) and also because some styles, such as the jheri curl, have required dripping hair, shower caps, and different types of sprays. Interestingly, locks have had a special appeal to African American women in academe.

10. Owens Patton, T. (2006), "Hey Girl, Am I More than My Hair? African American Women and the Struggles with Beauty, Body Image and Hair," *National Women's Studies Association Journal, 18* (2), pp. 24–51.

11. Mariame Kaba, "When Black Hair Tangles with White Power," in *Tenderheaded: A Comb-Bending Collection of Hair Stories*, (Ed.) Juliette Harris and Pamela Johnson (New York: Pocket Books, 2001), p. 106.

12. Ayana D. Byrd and Lori L. Tharps, *Hair Story: Untangling the Roots of Black Hair in America* (New York: St. Martin's, 2001), pp. 177–78.

13. Ann DuCille, *Skin Trade* (Cambridge, MA: Harvard University Press, 1996), p. 82.

14. Carla Peterson explains her use of "eccentric" in *Doers of the Word: African American Women Speakers and Writers in the North (1830–1880)* and in her "Foreword" to *Recovering the Black Female Body: Self-Representations by African American Women,* (Ed.) Michael Bennet and Vanessa D. Dickerson (New Brunswick, NJ: Rutgers University Press, 2000): "I have chosen to term the black female body 'eccentric,' insisting on its double meaning: the first evokes a circle not concentric with another, an axis not centrally placed (according to the dominant system), whereas the second extends the notion of off-centeredness to suggest freedom of movement stemming from the lack of central control and hence new possibilities of difference conceived as empowering oddness." *Recovering the Black Body*, pp. xi, xii.

REFERENCES

Byrd, A. D., & Tharps, L. L. (2001). *Hair story: Untangling the roots of black hair in America*. New York: St. Martin's.

Crawford, M. N. (2008). *Dilution Anxiety and the Black Phallus*. Columbus: Ohio State University Press.

DuCille, A. *Skin Trade* (1996). Cambridge, MA: Harvard University Press.

Kaba, M. (2001). "When black hair tangles with white power." In J. Harris and P. Johnson, (Eds), *Tenderheaded: A comb-bending collection of hair stories* (pp. 95-107). New York: Pocket Books.

Lee, V. (1996). *Granny midwives and black women writers: Double-Dutched writings.* New York: Routledge.

Morrison, T. (1992) *Playing in the dark: Whiteness and the literary imagination.* Cambridge: Harvard University Press.

Owens Patton, T. (2006). "Hey girl, am I more than my hair? African American women and the struggles with beauty, body image and hair." *National Women's Studies Association Journal 18* (2), 24–51.

Peterson, C. (1995). *Doers of the Word: African American women speakers and writers in the North (1830–1880).* New York: Oxford University Press.

Peterson, C. (2000). "Recovering the black body" (xi, xii). In M. Bennet & V. D. Dickerson (Eds.), *Recovering the black female body: Self-representations by African American women.* New Brunswick, NJ: Rutgers University Press.

Roberts, (1997). *Killing the black body: Race, reproduction and the meaning of liberty.* New York: Pantheon.

Williams, S. A. (1986). *Dessa Rose.* New York: Berkley Books.

3

Braiding My Place

Developing a Foundational Selfhood through Cross-Racial Mothering

Nancy Gibson

MY LIFE EXPERIENCE has been unique, because my family is unique. To understand my leadership development and the ultimate relationship that I had with my mother, you must first understand that I am an African American woman who was raised by Caucasian parents. I am the third child out of four children in an unusual family. I have a Caucasian brother (the natural son of my parents), a Hispanic brother, and a biracial sister whose heritage is African American and Italian. My Hispanic brother, my sister, and I were all adopted as babies, and we were born in different parts of the country—Minnesota, Colorado, and New York respectively. As a pastor, my father would receive a call to a new church, and he would move our family to a new part of the country. Curiously, my parents adopted children in each of these locations. We are certainly not a typical family by anyone's definition, and because of our uniqueness as a family we each had to deal with a variety of things ranging from racism to racial identity development, to how to fit into our community as a family composed of children who differ racially and ethnically from one another.

As an African American child of white parents I somehow always managed to stand out the most. With the help of my parents, especially my amazing mother, it always seemed like something I could deal with. Here I was—born in New York City and then adopted by this white couple, a Lutheran pastor and his wife, an elementary school teacher. From New York, they whisked me away to the mountains of Colorado, where I lived until the age of five. We moved from Colorado to a rural town in the Great Plains of Nebraska where we remained until I was thirteen.

In Nebraska, I actually think I was the only African American around for counties! People stared at me constantly and also stared at our entire family. The stares I received held an intensity that I was at a loss to comprehend at the tender age of five. To help me deal with this, my mother would always say to me, "If someone stares at you, just stare right back at them and smile . . . It will take them by surprise!" Amazingly, this simple advice worked, and I think that is why I smile so much to this day. Those simple words of instruction that gave me the confidence to stare right back at anyone became my first lesson in resistance to racial oppression. It took the form of silent messages from others that I "did not fit" into their picture of family, or their notion of belonging to the community, although for some it may simply have been just plain (albeit rude) curiosity. The fact that my early lessons in resistance came from my white mother is a testimony to how she tuned in to each of her children's particular needs based on our identities.

As young children in our multicultural family, we also had to learn about each other and how we each fit into the makeup of our family. We realized that we looked different from one another, but in time we also discovered that we had different personalities, characteristics, and dreams. Interestingly, we were all just about two years apart in age. In laughing, arguing, and playing together, we simultaneously learned about each other's cultures. Most poignant among these discoveries was the lesson that many of the negative comments we might have heard others say about us could be disastrously painful if you said them to your brother or sister. It was times like these when my mother would step in and help us understand each other and our unique family. I can remember a time when I was about six, and my Hispanic brother who was about eight called me the "n" word. My mother stepped in and scolded him and told him never to call me such a thing, because it was a hurtful and horrible word used back in the days of slavery and even now to degrade African Americans and make them feel unimportant. She reminded him that I was just as important as anyone else and that there also were horrible words out there used for Hispanic people and that those words would make him hurt just as much as this word was hurting me.

I can also remember one time when I was about six or seven years old and I went to the local swimming pool to swim. Upon my arrival, a little white boy said, "What are you doing here?" and I said, "Swimming, just like you!" He was stunned that I stood my ground, and he left me alone. That was evidence of the confidence that I had at such an early age. My parents made us deal with the issues directly. The outcome is that we were never scared to take a stand.

I saw my mother as the "Rock of Gibraltar" because she also faced adversity as a white woman with three "multicultural" children during the turbulent sixties and seventies. Somehow, because of the faith, love, and acceptance that we received from both of our parents, we never felt that we were strange; rather, we felt that others simply needed to become more comfortable about their own issues with who we were. Quite simply, she was my mother, and I was her child. I've always felt as if she had given birth to me, even though I look different from her. If I met my birth mother today I would feel uncomfortable calling her my real mother, because the amazing woman that raised me is the only mother I will ever know.

THE BRAIDING OF IDENTITY

My parents surrounded me with as much of my African American culture as white parents could, and I have appreciated that to this day. Some examples of the way that they helped to expose me to my culture occurred during my preschool years in Denver, Colorado. During that time, my parents had purchased a home in a multicultural neighborhood where I regularly had African American babysitters and many friends of different ethnicities and cultures. One of the stories I love to tell is that my mother even went to the trouble of learning how to braid hair. Some of the African American women in the neighborhood taught her. Every Saturday night (like so many African American mothers and daughters would), I would sit in the chair in the living room in front of the T.V. for hours, while she made the style of braids that I would request. She could do cornrows, French braids, and tiny braids with beads! Our hair braiding ritual gave us a chance to have time together to talk about life. Finding such one-on-one time could be difficult with a family of six people, so I treasured this time for contact and interaction with her. My mother's interest in my culture and me helped me to validate my identity. (After writing this chapter and telling the story of my mother braiding my hair, I came across a book on interracial adoption by Barbara Rothman (2006). When I saw the chapter entitled: "Hair: Braiding Together Culture, Identity, and Entitlement" (Rothman, 2006, p. 206), I smiled an "I knew that" smile to myself.)

One other significant memory for me that illustrates my mother's creativity was when there was a Bicentennial celebration in our small town in Nebraska. We decided as a family to participate in the festivities by being a part of the Bicentennial parade. My mother, being aware of how important each of our cultures was to us, came up with the idea that our family could walk in the parade as the United Nations. My sister and I wore dashikis, Afros, hoop earrings, and sandals, my brother wore the outfit of a Mexican dancer (sombrero and all), and my parents and oldest brother wore German and Norwegian outfits. I definitely felt special, and I think we taught our little town a life lesson that day, and as usual, I continued to be amazed by my mother's resourcefulness. She had the ability to transform the ordinary into the extraordinary or vice versa. In short, she had the uncanny ability of knowing how to turn a potential negative into a positive. Just as she had learned to braid my hair in Denver, Colorado, she had learned to braid each of us into our community. She seemed to know countless styles that took into account each person's needs, yet remained aware of the whole pattern. I always found my mother to be amazing in her ability to move between the details of day-to-day needs and the whole pattern of a project or organizational goal. Barbara Rothman's book *Weaving a Family* (2006) points to the importance of families transferring a sense of cultural pride and joy to the children. My leadership lesson does not stop with my mother's knowledge that cultural pride was needed by her multiracial brood. Rather my lesson extends to embrace the idea that she was so creative about how she did this. She made life resemble play, she epitomized joy, she effectively engaged in weaving a family, using an unlimited abundance of resources, ingenuity, and imagination. This I carry into my own leadership as an administrator in higher education. Ingenuity, imagination, and enthusiasm are among the strands I weave.

My mother taught me wonderful life lessons about respect, honesty, love, patience, faith, and understanding. She showed me how to just be myself. When I would get frustrated with something as a child and say, "But Mom, that's not fair," she would reply with, "Who ever said the world was fair?" and put me in my place. That simple statement has stayed with me to this day. In her response, not only would she address the issue that I was upset about, but she also made a powerful statement about the adversity in the world that I would continue to face. Sometimes it could be the simple things that she said that helped me understand the world and my role in it.

Because of our unique multicultural family composition, my very visible Blackness, and the very white environment we lived in, both of my parents helped me to develop a "thick skin" throughout my childhood and adolescence. There was a time when I was in high school in Lincoln, Nebraska, when I was doing community service by volunteering for a political campaign. One of my duties was to post campaign signs on the lawns of supporters. So one day after school I went to the home of a woman who wanted to have a sign in her yard and went to knock on her door. In the meantime, I noticed some white men standing over in another yard watching me. They began to yell things at me like, "You better leave you Black b—ch!" along with an array of ignorant comments. When I realized that the woman wasn't home, I promptly picked up my signs and went home to avoid the harassment and potential danger that I was in. When I reached the house, my father greeted me and clearly could see that something was wrong. After I told him the story, he wanted to head right back over there, but I feared for his safety. He asked me what I wanted to do. I said, "Hit them over the head with this hammer." But then I said, "I'd like to finish the job I started." So, I called the woman and asked her if I could stop by, and my father rode with me to put the signs up. I learned that day that regardless of how old you are, or how much you know, there is ignorance everywhere, and life will challenge you daily! Looking back, however, I also see how my mother and father were a team, sharing in their common vision that all of us kids would have the foundational support we needed to feel empowered despite the ignorance we encountered. Johnetta Cole and Beverly Guy-Sheftall share stories in their book *Gender Talk* (2003). They give examples of these "mothers and fathers who were somewhat gender-progressive in their child-rearing practices (Cole and Guy-Sheftall, 2003, p. 40). In my case their tag-team efforts resulted in support for all of us kids to find and express our strengths. For me, this was essential to my survival in the race-class-gender context of Nebraska. Looking back I see the emotional stronghold they helped me to build as the foundation of my leadership as well.

While my father clearly helped me create strategies to respond to racially charged incidents and structural injustices that I encountered, my mother was often someone I turned to for matters of the heart. It was with my mother that I shared those private musings and tender wounds that would be deeply etched in the soul of the girl on her way to womanhood. It was my mother who helped me get through all of the tough times of my teenage male/female relationships. In high school, I dated both African American and white young men. However, dating produced both happy and difficult times for me. For example, I dated one young white man whose family could not understand why he was dating a "black" girl and clearly disapproved of his choice. After much equivocation, he began to show signs that their disapproval was affecting his feelings for me. As a result, I decided that there was no need for me to put up with his ignorant parents, and we broke up. It was very difficult for me emotionally because he was someone that I really liked. Unfortunately, reactions like this were not new to me, but they still hurt. My mother was right there to comfort me and offer encouraging words of advice once again and to help me face ignorance and bigotry straight on. She said, "Honey he doesn't deserve someone as wonderful as you are. Clearly the ignorance of his parents clouded what he first saw in you, and I know he will always regret the day that he let them win!" These are conversations that I will never forget.

MY MOTHER/MY SELF

Now that I am an adult, I look back on my childhood with both its good and bad memories, and I realize that somehow I made it through *everything* without going crazy, harboring festering resentments, or wishing that I had never been adopted. Both my mother and father were the key to my reaching some level of normalcy within the uniqueness of my family situation. They helped me to realize my identity and gave me the internal confidence and the psychological "thick skin" that I needed to endure psychosocial hardships. As a result, I emerged knowing that there was absolutely nothing that I couldn't accomplish in life. As an adult African American woman, I now feel that I know who I am. Moreover, I am very proud of my culture even though I had to find out through experience exactly what my culture was to me. My childhood definitely served as a springboard for me to become an adult, a professional, and a mother.

As I look at my leadership development, I think that the most significant thing that I have realized is that leadership comes very naturally to me. Like my mother, I feel very comfortable bringing people together to get things accomplished. I too am a braider of many styles. I too give attention to each distinct braid yet ultimately produce intricate patterns. Even though I did not inherit any physical features from my mother, I definitely inherited learned behavior that I demonstrate to this day. Until her illness and death, my mother held leadership roles, whether it was within our family structure, in the parish, or on her job. When she took on a project or challenge she followed through regardless of setbacks until the work was finished.

My mother was always extremely organized. She was the one who kept us all on track, got us fed and clothed, *and* went to work to teach elementary students as well. She did all of this while my father was preaching and serving the parish as a pastor, day and night (a twenty-four-hour job). My mother was the true model of a working mother who somehow got her teaching work done *and* had dinner ready when I got home from school. To keep us organized as children, she would even have charts for who did what chore, whose turn it was to put the cheese in the macaroni or sit in the front seat of the car next to her. According to Martin Chemers, attention to *both* the pragmatic tasks and the relationship aspects of organizing are important skills in any leader (Chemers, 1995). These are skills that have helped me throughout my lifetime, and have also helped me to excel in my profession in higher education as a senior associate director of admissions.

My mother never failed to have a positive attitude! She consistently tried to see the good side of things or the good in people. I rarely heard her speak badly about anyone. As a result, I too live my life trying to have a positive attitude, and I encourage this in my own children, coworkers, and friends. Maybe this is my adult life translation of my mother's advice to "stare right back, and smile." As a result, I still benefit from seeing how people respond to my positive attitude in the face of any circumstance.

My mother was also a confident person. She almost had to be, given the extraordinary life that she chose to lead and the family she and my father chose to create. She would rarely let any adversity shake her or the family because of her confidence in herself and us. She could comfortably put herself in any situation and put us at ease as well. She demonstrated this same confidence as a teacher in the classroom with rambunctious elementary students. As the pastor's wife, she responded to many delicate situations and interpersonal conflicts among some members of my father's congregation. Some of the most sensitive situations were the times she was questioned about decisions my father made as the church pastor, or when members disagreed with my father's handling of an issue. My mother would use these times as an opportunity to teach (once again) or open the minds of the congregation to see the good that my father was trying to do. She was very skilled at getting people to see things in more expansive, generous, and gracious ways.

Through every facet of her life, she exuded confidence that I call "foundational selfhood." This is a trait that I consider my most treasured inheritance from my mother. I have had to be confident in myself from the time I was very young, through grade school, high school, college, and into my professional life. "Foundational selfhood" is my term for an unshakable belief that I can accomplish what I set out to do. And this belief in my ability to take effective action rests on a solid foundation of selfhood that my mother transferred to me. There is an African American cultural saying that Black women often speak of when working to develop confidence and agency in young Black girls whom these mothers, other mothers, and community mothers know will need the strength to face oppression. This saying is expressed as helping the girls develop: "a belief in self greater than anyone's disbelief" (Robinson and

Ward, 1991). This saying is an apt reflection of the kind of foundational selfhood that my mother helped me cultivate.

While I engaged in much soul searching and social and communal exploration during my college years to construct for myself a more elaborate sense of African American identity, I can truly say that without a core foundation of selfhood, little else would matter. Pride in cultural heritage must be integrated into a sense of the intractable dignity of self. For girls growing to womanhood, an effective gender role model is crucial. While a same race and gender mother, other mother, or community of such mothers would enrich and expand a gendered and raced identity development, having such a model is not the only way for a child to thrive. For me, my mother's individual bonding with each of us and finding singular ways to affirm and integrate us into our respective cultures was part of her "alchemical" gift. This gift sealed in me a cultural respect that became the framework for knowledge and experiences about my cultural identity that I gained in later years.

As I reflect on my life, I can see that early experiences formed the confidence and certainty that became a part of my self-trust and formed my foundational selfhood. By gaining a sense of self, I was able to develop a leadership style that I call "thick-skinned leadership." This is a shield that I naturally created for myself, which helped me to overlook what people said or how they reacted to me. Thick skinned leadership allowed me to cut through all of "the stuff," the issues related to the vulnerable areas around race and gender. I didn't give people time to dwell on what color I was or why I was there but instead focused on taking control and leading a group to get goals accomplished.

Another important part of my leadership style involved helping people move toward a goal by looking at the collective interests. I work hard to listen and understand the needs of the group in order to get the group's goals accomplished. As a leader in a group setting, I feel very comfortable with delegating duties, creating timelines, organizing processes, and developing procedures. Ultimately, all of these areas can be directly related to how my mother ran our family. I follow her example and her process of getting tasks accomplished; this was a very natural part of my development.

As a wife and the mother of two, I now see myself repeating many of the same actions and words of wisdom that my mother used with me. I find myself constantly encouraging my children to be themselves and to have confidence in everything that they do. I also think that I have taught them to love everyone regardless of the color of their skin in the same fashion that my parents did. My children found it very natural to have white grandparents and relatives who look different from them because that is all that they have known. It is my hope that they will continue to see the world that way. With my mother as the example, I have tried to raise my children to be honest, respectful, positive, and understanding. I have also stressed the importance of their faith in God, which has been the center of my life and existence.

It is reassuring how life can go full circle. When my daughter was little I found myself getting to know her, listening to her, and giving her advice as I braided her hair each day. It is my hope that I am passing on to her what I have learned from my mother and that one day she will look back on her childhood with fond memories of her mom and her wonderful grandmother and the life lessons that we taught her.

REFERENCES

Chemers, M. (1995). Contemporary leadership theory. In J. T. Wren (Ed.), *The leader's companion: Insights on leadership through the ages* (pp. 83–99). New York: Free.

Cole, J. B., Guy-Sheftall, B. (2003). Gender talk: The struggle for women's equality in African American communities. New York: Ballantine.

Greene, B., White, J. C., & Whitten, L. (2000). Hair texture, length and style: A metaphor in the African American mother-daughter relationship. In L. Jackson & B. Greene (Eds.), *Psychotherapy with African American women: Innovations in psychodynamic perspectives and practice* (pp.166–93). New York: Guilford.

Robinson, T., and Ward, J. V. (1991). A belief in self far greater than anyone's disbelief: Cultivating resistance among African-American female adolescents. In C. Gilligan, A. G. Rogers, and D. L. Tolman (Eds.), *Women, girls, and psychotherapy: Reframing resistance* (pp. 89–91). Binghamton, New York: Hawthorn.

Rothman, B. K. (2006). *Weaving a family: Untangling race and adoption.* Boston: Beacon.

PART II

The Foundations of Mother-Daughter Tutelage

>...African American woman
>Communal voice
>staking claim to her space/place
>...standing at the foundation and
>the center of the world
>human family
>—Bernice Johnson Reagon,
>*The Women Gather*

THE MOTHERLINE KNOWS that it must offer its daughters training and tutelage in crafting a black woman persona that can be a seaworthy craft for navigating the rigors of life in a diverse world society. Way showing, stories, fables, apocryphals, folk sayings, quips, instructions are the Motherline's tools. There is an old Motherline folk saying that captures the essence of the approach and its value: "You pay for your learnings, but your education is free." This admonition points to the Motherline as the master educator, task master, refiner, and finisher. The pieces in this section respond to the questions: What is actually being taught down this Motherline? What are the indications that there is an African philosophical worldview being transferred? How is such cultural insider knowledge transferred from mother to daughter? Three writers speak of their experience: Oare' Dozier-Henry, in "Ìdílé: The Power of Mother in the Leadership Tradition," Ceara Flake, in the poem "Hard to Define," and Toni C. King, in "Don't Waste Your Breath: The Dialectics of Communal Leadership Development."

At every turn, daughters are asked to embrace Motherline lore as a path to personal growth and contribution to the collective. Equally important, they are cautioned that rejection of Motherline wisdom is tantamount to self-abnegation and psychospiritual annihilation. To veer off course holds consequences. It can mean untold hardship, struggle, dreams deferred, false starts, midcourse corrections, and separation from core values, core relationships, and even the core of hope that keeps us going when all else fails. Like crazy quilts, the stories of these three women carry forward the larger design in a myriad of new ways. The first woman returns to a traditional African concept—'ìdílé'— to speak her truths. Oare' Dozier-Henry gives us a tangible sense of being wrapped in love by women who "modeled the qualities she came to associate with." Ìdílé "is the unbroken line of African women (and men) who breathe in us still, generations removed." Through her description of living in the working-class section of a relatively prosperous middle-class neighborhood in New York City called "St. Albans," we come to know the explicit behaviors the Motherline modeled daily to negotiate relationships and influence. Now, as an African American woman educator in academe, she has become a cultural negotiator—offering her students options ranging from individuality to communality and back again.

The second author in this section, Ceara Flake, speaks through poetry. The title of her poem "Hard to Define" points to additional difficulties in transferring leadership lessons across generations. Nowhere is the transfer more difficult than when it occurs with ancestral mothers who are no longer here to pass on their knowledge directly. To remedy this, Flake senses and surrenders to the presence of an ancestral mother, Fannie Lou Hamer, and in so doing she spans the life-death-life cycle so integral to black philosophical thought (Nobles, 1972). Within this paradigm, Flake guides us to see that through surrender to the inspiration of this civil rights activist, she receives—over half a century later—the impetus she needs for her own work as an attorney and activist.

The final author in this section testifies that her mother gave her a love of storytelling. In general storytelling is basic to preserving and passing on black culture. In the case of Toni King's own life, her mother used story to transmit leadership lessons. King writes that "[stories] are what my mother gave me to leave home before I was old enough to leave. They are what she gave me to set up home in the world, in spite of race, class, or gender oppression. And they are what I use to return home when the negotiations of the world erode my sense of well-being." By tracing the meaning of "breath" from an Africentric Motherline view, King shows us how her mother's adage "not to waste your breath" is integrated into her current leadership work. The messages she received from her mother, grandmother, and the communal circle of women in her life, she now applies in her work as an educator, scholar, and practitioner of organizational behavior to bring persons alone or in groups, in touch with their own life stories.

The leadership lessons that all three writers in this section express emerge from an ethic of caring that requires looking after both the collective and the self in the process of leadership. The Africentric Motherline worldview demands a creativity beyond either/or thinking. It emphatically refutes a "me versus you," "us versus them" approach. Nor does it permit binaries that bind women in either "I must sacrifice self completely" or "I must win out over all others." From Motherline teachings daughters have learned to take a nuanced perspective of the African philosophical cornerstone: I am because we are, and because we are, therefore I am." We tailor and elaborate this saying to describe an African centered, woman centered communal philosophy: "You exist in me; therefore I am; and because you exist in me, all the women who have gone before now live in me and give me strength."

REFERENCES

Nobles, W. (1976). African philosophy: Foundations for a black psychology. In R. L. Jones (Ed.), *Black Psychology* (pp. 18–32). New York: Harper and Row.

4

Ìdílé

The Power of Mother in the Leadership Tradition

OARE' DOZIER-HENRY

A LOVING OFFERING to the unsung generations of transplanted African women who instilled in us the values from home: faith in a vision that enlarges who we are and what we can be and the courage to step up and fashion our world. This chapter is a small tribute to my mother's incredible gifts and an exploration of what these gifts have meant in my life. This writing sends love across worlds to Mildred, Ertie, Jane, and others known and unknown.

> I am an African five generations removed
> Sister/daughter/womanchild
> Wife/mother-leader/custodian of the ancestors
> Committed to the liberation/restoration of the Spirit and
> well-being
> of African people worldwide.

As an African woman descended from ancestors forcibly transplanted in the Americas, I relate the power to serve and lead to a heritage transmitted through *ìdílé*.[1] In the mother tongue of my Yorùbá ancestors, *ìdílé* refers to family lineage and tradition. It is the unbroken line of

African women (and men) who breathe in us still, generations removed. *Ìdílé* links humans to immortality. *Ìdílé* is manifest in the power of Mother as a bearer and transmitter of tradition (Angelou, 2008; Ruiz, 2004; Hill Collins, 2000). It is preserved through memory, as the examples of cherished ancestors are honored in the names given children in contemporary times.

It has been my experience that when most African American "baby boomers" are asked to identify an important role model in their lives, mother is the first to be named. I believe this, too, is a manifestation of *ìdílé*. The ancestry of African-descended people in the United States is overwhelmingly West African with a majority coming from matrilineal, matrifocal societies such as Akan and Yorùbá (Clarke, 1996; Eltis, 2000; Franklin; 2000; Holloway, 1990, Nzegwu, 2001). *Womanism*, termed by a woman of African descent,[2] connotes the uniqueness of feminism among women of color and stresses the mother/othermother who acts a mentor for other, usually younger, women. In my life there have been many mothers/othermothers.

Moreover, as our first teacher, the magic of a mother's love is a crucible for what we can become. Her love is an imprint that molds and motivates us to be the best that we can be. Academics may be tempted to neglect the "sturdy black bridges that we crossed over on" in favor of singular women of merit celebrated by the larger society. This chapter honors aspects of leadership inherent in the choices made by ordinary women doing extraordinary things. Really loving someone or something is most extraordinary![3]

Like most mothers, my mother, Mildred Wilson Dozier, was my first and foremost teacher. Commonly, we learn trust and safety in the arms of our mothers. My mother's everpresent lap and sheltering arms let me know that I mattered and was loved. Seeing myself in the mirror of her eyes and in those of my grandmothers, aunts, and extended family members laid a strong foundation for belief in myself. These women's ways of walking in the world modeled the qualities I came to associate with leadership: grace, initiative, spiritual anchoring and inner direction, humility, transcendent self-confidence, and relationship agility. These were affirmed by "faith you could walk by rather than sight."

My mother was an extraordinary woman. She wore self-confidence like so many rainbow scarves. On her, pride was a sweet perfume that preceded her entrance into a room. She had flair and passion that spilled over in impeccable taste and style. It wasn't until years later in my adult life that I would actually learn some of the dreams that my mother held most dear. But when I was fourteen she began fulfilling one dream, and that was to travel. That year we traveled to Puerto Rico. Eventually my mother would visit more of the Caribbean basin, Venezuela, Europe, and Asia. These trips were always taken with me or in the company of women friends—rarely with my father. Here she flexed her independence muscle. She paid for these trips herself and did not ask permission to go.

Through *idílé* I was shown the inseparable equation of love, confidence, and competence that serves as the Petri dish for leadership. Through the generations (*idílé*), our ancestral mothers were animated by what is now recognized as feminine manifestations of leadership: the use of persuasion over coercion, spirituality over ego, foresight over control, listening over directing, and acceptance over judgment (Shugart, 1997). These qualities appealed to me, and I aspired to acquire them. They have served me well in the arena of family and immediate community; I seldom meet them in commerce or the workplace.

I consider myself a conjure woman. I work in the arena called "higher education," conjuring memories into futures and trafficking in the world of ideas. I enjoy the world of magic and transformations. The transformation/development of critical consciousness is what I enjoy most. Teaching is an art dedicated to transformation. Like magic, teaching doesn't get the respect it is due. Yet for me, it is a central core that informs the major themes in my life.

By most measures, I am considered a "success." I am a full professor in the Department of Educational Leadership and Human Services at an HBCU (historically black attended college /university). I have an enjoyable career with flexible hours and summers off, live comfortably, have traveled extensively, and am in the third decade of marriage with a man I very much love. We have two outstanding children engaged in careers in medicine and nanotechnology. Who could be more blessed?

By virtue of possessing a terminal degree, many in my community assign me the status of "leader." Yet my understanding of leadership is informed by a strong component of service. As such, authentic leadership is earned, not conferred. I study and teach theories of leadership with the determination that my teaching will energize a new generation of practice in communities and places dedicated to learning. In my teaching and scholarship, I critique and challenge the dominant Eurocentric paradigm because it disempowers and silences other ways of knowing and being in the world. Conspicuously absent are the voices of my mothers. The dominant paradigm localizes power, prestige, and privilege in a construct of leadership with a white male face. By contrast, choosing service over grandiosity and personal gain is what I learned from my mothers as leadership. This choice, which seemed as natural as air, was also the denominator of womanhood.

A "baby boomer," I grew up during what was for African people in the twentieth century, a "Golden Age" (late fifties-late sixties).[4] I was an only child in a household nurtured by the collective power of three generations of women and my father. We lived in the working-class section of a relatively prosperous middle-class neighborhood in New York City called "St. Albans." Divided by the Long Island Railroad, greater St. Albans was home to affluent African American entertainers such as James Brown and Count Basie, as well as a growing number of black civil servants such as my father and their families. Extended family groupings were the rule; siblings provided daycare, and the house had to be clean with all homework done by the time your working mama came home.

Formal schooling, which the family called "education," was important. My father stressed that an education (meaning college) would position me so that I could take care of myself and not have to depend financially on a man like most women had to during the fifties and sixties. This, of course, was seconded and encouraged by my mother. Good manners and etiquette protocols were considered very important. The adult women in our circle of family and friends were "othermothers" who had the authority to discipline and bless. None was as powerful as my mother, Mildred (known as "Sister" to her family),[5] Grandma Ertie, and Great Grandma Jane. One of "New York's finest,"[6] my father's Ogun[7] energy counterbalanced evenly the woman energy of the three females in our home.

In my home and surroundings women expressed themselves freely. My aged great grandmother and my maternal uncle's wife were the only women I knew while growing up who did not work outside the home.

Both grandmothers were domestics. My mother was one of the few high school graduates in the family and had a respectable job. Mommy's younger sister, "Baby," capitalized on her "sassiness" and became active in a union shop, eventually retiring as a successful labor organizer. The women surrounding me were not afraid to differ with menfolk and often did. Their wisdom and grace belied the "Sapphire" image stereotype of black women popularized on *Amos'n'Andy*.[8] Adept at her job as a purchasing agent for a manufacturing firm, my mother ascended to a supervisory position in an all white department. Treated well by supervisors and peers, she would eventually question my feelings during the Black Power movement. Yet she listened and did not judge.

Daddy's tolerance of feminine independence was at least partially credited to his upbringing where the ability of women to lead was not a debatable question.[9] The women on Daddy's side had a history of being mavericks; in the late fifties my great aunt was ordained as a minister. Daddy's mother was a "sporting" woman who enjoyed gambling and all night card games. She did not hesitate to pit her talents against those of the men in her social circle. The tradition of family importance was evident in the annual family reunions (initiated by a woman) and the constant support shown to family members (coordinated by women). While they proudly defined themselves as "colored women," my foremothers' African *ìdílé* came shining through all the same. Little did they know that their penchant for clubs mirrored their African foremothers' women's societies, that *susu*, which enabled them to save for vacations was a carbon copy of an African savings initiative, and that their devotion to family first rooted them in the African worldview.

I view the club tradition among diasporan women as an extension of gendered societies so prominent in traditional African life. My mother and othermothers were all club women. These were not the middle-class, politically oriented clubs identified in academic literature as "colored women's clubs" (Giddings, 1984; Knupfer, 1996, Zackodnik, 2007). These were locally organized clubs for fun and social purposes. In high school, my mother and several other girls organized the Beaumont Girls. These women were my mother's lifelong friends and my extended family "aunties." My mother followed her mother's footsteps as she had enjoyed the same relationship with my grandmother's club members when she was a child. This tradition continues in my life. I organized my first girls club at the age of ten and previously worked to restore African values in an organization of elder local women known as Yaa Asantewaa.

From my mothers I learned that sister friends are extremely important. They trusted one another. Their close friends were a perimeter in my life, always there to hail the least little success and forgive any failure. I could not imagine a satisfying life without this sisterhood. Moreover, my mother had male colleagues from work who would occasionally visit. This did not threaten my father. I realize now that this was a profound influence on my later relationships. I fully expected to have male and female friends as part of my life. This insistence caused me to forfeit several boyfriends who could not "go along with the program."

From my parents, I learned that negotiation was the communicative currency between men and women. I learned that human beings disagree and that men do not have inherent power over women. As my number one fan, my father believed and made me believe that I could achieve my goals. I will always be grateful for that. Mildred, Ertie, and Jane modeled and instilled in me a "can do" attitude and that no one was any better than I was. Thus, I did not hesitate in my early twenties to accept a supervisory role over a group of males in a correctional setting. The bearing I inherited from my foremothers enabled me to be the first civilian woman to walk the tiers of lower Manhattan's infamous jail, "The Tombs," and be respected.

The "circuits of power" of African American women (Clegg, 1988; Denton, 1990, McDonald, 2007) were circumscribed by the boundaries of family and community. Perhaps more than any other place, family was the arena where African American women's leadership was most visible. Family members were guaranteed hospitality, and their comfort was a priority. Watching my mother, I learned to forecast, plan, budget, and execute events. Though I have yet to acquire her prowess, I learned about diplomacy as I watched her bring together disparate family members and neighbors.

The African worldview generally is relational in its orientation (Ani, 1994; Asante, 1988; Diop, 1976; Dixon, 1978). Relationship agility is one of the strengths of effective leaders. Since there was no exile from family, maintaining harmonious relations was important. Mothers took the lead in this and emphasized the need to balance the relationship between earthly and spiritual obligations. Congruent with Christian values that guided us (as it was a way of life on both sides of the family), my foremothers' selflessness of service was demonstrated in many ways. There are countless examples of mothers taking in the children of the less able, cooking, cleaning, and caring for elders and friends, visiting the infirm, and sacrificing dreams on the altar of family advancement. I marvel at how (as) natural as breath these actions were.

As I struggle in the "sandwich" generation, I recall my mother's unswerving dedication to the care of her mother when she lost capacity and that of Grandma Ertie to her mother before her. Through it all, they never complained. Though she depended on her income as a domestic, my "sporting woman" grandmother dropped everything to come and care for my family after childbirth complications with my son. She stayed four months and is responsible for at least twenty of the pounds that I've needed to lose for the last twenty years!

Long before Robert Greenleaf's "servant leadership" (1970, 1977, 1979, 1980) and Lipman-Blumen's more recent concept of connective leadership (2000) offered leaders a way to move beyond competition or military metaphors, African women in the Diaspora energized a paradigm set forth by their foremothers. This model extolled African values, put service to others first, and urged gentleness, not rancor, as the path to power (Zackodnik, 2007). This gentleness is often tempered by a certain "sassiness." This courage to transgress is also discursively expressed in Black vernacular as womanish, bodacious, boldness, bogartin', actin' or bein' wild, and other terms that signify the courage of authenticity and the will to transgress subordinating social dictates (Hollies, 2003).

Sassiness has to do with self-affirmation in what may be perceived as vociferous terms. When it comes to sassiness, it is likely to be elicited by a perceived threat to an African American woman's person or family. To be genuine, it must be anchored in self-assuredness, not doubt. Physical gestures such as neck rolling, teeth-sucking, and hands-placed-on-hips may attend sassiness. Then again, it may be the erudite delivery in measured terms that rocks someone else's world. It is standing up for oneself, drawing a line in the sand, and establishing in no uncertain terms who you are and what the limits will be. It involves telling it like it "T-I-is!"[10] It is walking up to adversity and smacking it right in the face. This willingness on the part of African American women to take on the world and raise a family with or without a dedicated man in their lives fueled the demeaning myth of "Black matriarchy" (Moynihan, 1965). Through this lens, sassiness was transmogrified into a pathological matriarchy. Despite the associated imagery, as Maya Angelou says, "still we rise."[11]

I realize now that I learned from the women who danced through my life what it means to be a woman, a friend, a sista,[12] a daughter, and a mother; what it means to be whole, and by extension, what it means to lead and serve. Servant leaders dream, develop, heal, promote and evolve (Bennett, 2001; Williams, 1996). A mother's impetus is to guide the evolution of her child and in so doing, to etch a dream of possibility on the young consciousness. This is leadership par excellence. The Greenleaf Center for Servant-Leadership (www.greenleaf.org) identified ten critical characteristics that a servant leader should exhibit. These ten are by no means complete but do communicate important aspects of this leadership model. The ten characteristics follow:

1. Listening
2. Empathy
3. Healing
4. Awareness
5. Persuasion
6. Conceptualization
7. Foresight
8. Stewardship
9. Commitment to the Growth of People
10. Building Community.

Nonviolence, love, revolutionary patience, and the emphatic embrace of the good in life are things my mothers taught. Lao-Tzu observed, "True leaders are hardly known to their followers." More than my degrees and schooling, I am sure my foremothers would be surprised to learn how much more I credit their roles of cheerleader, listener, and mentor for my success.

These luminous women simply modeled in their everyday manner the best of womanhood. This womanhood was characterized by initiative and acceptance of responsibility and peppered with the sassiness born of self-confidence that compels some women to step up and lead. By being givers and not takers in society, my ancestral mothers stimulated my desire to make a difference in community. Ourmothers' selfless sacrifices for our well-being and postponement of dreams teach us much about duty and service. I cherish all the gifts I received from my mothers. On balance, I also acknowledge the baggage that attends the benefits of the model. Western society extracts high dues from sassy women, no doubt because it fears our boundless spirits. What is cherished in others (particularly white males) as assertiveness is demonized in African American women as "intimidating." Sassiness, our survival salve, can alienate those who've been socialized to disparage it. Unfortunately, many times these are our sisters.

I learned also, perhaps too well, to step aside, postponing my needs to attend to the needs of others. Others, namely my children and family elders, come first. The primacy of the collective exceeds personal preference. This very African view is riveted to the core of my being. Moreover, it is the only definition of Mother that I choose. Viewers outside the *ìdílé* allege that this is self-effacement and codependency. My response? Because leadership is an act of stewardship anchored in vision, and because family is a missive from God, the power of Mother is an indispensable ingredient in the leadership formula. As we strive to understand how the leadership phenomenon is created, let us acknowledge its beginnings. The power of Mother is at the source of who we are and is often the model for who we are to become. Growing up in the sunlight of the love of these transplanted African women made me strong and committed to both my immediate and my extended African family. It is a legacy of wealth and personal power. For me, and no doubt for many others, it has been a powerful impetus for leadership. This is *ìdílé*.

NOTES

1. *Ìdílé* is a Yoruba word meaning native son or daughter, bearer of tradition. By extension it refers to family/blood lineage.

2. The specification of womanism is credited to Alice Walker. See Walker's definition of "Womanist," "Definition of a Womanist," in *In Search of Our Mother's Gardens: Womanist Prose,* pp. xi–xii.

3. Loving and giving under the severe condition of oppression African women face is indeed extraordinary.

4. A termed coined by Oba T'Shaka and mentioned during a lecture at Florida Agricultural and Mechanical University (FAMU) in spring 2000.

5. The tendency to use relational names, *Brother* or *Bubba, Sister, Baby*, and so on, emphasized the primacy of family relationship in the African worldview.

6. A term of respect given to New York City's police force.

7. In Yorùbá cosmology, Ogun is a primal energy source associated with iron, hard work, and maleness and is the patron of policemen, soldiers, surgeons, and others who deal with metal implements.

8. Originally a radio show, *Amos'n'Andy* was the prototype for situation comedies based on stereotypes of African Americans, written and produced by Whites in the United States during the 1920s through the 1950s. http://en.wikipedia.org/wiki/Amos_%27n%27_Andy.

9. At least not within women's circuits of power: family, community, and church.

10. Slang terminology used in black culture to emphasize truth telling. Variations on this vernacular include "telling it like it T-I-is," with T-I spelled out followed by the word "is," or "telling it like it-is" with the word "is" pronounced emphatically as "TIS."

11. From the poem "And Still I Rise," by Maya Angelou in *The complete collected poems of Maya Angelou*. New York: Random House, (1994a). *www.poetryfoundation.org/archive/poem.html?id=175742*

12. The unique presentation of self black women commonly feel they must make to their peers and the world.

REFERENCES

Angelou, M. (1994). And still I rise. *The complete collected poems of Maya Angelou*. New York: Random House.

Angelou, M. (2008). *Letter to my daughter*. New York: Random House.

Ani, M. (1994). *Yurugu: An African-centered critique of European cultural thought and behavior*. Trenton, NJ: Africa World.

Asante, M. K. (1988). *The Afrocentric idea*. Philadelphia: Temple University Press.

Azibo, D. (1992). Articulating the distinction between black studies and the study of blacks: The fundamental role of culture and the African-centered worldview. *The Africentric Scholar, 1* (1), 64–97.

Bennett, J. L. (2001, March). Trainers as leaders of learning. *Training & Development, 55* (3), 42–45.

Carruthers, J. H. (1999). *Intellectual warfare*. Chicago: Third World.

Clarke, J. H. (1996). *Africans at the crossroads: Notes for an African world revolution*. Trenton, NJ: Africa World.

Clegg, S. R. (1989). *Frameworks of power*. London: Sage.

Clinton, M. J. (1991). *Behind the Eurocentric veils: The search for African realities*. Amherst: University of Massachusetts Press.

Coleman-Burns, P. (1989, July). African American women—Education for what? *Sex Roles: A Journal of Research, 21* (2), 145–60.

Collier-Thomas, B., & Franklin, V. P. (Eds.). (2001). *Sisters in the struggle: African American women in the civil rights-Black power movement*. New York: New York University Press.

Collins, P. H. (1998). *Fighting words: Black women and the search for justice*. Minneapolis: University of Minnesota Press.

Collins, P. H. (2000). Black women and motherhood. *Black feminist thought: Knowledge, consciousness, and the politics of empowerment* (2nd ed.). New York: Routledge.

Denton, T. (1990, December). Bonding and supportive relationships among black professional women: Rituals of restoration. *Journal of Organizational Behavior, 11,* 447–57.

Diop, C. A. (1978). *The cultural unity of Black Africa*. Chicago: Third World.

Dixon, V. J. (1976). World views and research methodology. In L. M. King, V. J. Dixon, & W. W. Nobles (Eds.), *African philosophy: Assumptions and paradigms for research on Black persons* (pp. 51–102). J. Alfred Cannon Research Conference Series. volume 1. Los Angeles: Fanon Center Publication, Charles R. Drew Postgraduate Medical School.

Eltis, D. (2000). *The rise of African slavery in the Americas*. New York: Cambridge University Press.

Fennell, H-A. (1999, May). Feminine faces of leadership: Beyond structural-functionalism? *Journal of School Leadership 9* (3), 254–85.

Franklin, J. H., & Moss, A. A. (2000). *From slavery to freedom*. New York: Knopf.

Gbadesin, S. (1991). *African philosophy: Traditional Yoruba philosophy and contemporary African realities*. New York: Lang.

Giddings, P. (1984). *When and where I enter: The impact of black women on race and sex in America*. New York: Morrow.

Greenleaf, R. K. (1970). *The servant as leader*. Cambridge, MA: Center for Applied Studies.

Greenleaf, R. K. (1977). *Servant leadership: A journey into the nature of legitimate power and greatness*. New York: Paulist.

Greenleaf, R. K. (1979). *Teacher a servant: A parable*. New York: Paulist.

Greenleaf, R. K. (1980). *Servant, retrospect & prospect.* Peterborough, NH: Windy Row.

Greenleaf, R. K., Frick, D., & Spears, L. (Eds.). (1996). *On becoming a servant leader.* San Francisco: Jossey Bass.

Hallen, B. (2000). *The good, the bad, and the beautiful: Discourse about values in Yorùbá culture.* Bloomington: Indiana University Press.

Hollies, L. H. (2003). Introduction: What is a womanist? *Bodacious womanist wisdom* (pp. 1–10). Cleveland: Pilgrim.

Holloway, J. E. (1990). *Africanisms in American culture.* Bloomington: Indiana University Press.

Kamalu, C. (1990). Foundations of African thought: A worldview grounded in the African heritage of religion, philosophy, science, and art. London: Karnak House.

Kambon, K. K. (1992). The African personality in America: An African-centered framework. Tallahassee: Nubian.

Karade, B. I. (1994). *The handbook of Yoruba religious concepts.* York Beach, Maine: Weiser.

Knupfer, A. M. (1996). *Toward a tenderer humanity and a nobler womanhood: African American women's clubs in turn-of-the-century.* New York: New York University Press.

Lipman-Blumen, J. (2000). *Connective leadership: Managing in a changing world.* Oxford, England: Oxford University Press.

Mbiti, J. S. (1990). *African religions & philosophy.* Portsmouth, NH: Heinemann.

McClaurin, I. (Ed.). (2001). *Black feminist anthropology: Theory, politics, praxis, and poetics.* New Brunswick, NJ: Rutgers University Press.

McDonald, K. B. (2007). The legacy of Black sisterhood: Deep collective roots. *Embracing sisterhood: Class, identity, and contemporary Black women* (pp. 33–63). Lanham, Md.: Roman & Littlefield

Moynihan, D. P. (1965). *The Negro family: The case for national action.* New York: New York Dept. of Labor.

Nzegwu, F. (2001). *Love, motherhood and the African heritage: The legacy of Flora Nwapa.* Senegal: African Renaissance.

Shugart, S. (1997). *Servant leadership: Robert K. Greenleaf's legacy and the community college.* ERIC (Education Resources Information Center)#: ED 407024.

Spears, L. (Ed.). (1995). *Reflections on leadership: How Robert K. Greenleaf's theory of servant-leadership influenced today's top management thinkers.* New York: Wiley.

Tedla, E. (1995). *Sankofa: African thought and education.* New York: Lang. Greenleaf Center for Servant-Leadership (www.greenleaf.org).

Walker, A. (1983). Definition of a womanist. In *In Search of Our Mother's Gardens: Womanist Prose* (pp. xi–xii). New York: Harcourt Brace.

Williams, L. E. (1996). Fannie Lou Hamer: The voice of the servant-leader. *Servants of the people: The 1960s Legacy of African American Leadership* (pp. 141–62). 2nd ed. New York: Palgrave.

Zackodnik, T. (2007). *African American feminisms, 1828–1923*. New York: Routledge.

5

Hard to Define

Ceara Flake

Stocky, poor, uneducated
Limp-walking
Sharecropping

A compelling public speaker?
A profound organizer?
A human rights activist?

Soaring beyond the limits set for her
God carried from "sharin' the crop to bogartin' the top"

Because of you
I am
Because you dreamed
I prosper
Because you ran
I am here
To receive your baton

Sweat from my temples
Tears from my eyes

Shielding the glare of the sun
I run

Looking back
I remember

>A mother—sacrificing her life for mine
>A sister—showing me the way
>A soldier—fixing her eyes on the prize

Her pace and stamina constant
I run

Though at times
She could barely see the light,
Fannie Lou continued to fight
When all hope was gone
Fannie Lou fought on!
Go on and fight on Fannie fight on!

6

"Don't Waste Your Breath"

The Dialectics of Communal Leadership Development

TONI C. KING

> The seamless web is one of my inheritances. My Mother taught me this. To know myself in the context of the web of life. To hear the heartbeat of the group.
> —Toni King, November 2000

I AM A COMMUNAL LEADER. I know this to be true. I have seen my mother participate in this communal web forever. And her mother before her. And her mother—whom I never knew. They were all a part of the circle of women that goes back in time. I feel these women in my dreams. They come for me and speak. One spits into the fire that is my hand. Another wraps me in a blanket she has woven from her tears. And in the center of this fire—their eyes flicker. Bringing me up. Singing me whole. Raising me from the dead.[1]

    I am a communal leader. A communal leader believes in the possibilities, strength, and wisdom of groups. A communal leader contributes to a group's development and wholeness by assisting the group in valuing and drawing upon the talents of all of its members to achieve an overarching vision that contributes to the group and to the larger society. As a communal leader there is within me a constant seeking of the life force as it swells from within communities. Everywhere in my upbringing I felt this ebb and flow, this rocking, this breath. My grandmother was Nona. She had healing hands that created order and beauty. My mother was Otissey. She blessed in me the spirit of creativity through the spoken or written word—nommo. She was both griot and trickster. My aunt, Wynona, my mother's only sister, taught me it was ok to create third space, to be what Alice Walker refers to as "in charge and serious" (Walker, 1983, p. 11) without being serious at all. She taught me to be a playful fighter—that it is hard to make war with Peter Pan, that reeds bend in the wind but do not break. And from Joan Marie, my only sister, I learned to tend well the stories that I want to tell so that I am heard before the looking glass queen can yell, "Off with her head!"[2]

And then there was the circle of women. Ever changing, ever moving, one becoming another, another becoming one. The women who passed me what I needed. Pulling from their pockets the last piece of bread when I thought I could not go on. Or pulling from the handkerchief in their bra, or pinned to their slip, the one thing I would need to get home.

> *Life is a seamless web, I sing.*
> *It is the thing that makes me mean*
> *It is the fire that cooks my food*
> *It is the way the world moves.*

STORYTELLING HAS EVERYTHING TO DO WITH LEADERSHIP

When I was little, my mother would tell us stories. Sometimes she would read them aloud. Like the summer she read us the story of *Heidi* while we stayed at our grandmother's house for four weeks. Every afternoon, in the heat of the day, before we fell asleep for our afternoon naps, she would read to us. I was mesmerized by this story that has captivated children for decades—the heat, the adventure, the loneliness of Heidi, and the longing of both Heidi and the grandfather. This was my world during these summer readings: falling asleep amid heat, the sound of Mom's voice, and the comfort and security of my grandmother's home, in the front bedroom with the green floral wallpaper and the mint green chenille bedspread.

So stories became for me the foundation for engaging self and others in the process of reflexivity—focusing the lens and method of inquiry on one's self.[3] This process of working through issues, sorting through experience, sense making, imaginary-role taking, values clarifying, empathy building, and identity construction were the "emotional technologies" that I began to develop, in part, through the love of stories that my mother planted in me. And these emotional technologies constitute my current leadership competency.

In particular, stories are useful for those with marginalized status in society. They help those from colonized cultures move toward a liberatory consciousness. Here I do not limit colonization to racial or ethnic groups but include any groups subordinated based on patriarchal hegemony along such dimensions as gender, sexual identity, or religion. According to Jungian psychologist Clarissa Pinkola Estes, women in particular need stories to identify, access, reclaim, and restore their instinctive or "wild" self. Of this she writes: "Fairy tales, myths, and stories provide understandings which sharpen our sight so that we can pick out and pick up the path left by the wildish nature. The instruction found in story reassures us that the path has not run out, but still leads women deeper, and more deeply still, into their own knowing" (Pinkola Estes, 1992, p. 6).

Stories are also important to the stability and development of a community, in terms of its cultural, historical, theological, and psychological health. Theologian James Cone confirms the importance to its spiritual ethic of a community knowing its own story. He says, "A community that does not analyze its existence theologically is a community that does not care what it says or does. It is a community with no identity (Cone, 1986, p. 8; Floyd-Thomas, 2006).

Stories and storytelling have played a fundamental role in the preservation of every aspect of black culture. In my life, this cultural salience of storytelling has become an essential tool of my leadership. Stories are what my mother gave me for leaving home before I was old enough to leave. They are what she gave me to set up home in the world, in spite of the race, class, and gender oppression I would face. And they are what I use to return home when my negotiations with the world erode my sense of well-being, and I need to "recover" from the degradation of stigmatized identity projected onto my person, either through interaction or by institutional action. Through stories and the process of storying, it becomes possible to return home, again, and again, and again.

LEADERSHIP LESSON NUMBER 1: THE LESSON OF THE SEAMLESS WEB

When I search for the roots of my matrilineal leadership development, I unearth a personal story about a childhood friendship I formed with a younger girl in my neighborhood—Candice Luper.[4] When I was ten, Candice was barely six, and she used to follow me to my Saturday piano lessons. During my lessons, she would inch closer and closer—as my teacher, Mrs. Payton, with the turquoise-highlighted silver hair urged me through my uninspired renderings of "Boogie-woogie Bill" or "On the Levee." Mrs. Payton was a gracious but firm teacher. She never failed to let me know that it was obvious I had not practiced. She never failed to let me know that she knew I was not applying myself. She expressed, with a grimace beginning at her ears, the pain she felt when my fingers went awry and stumbled onto wrong notes. I knew she was baffled by my amnesia.

And all the while, Candice inched closer and closer to the stool where I sat—almost toppling into us and whispering in her child-hoarse voice, the answers I was so slow to produce, such as the names of keys or the secret meanings of such things as EGBDF. She was spellbound by the magic Mrs. Payton released in coded breath—"Allegro. Or Allegretto, Toni, Allegretto!" Ultimately, I begged for a release. My pleas brought consultations serious enough to involve my grandparents. Their loving admonitions were to "consider long and hard child, how when you're an adult, you'll wish you could play the piano. Grandma and Granpa just don't want you to miss an opportunity. Are you sure this is what you want?"

And yet it was with great relief that those lessons ended. And there was only a twinge of remorse when Candice Luper replaced me on that stool. I did not walk her to her lessons as she had walked me. She went of her own accord, practiced between lessons, probably never made Mrs. Payton's ears move. And only now, when I consider the way of the seamless web, only now do I think of that trade-off, that passing of the batons, from me to Candice, and the unbroken line made when my mother spoke to Mrs. Luper to ask if Candice could take piano lessons.

That is leadership lesson number 1. I call it the "lesson of the seamless web." There was no big hoopla. Simply put, I stopped, and Candice began. Candice's mother didn't stop to fret about why my mother would want Candice to take lessons. They, in fact, laughed wholeheartedly about Candice giving me the answers that I could not think of, about Candice trailing me to lessons on a Saturday morning. Otherwise, according to Mrs. Luper, Candice (which she pronounced "Kanedis"), would normally have resisted being roused from bed. There was no ego, or false pride, or contest of wills in terms of whether this thing was okay or allowable or permissible. There was no competition around my fall from grace and Candice's rise to her rightful place as a budding pianist. Candice's much larger family of well-dressed, well-spoken, good-grades-earning children in which she was second, then third from the youngest could not afford lessons for *all* the various talents she and her brothers and sisters might demonstrate. But Candice's mother and father could and did provide much of the neighborhood with fresh fruit and vegetables from a thriving garden that filled most of their ample back yard. And none of the seven children at home ever went without anything he or she needed—love included. Somehow, they paid for Candice's lessons, now that the community mothers had worked together to address a need for one of "their children's" development. I have no doubt that with or without funds directly from her family, Candice's piano lessons would have been secured—whether by church, or neighbors, or a single benefactor. That was simply how the community worked.

Such were my lessons in community. While my mother opened a space for Candice, someone else opened a space for me. The world felt like a complex web. My grandparents' presence in the council of elders illustrates the communal process of raising children. They offered me the best of their wisdom and then left me to choose how I would weave my own fate. "Is this really what you want?" (in my case what I didn't want) they would ask. Moreover, it was also in the spirit of my mother's approach to allow me to make my own choices about some things, after hearing wise council. The piano lessons, I have since learned, had nothing to do with learning to play the piano. (To this day, all I recall of these lessons is the location of middle C.)

For me, this was an early girlhood coming-of-age lesson. Because piano playing was so important in my family (both my mother and sister played piano, and my grandfather had longed to play, eventually learning to play in the twilight years of his life), I struggled with the tension of how I would carry on family tradition. I also struggled with how to appreciate the class privileges such as piano lessons given to me that were denied to the many who had come before me. However, at the same time that I paid homage to tradition, it was necessary for me to come of age in my own time, honoring but not bound by the past. Since that time, my life has been a collage of both following tradition and departing from it, never knowing if I was getting it right, but always feeling that I had permission to choose. And this process of choosing and feeling the permission to "try it my way" has been a sacred offering for a black girl child from a small town in Oklahoma where many black girls lived their entire lives and the few who left felt it imperative to leave for good. My mother's gift to me was the "both/and" epistemology that made it possible for me to exist both within and without traditional communal templates for "good girls." I could choose how to make my mark on the world and still be the kind of "good girl" that black communities placed their hopes in.

In terms of leadership, the crucial process of choosing from some deep place beyond logic is an epistemology based on lived experience rather than on precepts, such as "I should because they did, or I must because they expect it." However, even when I claim this ability to choose in my life, I do not pretend to have the luxury of claiming choice without struggle or choices without costs.

But this ability to choose—this gift of "permission" that my mother extended to me—has become a part of what I do in my leadership with others. They call it "encouragement." I call it "permission." They call it "affirmation" to follow their deepest urgings. I call it "facilitating them in their ability to hold multiple paradigms in consciousness," allowing each paradigm an integrity, as well as allowing a playful relationship between the paradigms. For it is in this context of multiple paradigms that we can avoid binaries, dichotomies, and polarities. Polarities polarize.

Moving beyond polarizing ideologies requires the liberating adoption of what Mary Field Belenky (1986) calls "constructed knowledge" or the ability to "move outside of the given" (p. 133). This way of knowing involves understanding truths in the context from which they emerge, acknowledging the role of the knower as part of the known, and, finally, using the self as an instrument in the process of connecting so that there is passion and commitment to what and how we know (Belenky, 1986, pp. 133–42; Haraway, 1991; hooks, 1994; Palmer, 1998).

In order to engage others in the process of "permitting" one must be able to construct possibilities. We must be able to find what Audre Lorde calls the "source of the erotic" within ourselves: the place in which we think, feel, dream, envision a life tailored to the urgings of the soul. The source of the erotic is that which is most vital within us. Access to this source requires us to sweep away self-censorship or fear of communal shunning.

In finding a way to encourage others to have this freedom from being constrained to one paradigm alone, I often play a role in regenerating their vitality of soul. Thomas Moore explains our search for that which energizes and sustains us as a kind of "care of the soul" (in his book with the same title, *Care of the Soul*, 1992). Existential psychologist Rollo May discusses our pursuit of this freedom in the face of social oppositions (such as the need to conform, belong, or garner approval) as the "courage to create" (1975). Pinkola Estes, a Jungian psychologist who studies the adult development of women, speaks of this freedom as the "union of opposites between ego and soul" (1992, 272). According to Estes the process of creating this union produces a "spirit child," an archetypal character appearing in myth and story worldwide, who represents that part of ourselves capable of "Hear[ing] the far-off voice that says it is time to come back, back to oneself ... [I]t is the child ... that causes us to assert '[A]s God is my witness, I shall proceed in this way,' or 'I *will* endure,' or 'I shall not be turned away,' or 'I shall find a way to continue'" (Estes, 1992, p. 273).

I nurture the spirit child in others by encouraging a fluid imagination of identity. This is what Jessica Turk calls "tactical naming" (Turk, 1999). Cultivating such flexibility develops a capacity for and conscious use of our multiplicative identity (Lugones, 1990). Maria Lugones' term for this flexibility of identity is "playful world traveling." Gloria Anzaldua theorizes the process as "making face." Like the trickster, we are both clever and foolish, both protagonist and antagonist; we are rescuer and rescued, teacher and student, healer and healed. In my mind, this process is not only one of constructing knowledge that is both/and but constructing knowledge that has even more possibilities than allowing competing ideas to coexist. Perhaps this multiplicative approach to viewing the world is best captured as "both/both/and/and." I see the workings of this multiplicative epistemology handed down by my Motherline reflected in the concept of "holding." According to scholarly foremothers Carol Gilligan, Jean Baker Miller, and Judith Jordan, founders of the paradigm of relational cultural psychology, holding refers to "The effort to hold relationships across disagreement, to stay with someone in unknown territory ... [It is] a kind of care that keeps relationships going when there isn't any apparent common judgment, common experience, belief or reason to keep it going" (Robb, 2006, p. 212). Leaders from within the margins are often compelled to learn to "hold."

The Persistence of Dialectics

A communal leader is one who facilitates a group's ability to accomplish goals by drawing on each member's gifts and also helping each member grow in ways that benefit both the individual and the group. So yes. I am a communal leader but one who knows that the cost of communal integration can be a loss of the self; therefore, soul expression must be guarded as vigilantly as community. And in the process of tending the tender ties between community and personhood, between uplift and overload, between giving back and giving out. I have found that stories help a person, a group, or a community to see the complexity of issues and to embrace wholes rather than polarizing fragments. In such a community the spirit child thrives. So the seamless web is not simply the community that holds me but also my individual efforts to foster the community's ability to hold us all more humanely.

This is the way we construct a web. A web is a collection of intersecting threads. As a communal leader, I am both a weaver of the fine threads and a keeper of the big vision. The whole pattern can only be seen from without. But I, as Anansi,[5] weaver, spiderwoman, carry the whole design in my genes. And as a communal leader I bring this consciousness of the community's unfolding story back to the community members for their reflection and growth.

Sometimes the larger story of the community includes the pain its members have experienced or are experiencing. The communal leader also moves into the place of pain that the organization harbors. *This is not difficult for me a black woman. This is not difficult for me, a marginal woman. This is no more difficult than breathing. This is the place where multilayered oppressions push us. This is where and when we as black women enter* (Giddings, 1984). *In this place, we are "pushed back to strength"*[6]

Initially, I am not fine in this place. It is a place of pain, a place where I can see, but I cannot speak. However, silence also has its place. Mary Field Belenky also theorizes "silence" as a stage of knowing (1986). Audre Lorde (1984) speaks of silence as something that—if fully entered—permits us to transform our silences into action. These scholars treat silence (when it is actively engaged and examined) as a phase of recovery from social oppression. As a communal leader, I believe that honoring silence is vital in enabling both individuals and the collective to find voice. Here it is that my mother—a teacher who healed—has helped me. Here it is that my grandmother—a healer who taught—has helped me. Their gifts to me came from their own gifts.

Nona, my grandmother, was born in 1900 and lived to be eighty-five years old. She was a licensed practical nurse for twenty-five years, during which time she saw the end of segregated hospitals. In the last decade of her nursing career, she became one of the few black LPNs to move from the "Negro hospital" in Muskogee, Oklahoma, where I was born, to the newly integrated Muskogee General Hospital. (After integration, the original small two-to-three-wing white structure that had served the black population in Muskogee became a nursing home. (During our taunting years, my sister Joan loved teasing that I had been born in a nursing home for the aged!)

Once I asked my grandmother, who at the time lived in a nursing home, whether she had liked being a nurse. In particular, I asked about her around-the-clock care for my grandfather, who had gone blind in his forties from diabetes and who later had one and then the other of his legs amputated. Had she burned out in caring for others day in and day out, both at her place of work and at home with Pah-Pah? "Were you ready to retire?" I asked her. "Were you worn out?" From her wheel chair, with a look that said more than words, and in a voice that had grown soft and husky with age, she replied, "I loved nursing. I loved every minute of it."

My mother was a teacher. At first, she was barred from the public school system, so she took a job at a parochial school where she taught me in second grade. Later, when the schools were integrated, she taught English at the public high school. Still later, after earning her masters degree and certification as a reading specialist, she found a wonderful position as reading specialist at Guthrie Job Corps Center and soon after became director of their reading program. She loved working with these young and disadvantaged adult learners, and her salary as a reading specialist was good enough to trigger envy from my father. After my father died in a car accident, and my grandfather died from natural causes within a year of each other, my mother moved back to her home town of Muskogee, Oklahoma, and lived with her mother (my grandmother), Nona. Mother was hired in the public schools once again, although she took a significant cut in pay because of her years of teaching outside of the public school system. She began teaching high school English but was ultimately asked to work with younger children and to develop the school's literacy program, a program she directed for several years.[7]

As the granddaughter of a healer and the daughter of a teacher, I have had to synthesize. Two years ago, in search of the seamless web the two of them created for me, I raised questions as I journaled. What came back to me was from the collective imagination of my African heritage. One might say the archetypal storyteller in the form of Anansi responded from within me like this:

What is the difference between teaching and conjuring?
I asked before I was born
There is none, said my mother, you know that
What is the difference between teaching and healing?
I asked before I could talk
No difference toni-gal, now come on over here and give grandma some
  sugar
What is the difference between teaching and resisting?

I asked, before I could walk
But all the mothers gathered me up baptizing me in the name of the
  holy spirit.

My voice carries these teaching/healing/teaching rhythms. Sometimes one is the melody, the other the bass, or vice versa, speaking a multitongued leadership. The communal process is borne out in me this way. I listen for the wounding of the community or the place of pain. I set out on a mission to learn from the community what it knows about its own healing. I listen for its deepest desires, its unrealized dreams. I gather this knowledge like so much flax. I weave it in much the same way that the dwarf Rumpel-Stilts-Kin[8] demanded of the princess. Only I am not the golden-haired princess. I stare back with nappy edges, coarse locks, and a sweet smile. Already I know that my spinning is not for hegemonic consumption. I see the self-destruction of his tantrum before he does. My smile says, "You will soon go mad."

LEADERSHIP LESSON NUMBER 2: DON'T WASTE YOUR BREATH

Mother didn't have many sayings. I asked her about this when I was writing this chapter, she said, "I didn't have many sayings because I didn't give much advice. And I didn't give much advice to people because I didn't want people to give advice to me. Few things get on my nerves as much as other people's advice." But later, when I searched my memory, my reserves of history, I was able to recall one of her common sayings: "Don't waste your breath." This she would say when I wanted to convince her of something that she had already decided was not to be. This she would say when I wanted to change others or influence them to do or act as I wished. Inevitably I would share with her my frustrations at being misunderstood, or disliked, or not chosen, or any number of the other daily experiences a black girl might have in growing up. After our discussions about how I might approach these various situations, my mother would always encourage me to remember that others might still be oblivious to my efforts to explain, convince, or simply be heard. To let me know that there is a time to let go and move on, especially when I was getting nowhere, she would pull out her favorite saying: "Don't waste your breath."

There is a wisdom in this phrase that is intimately tied to my sense of leadership. Within the context of communal leadership, I am also a developmental leader. The developmental leader knows that life and growth take place over time, that growth, like listening, cannot be forced or hastened, that my desire for you to receive something of benefit according to my way of thinking cannot be determined by my rhythm alone, by my solitary sight, that the way your soul unfolds around you in the spiral of life is a sacred scheme that I can only enter with your permission. Thus, the role I play as a developmental leader requires your agreement. It may be that my mother was reluctant to give or receive advice because of the great temptation to give advice without the other's consent. The developmental leader must be good at acquiring such consent.

Just as the communal leader fosters the development and healing of the group so that it can promote the dignity and survival skills of all of its members, working as a developmental leader means focusing on the individual members: the developmental leader realizes that the individual members are also maturing as separate entities in their self efficacy and wholeness. The developmental leader assumes that individuals hold unlimited potential to work through limitation, pain, or psychosocial constraints to self-actualization. I would assert that many communal leaders also tend to the development of individuals (Belenky, Clinchy, and Goldberger, 1991; Evans-Winters, 2005). While the difference between these two kinds of leaders may seem small, in my view leaders who nurture the development of both groups and individuals have a profoundly complementary foundation for their leadership. This is reflected in the title bestowed upon civil rights activist Ella Baker. She was called the "*fundi*"—a Swahili word for someone who passes skills from one generation to another (Grant, 1981).

My mother's dictum not to waste one's breath provided one of her greatest lessons for me in my work as a developmental leader. In African cosmology, breath is the precursor to *nommo*, the sacred spoken word. For African philosophy, words are living things, and both thoughts and speech are forms of action (Nobles, 1976). Words are actions in and of themselves, and words have the ability to "translate silence into action" (Lorde, 1984a). Black women have developed a code of ethics that bases integrity upon the congruence between how one lives and what one says (Hill Collins, 1989). To think is to speak. Being clear about our thoughts allows us to "come to voice" (bell hooks, 1994a). The writer Edwidge Danticat is one of many creative artists who cosigns the importance of breath as the precursor to the sacred spoken word, indeed to consciousness itself. For Danticat, her matrilineal storytelling tradition depends upon "breath, eyes, memory." Telling the stories of her people's oppression in Haiti is her way of fostering intergenerational healing—her way of communal leadership.

WHAT THE GRIOT GAVE ME AND WHY THE TRICKSTER IS ON MY BACK

I was connected through breath to my mother's womb. I was connected by voice to my mother's thoughts. I was connected by blood to my mother's life. It was mother who gave me the spoken word through stories. But the *griot* (the African village storyteller) was also on my back. There were the stories she did not give to me. Those I strained to hear. Not content to lay my ear against the ground, I tugged on them like a rope caught on insights I could only grow into. Those were the stories I had to tug from underground, never sure I was hearing right. Tiring of the game, I would endlessly satisfy my need for voice and breath by joining in the lives of my friends. I played hard and long, until winded, breathless, sweaty, and fulfilled. I yelled and ran and was duly initiated into a vibrant neighborhood life. But underneath it I was trying to understand my family's story.

I both wanted and did not want the story of my mother and father. I both wanted and did not want the story of unhappinesses buried to the bone and at the same time surface sharp. And there were the stories I thought I knew but knew only with a child's mind. I thought I knew of the hunger for successes, the entrepreneurial dreams that my father swam in. I thought I had hold of the story of his rushing raft of energy against grim white waters of racism and classism. I thought I had hold of his apocalyptic approach to work as a contractor, landscaper, bricklayer, and carpenter. The sun-up to sun-down, hard handed, cement dust, chain smoking, customers-calling because-he-overbooked-his-jobs-and-they-had-not-see-him-in-weeks-so-what-could-they-do-about-the-patio-and-fountain-he-was-building-before-their-daughter's-backyard-wedding-next week?—father. And then, there were the weekend soirees beginning with deep blues and honky tonk jazz, smoke swirlin' in the family room (den) of the ranch style home that he built for us in the first black suburban development of tract homes in our town.

I tugged on these stories as I took "highballs" to Dad and the friend or two gathered with him before their nights out on Second Street.[9] I tugged on these stories while my mother sequestered herself in a back bedroom, earning her master's degree as a reading specialist—the thump thump bass of the stereo a persistent drum beat against her progress even with the door to the den closed.

And I tugged on this rope of untold stories during those suspiciously quiet conversations Dad would hold with Mom that would break into predictable arguments about money, culminating in that familiar unfulfilled look in his eyes. It was a look I would determinedly try to remove from the eyes of men I would date through my thirties. Ultimately, I liberated myself from this quest and married a man who did not have that look in his eyes.

My mother's untold stories had a deeper haunt. I was after all on the wrong trail. She brought consistency and focus to the family and did not pose such easy contradictions as my father did. Her sheer regularity was sanctity against my father's entrepreneurial storms. Her steadiness was sustenance to us and countered his penchant for spending money to further his business dreams first and paying bills later. I used my energies to follow his psychospiritual meanderings. I thought as children do that I could both find and fix the restless pace of his spirit that created all the excitement and magic a child might want in a father but that eroded a sense that the raft of fatherhood could be anchored against the rushing tide of dreams deferred.

To my mother I credit a skillful deflection and a sleight of hand. She did what any mother would do. She entertained me with whimsy. She enlightened me with moral teachings. She instructed me in flawless manners and civility. She bred in me the art of grace under pressure.

She rewarded me for living large whenever it could be politely done. But never, never was I to look too closely at the cobwebs under the bed. All feelings could be addressed except the particular pains and rages of her married life.

THEN AND NOW

And so dialectics persist. Both the stories my mother told and the ones she did not tell inform my current leadership identity. Currently, I stand at the juncture of two academic programs with a "joint appointment" in black studies and women's studies. I am told I connect two social movements that have not always seen eye-to-eye. A colleague reported, only half facetiously, that the two programs were connected across this "bridge called *my* back."[10] Gendered and raced as I am, it is not surprising to find myself doing bridge leadership. Belinda Robnett discusses bridge leadership as the ability to find intersections and weave shared visions that become increasingly inclusive and that ultimately foster ties between social movements and the community. These ties are based on authentic connection and the cultivation of an intimacy that humanizes (hooks, 2009). Black women in the civil rights movement created such bridges (Robnett, 1997, pp. 66–67). African women in the compounds created such bridges. I am their daughter.

Mothered and grandmothered as I am, this is where and how I play. *I laugh the laugh of Anansi. Crazy spider all them legs weaving he magic.* From my place in the organizational web, I weave home places for the sons and daughters seeking "balm in Gilead." For those who come upon me in this place, whether student, staff, or colleague, I teach them what to do with ruptured webs. I do what any mother of organizational vitality would do. I entertain them with whimsy. I instruct them in flawless manners, civility, and the performance of grace under pressure. Some call it "playing the game" of organizational life, I call it as bell hooks does "teaching to transgress" (hooks, 1994b).

I fuse the healer and the teacher. My mother's constancy makes me a weaver of continuity and stability. My father's ability to dream and create and dream again helps me nourish the seedlings of my students' tentative visions into flourishing projects, goals, career paths. My mother's ability for both playfulness and authority becomes the seamless web that holds offerings created by my own hand: humor, validation, and imaginings of our larger role. Reminding of a divine anointing is the balm I bring. When those I am invited to engage begin to see their place in a cosmology, a web going back forever, and affirming that "everything that has gone before has brought us to this place,"[11] we are then ready to begin. We imagine what can be done, what truths can be articulated, what silences transformed into what kinds of actions (Lorde, 1994a). As Lorde admonishes, we do not treat poetry as a luxury but as an act of survival, restoration, agency. *Now Anansi, he be laughin' hard now. Cause here is where the trickster turn me loose. Mother, grandmother, othermothers*, syntheses of the mother/father complement—all take root anew in my life. All come together to produce a new design.

In organizations, I use the web of my multiplicative identity. Having sought my mother's shadows and my father's shamings, I have learned to look closely at the cobwebs under the bed. I have learned to go after the hidden story. I become a guide and provocateur in the search to examine, assess, analyze, and interpret. I use a relational model and an ethic of care (Noddings, 1984; Robb, 2006) so that there is trust for such a search as this. In this context of trust I weave mutuality of support that permits me and others to pull up truths of organizational life. We pull as if it is our soul salvation. We pull until our scrutiny exposes our own weaknesses, inadequacies, fears and anxieties. We pull until the rope comes free. Disentangling our personal issues from the past and present events within the organization, exposes truths, discoveries and understandings about organizational agendas.

And when we know ourselves in relation to the issues that have ruptured individual and collective personhood, then and only then have we found the "true real" or the "true true"—a constructed reality that includes what is most meaningful with respect to living out our values. From here we prepare to speak "truth to power"[12] either in word or action. For now we have created liberatory space (bell hooks, 1994b) and sites of the possible. This is the "erotic" that Lorde (1984a) speaks of, the radical creativity that James Cone (1986) signifies. Is this the transformational leadership of scholarly leadership theory (McGregor Burns, 1995), a leadership that generates commitment to a goal larger than the individual and characterized by an enduring purpose in which leaders and followers raise one another to higher levels of motivation and morality? (McGregor Burns, p. 101).

Anansi be laughin' wild, now! Laughin' so hard he giddy. As a communal leader, I bring this process of web making to the group. As a developmental leader, I bring this process of web making to the individual. As a communal leader, I activate these cycles of healing, teaching, healing within the life story of the organization. As a generative leader, I position the individual's personal story within his or her familial, cultural, and intercultural mythology. *Back before the Mayflower. Back before the Amistad.*[13] *Back before the Nina, the Pinta, and the Santa Maria.* I have participated within this web forever. Each heartbeat, a story. Each story, a ritual, the web growing stronger, connecting, reconnecting, pulling away, and beginning again. In this way I make sure *never* to waste my breath. And in this way, I make sure *no* breath is *ever* wasted. *Ahhhhhhhhhhhhhhhh!*

NOTES

1. Italicized passages in this chapter signal a difference in consciousness. These passages derive from a phenomenological process of meditation, poetry, or journaling. In the tradition of phenomenology, and the use of writing as a form of inquiry, I engaged in free-form journal writing in response to questions I posed to myself about matrilineal leadership. See Laurel Richardson's "Writing: a Method of Inquiry," in *The Handbook of Qualitative Research*, 1994.

2. It is actually the Queen of Hearts who screams, "Off with her head" in response to Alice's outspoken answer to her queries in the popular children's classic, *Alice in Wonderland,* by Lewis Carroll, p. 128. However this scene takes place in part 2 of the unabridged version of the book *Through the Looking Glass*—thus the association in my memory between the Queen of Hearts and the looking glass [queen].

3. Fonow and Cook (1991) define reflexivity as reflecting upon, critically examining, and exploring analytically the nature of the research process. They further contextualize it as a "tradition of reminiscence about fieldwork experiences by sociologists and anthropologists," (p. 2).

4. All names of friends are fictionalized to maintain the anonymity of those referred to in this chapter. All family names are accurate.

5. Anansi is a character in African folk tales throughout the African Diaspora but particularly prominent in stories from West Africa and the Caribbean.

Anansi represents the traditional trickster of African lore and is most often represented in the physical form of a spider. Associated with the role of storyteller, Anansi is the main character in morality stories that depict him in a variety of roles, communal scenarios, and problematic dilemmas that require him to use his wit to resolve the issues at hand. Sometimes he cleverly outwits his opponents, and at other times he is fooled by his efforts to outwit. Either way he conveys important cultural lessons in community. See *Traditional Folk-Tales of Ghana,* by Emannuel V. Asihene.

6. *Pushed Back to Strength* is the title of a book by Gloria Wade-Gayles, which explores a black woman's coming of age in Memphis, Tennessee.

7. Upon retirement my mother became the storyteller in residence for the Muskogee Public School system and continued to inspire a love of stories and of reading in the schools and community.

8. Rumpel-Stilts-Kin, a classic from *Grimm's Fairy Tales*, is the story of a maiden who was given the power to spin straw into gold if she would promise to give her firstborn child in exchange. When she outwits Rumpel-Stilts-Kin at his own game, he flies into a rage. See *Grimm's Fairy Tales*, 1988, pp. 165–67.

9. Second Street, in my home town of Guthrie, Oklahoma, was known for its thriving nightlife geared toward the African American population of the town.

10. Title of a book by Cherrie Moraga and Gloria Anzaldua: *This Bridge Called My Back. Writings by Radical Women of Color* (Watertown, MA: Persephone, 1981).

11. This is a quote from the movie *Amistad*.

12. *Speaking Truth to Power* is the title of Anita Hill's 1997 book. In it she analyzes implications of her controversial testimony in the 1991 U.S. Senate hearings in which she described her experience of sexual harassment by Supreme court nominee Clarence Thomas.

13. The *Amistad* was a slave ship seized by fifty-three illegally enslaved Africans in 1839. After they took control of the vessel, the ship was intercepted and seized by the United States Navy, whereupon the Africans were imprisoned and forced to stand trial. Their case ultimately reached the Supreme Court, which not only acquitted them but also arranged for their passage back to the West Coast of Africa. See *Black Mutiny* by William Owens, 1997.

REFERENCES

Anzaldua, G. (Ed.). (1990). *Making face making soul/haciendo caras*. San Francisco: Aunt Lute.

Asihene, E.V. (1997). *Traditional folk-tales of Ghana*. Studies in African Literature, vol. 5. Lewiston, NY: Mellen.

Belenky, M. F., Bond, L. A., & Weinstock, J. S. (1991). A *Tradition that has no name: Nurturing the development of people, families, and communities.* New York: Basic.

Belenky, M. F., Clinchy, B. M., Goldberger, N. R., & Tarule, J. M. (1986). *Women's ways of knowing: The development of self, voice, and mind.* New York: Basic.

Carroll, L. (1993). *Alice in Wonderland.* Boston: Barefoot.

Collins, P. H. (1989). The social construction of black feminist thought. *Signs: Journal of Women in Culture and Society 14* (4): 745–73.

Cone, J. (1986). *A black theology of liberation.* New York: Orbis.

Danticat, E. (1994). *Breath, eyes, memory.* New York: Soho.

Estes, C. P. (1992). *Women who run with the wolves: Myths and stories of the wild woman archetype.* New York: Ballantine.

Evans-Winters, V. (2005). *Teaching black girls: Resiliency in urban classrooms.* New York: Lang.

Floyd-Thomas, S. M. (2006). *Mining the motherlode: Methods in womanist ethics.* Cleveland, Ohio: Pilgrim.

Fonow, M. M., and Cook, J. A. (1991). Back to the future: A look at the second wave of feminist epistemology and methodology. In *Beyond methodology: Feminist scholarship as lived research* (pp. 2–15). Bloomington: Indiana University Press.

Giddings, P. (1984). When and where I enter: The impact of black women on race and sex in America. New York: Bantam.

Grant, J. (1981). *Fundi: The story of Ella Baker.* Icarus Films.

Haraway, D. J. (1991). Situated knowledges: The science question in feminism and the privilege of partial perspective. In *Simians, cyborgs, and women: The reinvention of nature* (pp. 183–201). New York: Routledge.

Hill, A. (1997). *Speaking truth to power.* New York: Doubleday.

hooks, b. (1994a). *Sisters of the yam.* Boston, MA: Southside.

hooks, b. (1994b). Theory as liberatory practice. In *Teaching to Transgress* (pp. 59–75). New York: Routledge.

hooks, bell. (2009). Returning to the wound. In *Belonging.* New York: Routledge.

King, T. C., & Ferguson, S. A. (1996). We are, therefore I: Clinical interpretations of communal experience among African American professional women. *Women & Therapy 18,* 33–45.

Lorde, A. (1984a). Poetry is not a luxury. In *Sister outsider* (pp. 36–39). Freedom, CA: Crossing.

Lorde, A. (1984b). Uses of the erotic. In *Sister outsider* (pp. 53–59). Freedom, CA: Crossing.

Lorde, A. (1984c). The transformation of silence into action. In *Sister outsider* (pp. 40–44). Freedom, CA: Crossing.

Lugones, M. (1990). Playfulness, "world"—travelling, and loving perception. In G. Anzaldua (Ed.), *Making face, making soul/haciendo cara: Creative and critical perspectives by women of color* (pp. 390–402). San Francisco: Aunt Lute.

May, R. (1975). *The courage to create.* New York: Bantam.

Mbiti, J. S. (1970). *African religions and philosophy.* Garden City, NY: Anchor.

McCombs, H. G. (1986). The application of an individual/collective model to the psychology of black women. In D. Howard (Ed.), *The Dynamics of Feminist Therapy.* Binghamton: Haworth.

McGregor Burns, J. (1995). Transactional and transforming leadership. In J. Thomas Wren (E, *The leader's companion: Insights on leadership through the ages* (pp. 100–07). New York: Free.

Moore, Thomas (1992). *Care of the soul: A guide for cultivating depth and sacredness in everyday life.* New York: HarperCollins.

Moraga, C., and Anzaldua, G. (1981). *This bridge called my back: Writings by radical women of color.* Watertown, MA: Persephone.

Nobles, W. (1976). African philosophy: Foundations for a black psychology. In R. L. Jones (Ed.), *Black Psychology* (pp. 18–32). New York: Harper and Row.

Noddings, N. (1984). *Caring: A feminine approach to ethics and moral education* (pp. 40–48). Berkeley: University of California Press.

Owens, W. A. (1997). *Black mutiny: The revolt on the schooner* Amistad. New York: Plume.

Palmer, P. (1998). *The courage to teach: Exploring the inner landscape of a teacher's life.* San Francisco: Jossey-Bass.

Reinharz, S. (1992). *Feminist methods in social research.* New York: Oxford University Press.

Richardson, L. (1994). Writing: A method of inquiry. In N. K. Denzin & Y. S. Lincoln (Eds.), *Handbook of qualitative research* (pp. 516–29). Thousand Oaks, CA: Sage.

Robb, C. (2006). *This changes everything: The relational revolution in psychology.* New York: Picadoor.

Robnett, B. (1997). *How long? how long? African-American women in the struggle for civil rights.* New York: Oxford University Press.

Rumpel-Stilts-Kin. *(1988). Grimm's Fairy Tales* (pp. 165–67). New Jersey: Children's Classics, Dilithium.

Turk, J. (1999). *Subverting stagnation: Women of color, identity and a just feminist movement.* Senior Research Project, Denison University.

Wade-Gayles, G. (1993). *Pushed back to strength: A Black woman's journey home.* Boston: Beacon.

Wade-Gayles, G. (1995). *My soul is a witness: African-American women's spirituality.* Boston: Beacon.

Walker, A. (1983). Definition of a womanist. *In Search of Our Mother's Gardens: Womanist Prose* (pp. xi–xii). New York: Harcourt Brace.

PART III

Visions of the Motherline— Templates for Daughters

> There is a tremendous amount of teaching transmitted by Black mothers to their daughters that enables them to survive, exist, succeed, and be important to and for the Black communities . . . Black daughters are actually "taught" to hold the Black community together.
> —Patricia Hill Collins, "The Meaning of Motherhood in Black Culture and Black Mother-Daughter Relationships"

THE QUESTIONS FOR THIS SECTION take us further in our journey along the Motherline. The first section, "Roots and Significance of the Motherline," considers the significance of the Motherline in providing black women with cultural grounding so as to resist oppression. The next section, "The Foundations of Motherline Tutelage," focuses on the philosophical underpinnings of an African-centered worldview and its transmission to daughters and, subsequently, to us. In this third section, four more women write the Motherline. Some questions raised include: What kind of leadership emerges from the Motherline? What kind of leadership do mothers envision for their daughters? What roles will the daughters play in the world? And how do mothers enable leadership in their daughters—what actions, admonitions, and adages are effective in creating leaders?

Themes in this section resonate with those of previous authors. These narratives look closely at day-to-day Motherline negotiations and the purposes of Motherline apprenticeships. Each of these authors views the mothers who are "home and community level visible" as critical to the cultural stability of black communities and to the production of the next generation of leaders. The papers also show us that the traditions that help develop leadership in the black community may not be recognized in mainstream leadership theory but that black mothers and daughters know them well and have named them.

In the first chapter, "I Earns My Struttin' Shoes," Judy Massey-Dozier shows us how she was given a template by her mother for developing a healthy sexual identity. She was taught how to enjoy woman-centered pleasures of sensuality/sexuality/intimacy without being preyed upon in a sexist society. She uses the symbolism of "struttin' shoes" to illustrate a woman's healthy autonomy, worth, and sexual pleasure and to counter patriarchal control. Massey Dozier shows us how her mother bequeathed to her a wholesome sexual identity in a world that thwarts women's psychosexual development and disparages women's sexual agency. The author, who is now an associate professor of English and chair of African American studies at Lake Forest College, credits her cultural training to these models of "independent, sexual women focused on their own actualization in every area, not passive appendages to men" (Massey Dozier).

The second author, S. Alease Ferguson, frames her mother's tutelage as "Thelma's every tub paradigm" from the adage "every tub must stand on its own bottom." This adage of self-sufficiency "spawns a perception of self as a dreamer, creator and actor/director in one's own life" (Ferguson). Ferguson describes her mother's teachings as clear, appropriate to each stage of the daughter's growing up, and highly interactive and experiential. She writes: "Always a teachable moment would be followed by discussion, queries, and the imagining of viable alternatives" (Ferguson). Currently, the author follows a career in social services administration, organizational consulting, teaching within higher ed, and activism. She applies her mother's teaching to her clients who suffer from domestic abuse, incarceration, substance abuse, mental illness, and the grinding stress of poverty.

In the third chapter in this section, Rhunette Diggs remembers her mother as a no-nonsense disciplinarian; the mother of nine children held to a mantra that "abundant love brooks no disrespect." Although her method might be called "tough love," she was no "ordinary" mother, but one with abundant energy for raising her children to act always in good character and to strive for excellence in all aspects of life. Diggs refers to the leadership her mother modeled through her commitment to family and community as "*drylongso*," leadership, and calls the approach of infusing character into ordinary everyday acts as "*ajabu*" leadership. Diggs, now a scholar/educator and cofounder of a nonprofit organization, acts upon this call to bring her highest self into each moment, each setting, each relationship.

The fourth contributor to this section, Simona J. Hill, received a call to what she considers "legacy work." Simona draws upon two key Motherline women—her mother, Mildred, and her godmother, Ione, and shows us what she has internalized from their leadership visions. Both women were active in their communities. Mildred was an exemplar of community development and Ione as a community level political activist. Although "Mom-Mom Ione" was enmeshed inextricably in an alcoholic marriage, she reached beyond the home to the public sphere where she worked to connect people seeking employment to opportunities and where she participated in the founding of several service organizations.

African American mothers are legendary for passionately nurturing their visions and transmitting them to their progeny. In *On Becoming a Leader* (1994) Warren Bennis, an Organizational Behavior pioneer, employs the term "synesthesia" to refer to any mode of leadership transmission that is made palpable and perceptually available for ready application. It refers to a guide's capacity to powerfully translate and share a vision so crisp and clear that others can understand and follow easily.

Black women often take leadership when faced with the need to give immediate assistance or aid to others. Other times their leadership involves vision and long-range planning required to shape the life of a human being, to cultivate a career, or to show how to thrive in a society characterized by oppressive race, class, and gender barriers. The snatching of a fellow human being from the jaws of danger, pursing excellence in all phases of a job, defending against being the "throw away" people, conferring of the dignity of work, and infusing of mindfulness "regardless"—these are the lessons of the Motherline for their daughters. In this section we see that black women's intuitive sensibilities have been honed to view all aspects of life as expressions of leadership. No need is too small when one considers the vast influence and reach of hegemony and the dehumanizing social ills it spawns. In the machinery of oppression, the Motherline insists upon social uplift, problem solving, and psychosocial agency. The contributors to this section are our eyes for seeing the visions of the Motherline. They give us a dreamscape motif for a world in which every act is one of mindful, intentional excellence, steeped in an ethic of care, and available to any eventuality.

REFERENCES

Collins, P. H., Bell-Scott, P., Guy-Sheftall, B., Royster, J. J., Sims-Wood, J., DeCosta-Willis, M., and Fultz, L. P. (Eds.). *Double stitch: Black Women write about mothers & daughters* (pp. 42–60). New York: Harper Perennial.

7

"I Earns My Struttin' Shoes"

Blues Women and Leadership

JUDY MASSEY-DOZIER

> We have been raised to fear the yes within ourselves, our deepest cravings... The fear of our desires keeps them suspect and indiscriminately powerful, for to suppress any truth is to give it strength beyond endurance.
> —Audre Lorde, "Uses of the Erotic"

IN THE EPIGRAPH ABOVE Audre Lorde insists that the erotic in women has been suppressed and confused with pornography. She explains that it is because of our internalized fear that we are unable to grow and resolve the distortions we encounter within ourselves that ultimately leads us to become submissive to the external definitions of society. Thus, women have tended to shy away from a bold expression of the erotic, the sensual in themselves. Black women, having been defined as promiscuous as early as from missionary accounts in Africa and thereby excluded from the nineteenth-century ideology of the "cult of true womanhood," have chosen either to define themselves against the stereotype or to disregard the stereotype in favor of their own (re)creation of themselves as sexual beings. The latter have functioned as models for me. And they, either consciously or unconsciously, taught me that when we embrace the sensual in ourselves, we emerge whole and empowered and capable of leading others.

MOTHERS AND OTHERMOTHERS

Many women raised me. Outside my birth mother were extended family members who felt raising children was not the sole burden of only one mother, an approach to child rearing that resembles traditional West African culture. Patricia Hill Collins appropriately identifies these women as "othermothers." Oyèrónké, Oyěwùmí makes clear that in many African communities the female's mobility was often enabled by "a multiplicity of mothers and fathers, [which] meant that child-rearing was not an individualized experience that devolved only to mothers" (1997, p. 73). According to Collins, this tradition continued in African American communities. She explains, "African and African American communities have also recognized that vesting one person with full responsibility for mothering a child may not be wise or possible . . . The centrality of women in African American extended families reflects both a continuation of West African cultural values and functional adaptations to race and gender oppression" (p. 119). Such a sense of group mothering did not arise out of the father's absence in the home. Many were still present, and even fathers divorced from the bloodmother, like my own, were constantly on the scene.

My mother worked during the day at the United States Post Office. She was one of the few women on our block who did work during the day. During my prepubescent years, my mother left strict instructions that I was not to comb my hair on the porch (this was considered to be "country" in the south suburb of Chicago), I could not emerge from the house for play until the afternoon, and I was never to leave the house with my hair uncombed. It didn't matter that my mother was at least twenty-five miles away during the day and would not be able to see me violate her rules because I knew that the women on the block would be her eyes. Not that she had asked them to participate in the reinforcement of her mandates; this was unnecessary. My mother would not have raised an eyebrow if they had scolded me or even whipped me. And they knew this. When my mother wasn't around, I could feel their eyes on me as if I were one of their own.

RED POLISH AND ANKLE BRACELETS: SYMBOLS OF FEMININE POWER AND PERFECTION

Such overseeing wasn't always negative or one-way. I watched them, too, particularly the two women who lived next door. One of them always wore bright red nail polish on her fingernails and toes. Whenever she sat down in the evenings to talk with my mother, she would bring her fingernail polish and touch up her nails. They were always flawless.

When this woman decided she would go back to school, one of my mother's sisters ridiculed the woman in conversation with my mother for wanting to do such a thing at this stage in her life. My aunt insisted that at fifty this woman could not possibly finish high school and go on to get an undergraduate degree. She was making a fool of herself, according to my aunt, and would suffer an embarrassing fall. Perhaps I watched this woman as a result of my aunt's words. Otherwise, the entire lesson I was destined to learn might have fallen outside of my observation. After all, they were grownups whose lives held very little interest to me. However, I must admit that I couldn't wait to wear an ankle bracelet like the one this woman wore, and when I began to wear fingernail polish, it was with the meticulousness I had observed as a child. In fact, such perfection has continued to permeate everything I have done in my life.

So my othermother returned to school. I watched her perfectly manicured nails turn the pages of books, type papers, and finally reach for, first, a high school diploma, then an undergraduate degree, and finally a graduate degree. Pregnant at sixteen, this woman decided, as my mother stated to my aunt, "to do a thing, and did it." Her only child, another polish-perfect othermother, even returned to college with her mother. For me the symbols of my othermother's ankle bracelet and fingernail polish represented a woman who acted against the odds. I knew as I watched this woman walk that she lived fully in her body, that she denied nothing about herself. And before she ever spoke a word, her love for herself was evident. She was sexual and strong enough to resist the restrictions on her display of her sexuality.

The ankle bracelet and the red polish became for me the symbols of the power and the creativity to make oneself over in one's own image. For these and other reasons, I refer to my othermothers, including my blood mother, as "blues women." Like the blues singers, they were determined to define their own sexuality.

INDEPENDENCE AND SEXUAL CHOICES

The other women I watched were my mother and her friends at work, all of whom had good paying jobs at the United States Post Office. Most of them were divorced and very independent. They made enough money to support themselves and their children whether the child support arrived or not. None would have dared jeopardize that good government job in order to enter college. Instead they managed to have some fun on weekends. These blues women partied together, cussed, smoked cigarettes, and told dirty jokes. They formed close, supportive relationships, and they were consistently there for one another: cosigning loans, tiding each other over until a check came for an unexpected expense, sharing rides to and from work. Once during my teenage years, I rode with my mother to pick up one of her friends. My mother drove up to a house unfamiliar to me, and we waited. In moments, my mother's friend emerged from the house, kissed a man goodbye, and ran to the car. I knew this man was not her husband, and this image is a vivid memory even now. There was really nothing unusual about this encounter. My mother's friend was not married. But somehow, prior to this sighting, I hadn't imagined my mother or her friends as sexual beings. They were mothers, for goodness sake!

Nonetheless, after this new awareness, I looked for more signs of sexuality. Here were women who joked about sex. References were obscure, but a curious teenager could read between the lines. I discovered from these women that sexuality was nothing to be ashamed of. Sex was not being misused by them, but it was a necessary element of living, vital in fact, to a full knowledge of oneself. There were no discussions of tolerating sex because they owed their sustenance to some man. Instead these women could and did choose their partners. And they chose to have sex, not as a favor or as an obligation, but as an answer to the desire of their bodies. However, these women were not promiscuous as black women were considered to be back in the fifties and sixties, and even today still. It's just that these Post Office women were comfortable in their bodies. And they loved entertainers who were too. I sang along with my mother to the lyrics of Sarah Vaughn with her husky, sensuous voice and also joined in singing along with Ella Fitzgerald, Della Reese, and Dinah Washington. At nine, I remember walking around singing the lyrics to *This Bitter Earth* as if I had actually been through something.

My mother cautioned against having sexual relations too early, as did her friends with their daughters. My othermothers, too, imposed sexual standards on their daughters, but the approach, at least if my own mother can be considered typical, was different from the repressive sexual expectations the larger society held girls and women to during the fifties and early sixties. For instance, my girlfriend who lived around the corner had a stay-at-home mom. When it was time to tell her about sex, her mother told her to remember that boys don't respect girls who aren't ladies or something to that effect, something elusive and indirect. My friends and I translated her message to mean that if we had sex with a boy, he would not respect us. This told us nothing about the actual sex act and plenty about caring more for the way we appeared under the male gaze than about making choices for ourselves based on knowledge of our bodies. So when my mother gave me her pitch, I shared it with my friend who was waiting with bated breath to hear the "real deal" that we had come to expect from my Post Office mother.

In a nutshell, my mother told me that I was at an age when I would experience sexual feelings. She insisted that these feelings were nothing to be ashamed of; in fact, I should own them as a part of my being. She explained exactly what the sexual act entailed and told me that since I was young, the chances of my getting pregnant were extremely high, no matter what a little boy might tell me. Practical, sensible, rooted in the reality of her experience, my mother only mentioned the boy to dismiss his falsehoods; the rest of the conversation was all about me. Knowing my mother as I do, I'm sure she never once thought of telling me to maintain my sense of "ladyness" in the eyes of the young boy.

BLUES WOMEN AND LEADERSHIP

Anyway, I grew up around these two classes of othermothers: blues women who took chances and made their own decisions and choices about their sexual identities. Fueled by their sense of the erotic, the women I watched seemed to conform to Lorde's sense of the erotic as creative power and energy. Lorde explains: "The very word "erotic" comes from the Greek word "*eros*," the personification of love in all its aspects—Born of Chaos, and personifying creative power and harmony. When I speak of the erotic, then, I speak of it as an assertion of the life-force of women; of that creative energy empowered, the knowledge and use of which we are now reclaiming in our language, our history, our dancing, our loving, our work, our lives" (1984, p. 55).

This sense of my othermothers' own sexuality moved beyond sexual relations. Their willingness to respect the erotic in themselves was manifested in a self-love displayed in the confidence of their movements, their speech, and their independent actions. They approached every activity in their lives with enthusiasm and pleasure. As far as I could tell, my mother and my othermothers had adopted none of the Western ideology that bound women to a repressed sexuality, an ideology that insisted a "true woman" was only one who was virtuous, dependent and asexual. This nineteenth century legacy of "the cult of true womanhood," which excluded black women as women and identified them as the antithesis of true womanhood, was lost on these women. Instead their resistance to the dominant ideology derived from ways of living in the body that originated across the ocean. According to Eugene D. Genovese,[3] sexuality was viewed in West Africa so differently from the West that Europeans were unable to understand or objectively evaluate the differences that they witnessed among the natives. Sex as "delightfully human and pleasurable" contrasted deeply with the European view of sex as "sinful, dirty" (Genovese, 1974, p. 459). Responding to the Africans' "different standards of behavior," Europeans concluded that these people were amoral, since the absence of taboos seemed to mean the absence of restraints on sexual behavior (Genovese, 1974, p. 458). Genovese explains: "[I]n fact West Africans demanded chastity in their youngsters and severely punished adultery; but since these same Africans had the audacity to define chastity, adultery, and other relevant terms to suit themselves, and since *their views of sexual freedom largely applied to women as well as men,* they continued to be regarded as amoral by Europeans" (pp. 458, 459; my emphasis).

The European insistence upon the repression of sexual desire located woman's fulfillment within the context of nurturing her family. In contrast, West African mythology contains gods, who, as divine temptresses, relish sexual enjoyment.[1] For instance, Yemaya is not only the god of rivers and springs but "Yemaya is the sea itself" (Jahn, 1989, p. 65). According to Jaheinz Jahn, "In Africa . . . she appears full of virtue, she is the wife and mature woman, and yet she is sometimes wild and sensual, [since according to Fernando Oritz] '. . . the Africans do not consider virtue and sensuality incompatible'" (p. 65). Similarly, Oshun, the wife of Shango, is both devoted wife and seductive temptress. Within this pantheon, Oshun is very much like Erzulie, another sea god who presents herself seductively to the man she would possess, demanding his total sexual allegiance. While Oshun has these seductive dimensions, she is not dichotomized as dangerous or evil as is the pattern in Western thought. Rather, she is described as the "embodiment of feminine beauty and grace" (Jahn, 1989, p. 45), Marjorie Shostak translates the words of Nisa, a member of the !Kung tribe in West Africa, who explains that "[w]hen the gods gave people sex . . . they gave [them] a wonderful thing. Sex is often referred to as food: just as people cannot survive without eating, the !Kung say, hunger for sex can cause people to die (1983, p. 108).

As I watched my othermothers in their daily activities, I recall absolutely no sense of rebellion against the way American society represented them; they were simply carrying on in a manner that pleased them, consciously or unconsciously continuing a sense of the sexual that bears more similarity to West African tradition than to the restraints on sexuality fostered in the West.

EMBRACING ONESELF WHOLE, LOVING ALL THOSE FEELINGS

The women I grew up around placed few censors on anything that moved them. They loved and accepted themselves in the face of a society that denied the sensual public display. In contrast, these women, empowered by the sensual, spoke their minds. As Lorde makes clear, "In touch with the erotic, I become less willing to accept powerlessness, or those other supplied states of being which are not native to me, such as resignation, despair, self-effacement, depression, self-denial" (Lorde, 1984, p. 58).

What fascinated me most about my cultural training was the fact that so many of my othermothers were women who did not worry about being "ladies" as women in the West typically did. Rather, they were led by a sense that sensual union was more in line with what the blues singer Shug Avery, in Alice Walker's novel *The Color Purple*, claims about "God lov[ing] all those feelings" (p. 191). These women did not defend themselves against becoming reservoirs for male release but rather took charge of their sexuality as active participants in the realization of their own bodily pleasure. These are the women I remember from my childhood—independent, sexual women, focused on their own actualization in every area, not passive appendages to men (Crawford, 2006). Refusing to conform to external definitions of themselves, these women grew beyond any limitations to embrace their sexuality as an empowering aspect of their being (Thompson, 2009).

My decision to leave a career in advertising to return to school in my forties was met by exclamations from my friends about my courage. Since I didn't feel very heroic, I began to ponder my past to pull together where such courage originated. I remembered the othermothers who, right before my growing eyes, sat on the front porch in the evenings and talked of their education. Undoubtedly, my decision stemmed from the subconscious remembrance of the woman who at a mature age thought nothing of stepping back into a classroom. Rooted in my memory also were all my models who maintained a home, a job, and their sensuality without complaint or self-doubt. I had watched and listened to these women as I followed their successes. My othermothers made choices and changed their minds; they did what it took to move to another phase in their lives. And these were women who represented the importance of sensuality and its connection to power. The ability to say yes to the fullness of one's self, one's feelings, one's sensuality carried over into their decisions to take charge of their lives. The ability to adorn one's own body boldly and to speak unrestricted about one's sexuality enabled the courage to act on dreams and make them a reality

(Kinser, 2008). I found in their examples the necessity of accepting all of one's self, listening confidently to the wisdom of one's own inner directives. To deny any aspect of oneself was to risk disempowerment. One might lose the ability even to see clearly, much less to create oneself in one's own unique vision.

I hear similar messages in the lyrics of many young women's music today. Coming-of-age promptings from innovative artists such as India.Arie,[2] who adorns herself in sensual fashion emblazoned with the phrase *love yourself* across her chest as she sings of the importance of loving the physical and accepting the emotional that we are. Queen Latifah became popular espousing an acceptance of herself physically. Both Latifah and Arie remind young women that they are queens. Lauren Hill's sensual dance movements showed how to be comfortable physically as she too sang of the importance of self-initiated creativity and personal acceptance. Each of these self-defined women in their own traditions—be it neosoul or rhythm and blues—echoes the traditions of blues women who showed us how to "embrace ourselves whole."

The risk to young women who are unable to fully accept their sensuality as empowering is that they may choose early mothering as a measure of one's power, seeking external affirmation from men. Sensuality is too strong an aspect of our being to be denied. Too often, without the knowledge of the magic of its creative potential and its channel to the power within ourselves, young women look for themselves in the eyes of others. This choice is an obstacle to the knowledge of themselves as future leaders.

My development as a leader began very early. My mother recalls how "bossy" I was with the other children on the block; I always needed to lead the way. My favorite uncle looked out at me at play one day and responded to my mother's criticism; "she's a leader," he smiled with pride. And I am. I take this role seriously, and I spend lots of time outside of the classroom sitting and talking with many of my young black female students. During the time that they attend Lake Forest College, I am at times their "othermother." Not that these brilliant young women need watching, but rather my position at this stage of their lives provides them with the comfort of knowing there is someone they may call on who knows, among other things, how black hair tends to act, what it feels like to lose a boyfriend and watch him walk on campus with someone else on his arm, where to get a boost to the confidence they already hold about themselves and their possibilities. And perhaps most important, I show them where to read in literature about the othermothers in their experiences. These readings, created by their literary othermothers, lead these young women to the spaces they carve for themselves, as they step fully into their own empowering self-definitions with bold confidence and sensuous stride.

NOTES

1. According to Oyĕwùmí, since *orisas* are not gendered in Yoruba, female *orisas* are also referred to as gods not goddesses (p. 174).

2. This artist spells her name "India.Arie" as multiple online popular culture sources confirm: http://en.wikipedia.org/wiki/India.Arie.

REFERENCES

Crawford, N. (2006). Good, bad, and beautiful: Chester Hime's femmes in Harlem. *National Women's Studies Association Journal, 18* (2).

Genovese, E. D. (1974). *Roll, Jordan, roll.* New York: Pantheon.

Jahn, J. (1989). *Muntu.* New York: Grove Weidenfield.

Kinser A. (2008). Embracing the tensions of a maternal erotic. In A. Kinser (Ed.), *Mothering in the Third Wave,* (pp. 119–26). Toronto: Demeter.

Lorde, A. (1984). Uses of the erotic. In *Sister outsider* (pp. 53–59). Freedom, CA: Crossing.

Oyèrónk , O. (1997). *The invention of women.* Minneapolis: University of Minnesota Press.

Shostak, M. (1983). *Nisa: The life and words of a !Kung woman.* New York: Vintage Books.

Thompson, L. B. (2009). *Representing the sexuality of black middle-class women in contemporary popular culture.* Chicago: University of Illinois Press.

Walker, Alice. (1982). *The Color Purple: A Novel.* New York: Harcourt Brace Jovanovich.

8

Thelma's Self-Sufficiency Paradigm

Every Tub Must Stand on Its Own Bottom

S. ALEASE FERGUSON

INTRODUCTION

MA HAD BATTLED the ravages of cancer for almost two years. December 9, 1992, was the last day that my mother was lucid and able to speak before she passed on. For that one day, she came back to herself. She rose from the hospital bed, walked about, talked, and giggled with visiting girlfriends and took time with Daddy and each of us to say farewell. Sitting side by side on the edge of the bed, we hugged, swung arms like we had done hundreds of times walking along together in the park, or coming out of a restaurant, or strolling down a mall. On that last day, she said, "Thank you sister-friend, you are the best daughter, friend, and woman any mother could ever hope for. You've taken the best of my love, my examples, my hopes and dreams to become a *self-sufficient* human being. She asked: "Please never stop helping others to become self-sufficient wherever you can. I love you."

Post Script: This stamp of approval meant more than words could say. It was a golden moment for each of us. It was our last sharing of affection and the appreciation for the gifts given. From that point on, once she left this physical plane, the potency of the thirty-seven years of self-sufficiency leadership training would be tested by my ability to continue myself as a tub standing on its own bottom.

My mother used "self sufficiency" in the classical sense, much in the same way as Thoreau talked about "self-reliance." She took on self-sufficiency leadership as a personal mission long before it was in vogue in the welfare reform world to usher people off public assistance, while expecting them to miraculously evidence self-sufficiency and financial independence without the benefits of work opportunities or mentorship to acquire and perform in the workforce. Her approach was at once systematic and developmental. She aimed to create sustained resistance to patriarchal authority and to prevent spiritual and financial poverty. Foremost, she tried to help a sister care for herself lovingly and responsibly and to stay buoyant and alive even in the worst of times. To my mother, self-sufficiency demonstrated complete faith in God's abundance for those willing to do their part.

I coin my mother Thelma's style of leadership as the original "self-sufficiency model of feminist leadership." The model's raison d'être for self-sufficiency is grounded in the Maslowian hierarchy of needs and self-actualization. Essentially, Ma encouraged people to gain the skills and engage in the activism needed to take care of one's basic creature comfort and needs: food, rest, shelter, and also belongingness, love, and spiritual support. The method of application is much like the Zen notion of "chop wood, carry water"—the practice of ordinary work and the ordinariness of everyday life. She taught us that when you apply a focus to everyday acts such as folding the laundry, cleaning the bathtub, or preparing a salad, you are empowered to live in the now. From there, seeing the unfolding of a task brings the doer in contact with the mysteries of purpose, accomplishment, beauty, order, and the joy of discovering one's own transformative powers.

Overall, self-sufficiency leadership is also about learning the arts of everyday self-care and individual responsibility in order to fulfill personal and career aspirations. My mother also believed that children require conscious adult guidance and rigorous home schooling on the how tos, the tools, and the coaching supports for accomplishing everyday tasks. Ultimately, the continual presence of the active adult guide and repetitive and progressive practice of new skills reinforce the child's cultivation of intuition, ingenuity, and desire for self-sustenance. My mother maintained that teens or adults deprived of the opportunity to develop life skills as children required a modified resocialization training in order to engage life fully and to be able to spread their wings.

This approach to leadership draws from a vast world lineage of women determined to do something to improve the condition of their lives and that of others. You see, Ma really "walked the walk and talked the talk" of self-sufficiency. Some of the hallmarks of her brand of leadership and resistance to oppression began in the late 1940s and early 1950s. In her late adolescence, she worked summers at Connecticut's Shoreham Club to put herself through college and earned a bachelor's degree in biology from North Carolina Agricultural and Technical College on time. Fresh out of college, she worked for four years at a New York City biology laboratory and prepared histology textbook drawings. Driven out of that job by sexual harassment, she reinvented herself by taking a cross-country trip with college chums, moving to Cleveland with her sister and brother in law, and entering into training to become a licensed practical nurse. In her late twenties, she married, became a financially independent woman, a home and property owner, a culinary artist, and a superb gardener and caretaker for a mentally ill husband.

Her stellar accomplishment was the singlehanded nurture of three self-possessed, professionally competent, and financially independent daughters. By their midtwenties, the daughters had earned professional degrees to become, respectively, a psychologist, an exercise physiologist, and an attorney. Through my mother's willfulness and ingenuity, I and my sisters, Sharon and Leah, along with scores of women friends, neighbors, and aspiring young nurses and neighbors were the beneficiaries of this highly physical, strategic, energetic and activist style of mentoring. Note none of these things was a small accomplishment for a mocha chocolate brown girl born in Chester, South Carolina, in the 1920s.

THE ROLE AND FUNCTION OF MY SELF-SUFFICIENCY S/HERO

Structurally, Ma's role as a self-sufficiency leader can be likened to the preparatory works of the women ritual specialists and mystery school leaders[1] charged with the passing on of sacred women's knowledge concerning menstruation, womanhood, marriage, birthing and motherhood, and croning and death. Rituals in which women provide the psychospiritual nurturing of personhood across the life span are chronicled in Zora Neale Hurston's *Tell My Horse* (1938, p. 14), an anthropological study of Jamaican and Haitian cultures. Ma's demonstrated self-sufficiency and liberationist strides also resembled the life work of Harriet Tubman, Ida Wells Barnett, Fannie Lou Hammer, and the work of an unknown woman farmer-merchant in Zimbabwe or a young woman Peace Corp worker teaching irrigation to farmers in an underdeveloped country. Her style of self-sufficiency leadership was indicative of what bell hooks (1994a, pp. 151–59) calls "construction and preservation of the homeplace," a mother-created safe haven for nurture and protection against the violence of racism. Ma could turn any site or setting into a veritable homeplace through the outreaching of others to impart the knowledge, insight, and belief. Ma's strategy involved a warm, hands-on support of people, families, workplace teams, church activities, a new enterprise, a crucial community project, or an activist goal.

OUR ORIGINS IN SELF-SUFFICIENCY LEADERSHIP

The belief in self-sufficiency ran through every fiber of Ma's being and that of her sisters and her female forebears. I attribute the quest for perfecting self-sufficiency to the fact that women in three consecutive generations of our maternal lineage were orphaned before the age of twelve. Amazingly, the surviving daughters surmounted the grief and betrayal of mother loss and the differing support each was receiving within her kinship care network to help one another attend college and mount careers in the industries of education, medicine, and the arts. Those early losses fostered fire, tenacity, gumption, and resourcefulness in successive generations of women. The visceral warmth of Ma's daily actions and care taking counterbalanced the painful cellular memories of those ancestral struggles. Lovingly, Ma shared every practical skill and talent that she herself had attained, through story, advice, and daily lessons.

From our mother's messages—spoken, sung, demonstrated, and manifested—my sisters and I took her instructions to heart as truisms about our lives as African American women with bright futures. Over time she gave us glimpses into the evolving lives of women; racism; sexism and chauvinism; male infidelity; sexual harassment; black-woman-white-woman relationships; workplace discrimination and stereotyping; the hardships faced by women who were unable to extricate themselves from the tendrils of depression, drugs, and alcohol; domestic violence; the welfare state; the possibilities and perils of desegregation; and the ongoing realities of internalized oppression (Galvan, 2006, p. 263; Nadasen, 2002, pp. 271–72)

Being touched by this legacy has empowered me to uplift myself and also provide developmental support to others. In time, the experience of my mother's self-sufficiency work has been integral to my life's work as a community-based psychologist and social work administrator. My lifetime working with self-sufficiency has made it possible for me to create, fund, and deliver services that reinvoked the sharings of the Sister Circle—my closest women friends. My work has widened alliance vistas and taught men, women, and children how to do their own fishing, how to stand as tubs on their own bottoms (Johnson, 2004, pp. 101, 114–16).

THE RATIONALE FOR SELF-SUFFICIENCY LEADERSHIP

> Life for me ain't been no crystal stair . . .
> But all the time
> I'se been a-climbin' on.
> —Langston Hughes, "Mother to Son"

The poignancy of these lines from the oft-quoted above poem speak of both hardship and struggle. In this message Hughes imagines a mother's message to her son, but he also depicts a mother's reflections on her life philosophy. His poem speaks not only of a stairway with tacks, splinters, and bare rough wood, but of the mother's continued efforts to carry on in order to make a way out of no way. This message has currency for me as time goes on and speaks to the philosophy of self-sufficiency that my own mother taught me.

In practical terms, Ma saw self-sufficiency leadership as a sort of life contingency plan of making the way straight behind and before. She used to say: "Know that you cannot control the hand life deals you, but you can do your level best to prevent the hardships that can arise from sloth or irresponsibility. So in all cases, learn all you can to take care of yourself, solve your own problems, and seek the appropriate help needed." Essentially, the life contingency plan was a road map for building the muscles for self-support, adaptability to change, and a readiness for moving out and acting. One must establish a vision and find an orientation toward the future. The individual must find an anchoring in order to sustain the self and contribute to others, for the anchored individual has the resilience to be successful, to overcome obstacles, and to avoid total devastation in the face of turmoil and loss. The contingency plan helps to set in motion a reality-based assessment that includes querying: What is my current situation or problem? What skills, resources, and supports do I need to improve or resolve the matter? What can I do both long- and short-range to take myself to another level? How can I anticipate and avert danger? These questions point one to taking the first steps of a thousand-mile journey. Overall, the life plan requires developing competencies for successfully navigating and orchestrating the day-to-day. It requires what Ruth Trinidad Galvan (2006, p. 252) refers to as "operating in a pluralistic mode" to respond to the everyday, the diverse, and the unexpected.

The rationale for promoting self-sufficiency leadership training with young African American girls is two-fold and linked to communal cultural rites of passage and the parenting socialization. The rationale for promoting self-sufficiency training with African American girls is twofold and is linked to communal rites of passage. In the Americas, there is the urgent need for such training as a rite of passage because of the reality that by their midtwenties most black females have encountered the triple whammy of race, gender, and class. The firsthand understanding of the marginalizing impact of institutional racism makes it imperative that young black girls and women learn the basic principals of self-sufficiency. This approach is a mechanism for developing self-esteem, basic life skills, physical heath and fitness, personal and intellectual capabilities, skilled trades, a spirit of opportunism and enterprise, and an ethic of care for facilitating the development and improved life chances of self, family, and their cultural group of origin. According to Betsch Cole and Guy-Sheftall (2003, p. 70), the sharing, telling, retelling, and writing of individual struggles against racism and poverty are also critical ways of fending off patriarchy.

From the perspective of psychosocial and emotional development, Jungian psychologist Clarissa Pinkola Estes (1993, pp. 219–22) suggests that when parents provide the girlish maiden with knowledge of large looming dangers and pitfalls, they support their daughters' transition into womanhood and self-sufficiency and self-advocacy. Warnings, red flags, myths, and stories signaling danger serve to break the spell of maiden innocence and potential victimization. Such support helps to transport the girl from Maiden to Warrior Heroine and self-advocate. Pinkola Estes (1992, pp. 97–98) and Valentis and DeVane (1994, p. 49) also warn that failure to provide this kind of realistic teaching can stultify growth, self-nurturing, and the capacity for self-sufficiency.

THE INTENTIONAL MODE OF TRANSMISSION

Ma's process of cultivating self-sufficiency-oriented leadership in her children was a highly intentional and interactive style of parenting. She employed the elements of role-modeling and demonstration, instruction, storytelling, and the sharing of adages and apocryphal tales. To be of service the knowledge presented is always age-appropriate, graduated, and a progressively complex conceptual schema relative for problem solving and decision making. Her method of instruction exemplifies what bell hooks (1994b), Paulo Freire (1980), and Chodron (2005, pp. 237–39) define as "praxis," the use of reflection and positive action upon the world in order to change it. At no time were we the passive observers or listeners. Always a teachable moment would be followed by discussion, questioning, and the imagining of viable alternatives.

Ma's voice led as the instrument of healing, instruction, and correction. Like a West African Griot, Ma told stories to transmit knowledge, to prime the young ones for listening and remembering, and to establish a base of cultural values. Wherever Ma told stories there was the aura of a campfire. We attuned our ears to listen, as we knew that the stories were important and held mystery and surprise. Always, the stories were purposeful and germane to the moment. They highlighted the accomplishments of legendary Africans and African American figures, ancestral and family lineage tales, and her own accounts of growing up. She told work stories, payback stories, man–woman stories, and death/near death stories. The stories included profiles in courage or in guile and trickery; they illustrated the consequences of actions; and they instructed us about successful and unsuccessful methods of solving problems. Overall, these stories were told to provide us with a sense of place within the grander scheme of the community and the family.

The knowledge gleaned from the various stories was fortified by the use of a series of adages. Some of the most potent examples of self-sufficiency leadership include the following: every tub must stand on its own bottom; if you teach a man to fish, he will have food for a lifetime; no cross no crown; and if you educate a woman (or a mother), you educate a nation. She would also say that whenever you get lemons, you make lemonade, and the Bible verse, "I can do all things through Christ who strengthens me." All told, these pearls of wisdom provided us with an almost visible and visceral sense of what it means to be self-sufficient.

Ma's potency in this work rested on her life experiences of the troubles and beauties of the world. She tested her own mettle and prevailed; struggled, fell, got up again; and was renewed by grace and the desire to assist others. If I could distill her method into a formula, it would begin with these requisite components: first, a mother or elder woman presenting herself as a loving, insightful, and purposeful catalyst for growth in the life of a younger female; and second, the elder woman's demonstration of self-sufficiency competencies at a variety of levels. With this realization of having gifts to share, the elder woman teaches and coaches via life lessons presentations, skill demonstrations, and cocreative activities. She provided models of goal fulfillment and examples of the power of persistence and prayer in yielding results. The ten essential elements of Thelma's paradigm follow:

1. The acknowledgment of the rigors of being a black woman and all of the complexities of managing race, gender, and class demands; the willingness to take a preventive and proactive stance in infusing the next generation with adaptive skills for self-mastery, self-sufficiency, and contingency planning across an array of circumstances.

2. The capacity to project and anticipate various stress-laden scenarios or crises that may challenge one's emotional and economic stability such as illness, death, violence against a family member, loss of employment, financial ruin, or the absence of support from family, mate, or social linkages.
3. The investment of intensive support and help giving where students show genuine motivation, vigor, and the active pursuit of a goal.
4. The expression of loving touch, adoration, and verbal kindness as bolsters to self-esteem.
5. The adornment of the feminine so as to promote love and care of the body and acknowledgment of its changing contours and imperfections as a map of one's journey.
6. The encouragement of nonsex-typed skill development in the belief that both a woman and a man should be able to fix a leaky sink, paint, care for the lawn, plant a flower, cook a meal, wash and iron clothes, balance a checkbook, shrewdly buy or sell property, purchase a car, and travel freely.
7. The preparation for presentational opportunities, for example, standing in the living room in your patent leather shoes and reciting your Easter Speech over and again while your Easter dress is being pinned; reciting your Martin Luther King Day speech while your mother cooks dinner; or practicing a piano piece (or any art form) as a means of understanding the nature of process. Preparation and practice are crucial ingredients to success.
8. Role modeling and tip giving such as, "Sit right here on this stool, and watch me make these sweet potato pies; here's how you fold a hospital corner on a bed sheet; do not open and close the oven door while the rolls bake because the draft will make them hard."
9. The blending of work with play was a catalyst to gaining practical know-how and a place as a citizen of the world. Our involvement in the extracurricular activities of art, music, modern dance, gymnastics, and softball provided us with an exposure to a cultural aesthetic; to competitive and

collaborative team-group experiences; and to knowledge of rules and technique. Involvement also developed our bodies and minds.
10. The encouragement of dreaming your wildest dreams because with hard work and persistence they can come true.

Through this program, my sisters and I were stretched and molded into tubs that could stand on our own bottoms. To make us into sound vessels, Ma hammered, twisted, shaped, sanded, glazed, painted, washed, scoured, and anchored us.

BUILDING A BASIN OF RECEPTIVITY, REFLECTION, AND ACTION

> Auntie: "Where are you going with all those pretty dresses, honey?"
> S. Alease: "Mommy is getting me ready for college. In two days I'm going to college."
> Auntie: "You're only five Sheil, so you have to go to kindergarten first and all the way through grade 12. Then you can go to college."
> S. Alease: "Auntie, I *can* read and write, and I'm ready to go to college."
> —Me and Auntie, 1960

I believe that long before my conception, my mother had a vision of how to rear a child. She had a flawless knack for choosing our most receptive times to impart her wisdom. She seized opportunities daily. Evenings, Saturdays, and summers provided the best spaces for Ma to really give of herself in the home schooling of self-sufficiency leadership. During these times, she encircled her three little captives in the embrace of her encyclopedic knowledge. She would speak on all manner of topics: living, loving, mothering, womanhood, scholarship, herbal and hands-on-healing, the culinary arts, decorating, horticulture, animal husbandry, the secret life of insects, relationships, sizing up people, managing your assets, and world travel. To prepare us for a self-sufficient life, she filled virtually every minute of our young lives with purposeful interactions and opportunities. She could even transform the work of weeding the garden, dusting, washing the baseboards, canning, baking, studying, mending the broken wing of a bird, or sitting out back sipping lemonade under the elm tree into a lesson, a story, or an adventure. She would make connections among the tasks, the stories, and the characters to create a rich tapestry of ideas.

Now as a parent, grandmother, and clinician, I see her method as a precise and deliberate art—its own Zen. She knew just what help a girl needed to build competencies and self-esteem at every turn of the road. At the same time she stimulated a level of reciprocal interaction much in the same way the old folks would nurture a premature baby by swaddling, holding, feeding, and singing to the infant in front of a warm oven or cook stove or would nurture a house plant in the dark of winter by providing water, air, sunlight, pleasing music, and a daily talking to.

Throughout childhood, my mother was my prime model for womanly self-sufficiency. By my high school years, I would have two very powerful outer world representations of how feminine self-sufficiency could aid in accessing girl power and the wider world. When I was in the ninth grade, my biology teacher, Ms. Clarissa Sherard, organized a summer trip to Italy, Switzerland, and England. She not only organized the trip, but she guided us through a year of preparations, planning, and intercultural study. Only three girls took on her offer, so for nine months Dennette, Debbie, and I and our mothers sold barbecued rib dinners, greeting cards, cutlery, and candy to pay our World Academy Travel Tour passage.

That trip to Europe was a life-changing demonstration of how the community of girls and women could take hold of a vision and engage all of the steps needed to reach the goal. The trip was wonderful; we flew from Cleveland Hopkins to JFK, met the other World Academy students, and boarded a plane for Rome. We toured Rome, Venice, Florence, and the Tuscan province. From there we traveled on to Zurich and Geneva, Switzerland. On the third week of the one-month tour, we were notified that our final week in England would be cancelled as the World Academy had gone bankrupt. We were allowed to finish the third week in Geneva but then left for home from there. As disappointed as I was, I had been enriched and changed by the year of planning and by the architecture, food, gardens, artistry of Michelangelo, radiant Italian sun, and rarefied air of the Alps and the Pyrenees that I had encountered on the trip. I felt the awe that centuries before our visit, Hannibal of Carthage had brought the elephants across the mountain passes.

In Europe, I had encountered a world bigger than Cleveland's Lee Harvard neighborhood and more diverse than Cleveland's black community, and I knew my life would never be the same. I asked my mother to enroll me in a private school. Without saying so, she recognized that I now needed more stimulation, rigor, and exposure to diversity. With lightning speed, my mother enrolled me in the Beaumont School for Girls, a school founded by the Order of Saint Ursula. I had been accustomed to coeducational classes, but I soon learned that going to an all girls' school offered me something special. When the junior class presented a production of *Oliver Twist*, I was intrigued to see girls playing all of the male as well as the female roles flawlessly. I understood then that girls could do anything.

THE LIVING LEGACY: A POST SCRIPT

During my mother's life, there was nothing imperious, clandestine, or exclusive about her work as a self-sufficiency leader. She was committed to promoting its value beyond the bounds of her kinship network to instruct anyone, including males. Since Ma's passing, my sisters and I have gleaned that her highly reflective approach to mothering came from a desire to enrich every area of our growing and thinking. To Ma, it was unthinkable to omit pertinent information on how to do something, what not to do, or the best way to do a thing. One illustration of Mom's foresight is reflected in the words of Kahlil Gibran as sung by Sweet Honey in the Rock:

> Your children are not your children.
> They are the sons and daughters of Life's longing for itself.
> They come through you but not from you,
> And though they are with you yet they belong not to you.[2]

Mom knew that we would live in a world well beyond her physical and temporal existence, and she armed us with knowledge, skills, and preparation for what we could not yet imagine.

Early on, the most important message she shared was that my life was my own little garden patch to tend; that I—and my offspring—would depend upon my capacity to become a self-sufficient individual. I should form a covenant between myself, God, and the family that was never to be broken. In preparation, I was given an array of experiences and tools to support my capacity to meet life's demands. Mom gave me these tools at progressive levels of my development so that I would be emotionally and mentally ready to utilize them. I practiced being a decision maker, planner, strategizer, and expediter who could be responsible to myself and others. In particular, she taught me to always consider and tend to my emotional, physical, and spiritual self. Areas of practice included academic and career pursuits, financial planning, mating relationships, and large life choices. In short, Thelma taught me how to "carry my own burdens in the heat of the day." Her wise-woman advice was integral to my learning to love life and to operate as a vital and strong link within the communal chain.

KEEPING THE KEYS TO YOUR OWN HEALTH AND WELL-BEING

Q: Where has all of this preparation led?
A: I have my existential challenges like anyone else. However, I do feel that I am the captain of my ship and the master of my destiny while giving God the glory too.

Thelma's gift of self-sufficiency leadership was priceless. It enriched my day-to-day living, my physical health, and my functioning in the world as a person and as a career woman. She gave me a spirit about life that says I can do for myself and commit acts of *sevaa* (service).[3] I am thankful to be able to do for myself and those members of my family who are either too young or too old and frail to care for themselves.

The motif of self-sufficiency permeates all aspects of my personal care taking and management of the homeplace. Ma always stressed the benefits of home cooking, no matter if a woman was single or married with children. She would say: "Any tub that is gonna' stand on its own bottom's got to be nourished. Feeding yourself is an act of empowerment and self-sufficiency. To keep yourself physically and emotionally alive you must make a commitment to feed yourself good food first, three squares and snacks all nutritionally balanced; then good friendships; and then good experiences." I have firmly adopted her belief that the preparation of a meal is an act of self and communal nurture. For the last thirty-four years, I have cooked at least twice daily, unless I am on vacation or working out of town. Cooking for oneself and one's family makes a statement about *caritas*, health, sound nutrition, and disease prevention. In preparing food, I savor the connection between food and the sensual, between food and mother nature. Cooking provides a regrounding with God's bounty.

Passing on the legacy of self-sufficiency and the Zen of ordinary everyday life to sons was not so easy. During my parenting years of the 1980s and 1990s, I battled the outer forces of the media, what classmates' families did and did not do, and the chauvinism and strict role type casting of their Daddy's upbringing. Teaching boys to wash, iron, cook, bake, change a tire, assemble furniture, plant the flower and vegetable gardens, and care for the lawn was a challenge. Yet after all the exasperating moments of battling, explaining why a thing must be done now and in the future, two male people have managed to learn how to do a lot of basic everyday tasks well, and in some cases, elegantly. I am thankful and tickled now to see that they really got it. When I stop by their homes, they are clean and tidy. To be offered a warm hors d'oeuvre, roast beef au jus, red-skinned potatoes, and sugar peas with sprigs of fresh parsley and rosemary or Pommes Anna with a tangy ketchup and spicy mustard or a slice of German chocolate cake is a delight. All I can think of is, these are the two little curmudgeons who griped and grumbled that everyone else's mothers bought fast food three times a week and never under any circumstances prepared a gourmet meal; or sent their clothes to the laundry, or had a gardener to do all of the dirty work. Thank God, it seems that now I've got it! And I am still growing.

THE PEER-TO-PEER AND THE INTERGENERATIONAL INTERSECTIONS

> I am a point of light within a greater light; I am a strand of
>   energy within
> the stream of love divine. And thus, I Stand.
> —Alice Bailey, *Affirmation of the Disciple*

It has been said that there are no accidents in the universe, that everything happens for a reason and is a part of a larger, more divine plan. Since my twenties, I have been a counseling psychologist, social services administrator, and nonprofit consultant serving adolescent girls and women. Mesmerism, attraction, or the energetic propulsion of an intergenerational family vocation—whatever the reason, I have always had a need to empower other females and to help them strive for self-sufficiency and control over their own lives. In any case, this need is a natural outgrowth of being born to a maternal self-sufficiency leader. Witnessing Ma teach leadership in peer-to-peer woman relationships, across the generational divide of parent and child and that of neighbor elder to child mentee has had the greatest impact on my own style of leadership. Retrospectively, I have been able to do the work through my own distilling of her self-sufficiency leadership model.

The majority of my work has involved providing direct therapeutic services or designing prevention education and remedial/corrective counseling programming for women and adolescent girls. Many of my clients confront such issues as a fragmented family system, drug addiction, obesity and weight management, divorce, sexual violation and rape, domestic violence, unassertive and victimized identities, academic failure, unplanned pregnancy, parenting difficulties or child custody problems, agoraphobia, homelessness, joblessness, dropping out of school early, criminal history, welfare subsistence, work-life dilemmas, and other challenges. Interestingly, in each of these crises, clients have needed help in reconstituting their identities and gaining control over their lives. Beyond addressing the problems that these clients present, my work involves assisting them to gain access to their own inner core of strength and to take responsibility for themselves for transcending the problems.

IMPLICATIONS

"Thelma's every tub paradigm" is a worldview that spawns the perception of self as a dreamer, creator, and actor/director in one's own life. I cannot tell you how indispensable this perception has been in every area of my life. As a woman who is a wife, mother, grandmother, family elder-care giver, and sister circle friend as well as a social worker and community activist this value stance has helped to fulfill a rich tradition and belief in what both Thelma's paradigm and by the song "Sisters Are Doing It for Themselves" by song writer and singer Annie Lennox. James Brown's more playful rendition is still intended to convey a serious message of self-sufficiency when he sings "I don't want nobody to give me nothin'. Open up the door, I'll get it myself."[4] Thelma's every tub must stand on its own bottom paradigm is a template for forging self-sufficiency leadership skills at the individual, family, and communal levels. At this juncture in history, her brand of wisdom is urgently needed as a large segment of African American society is ailing, transitioning through welfare reform, shattering under the strain of poverty, substance abuse, HIV/AIDS infection, domestic violence, and the neglect of children. There is value in my mother's lessons on forging the intergenerational bonds that cultivate self-sufficiency-oriented leadership. These relational and instructional strategies must be decoded, articulated, preserved, and made formulaic to facilitate personal mastery, child and adult care-giving leadership, pedagogy, mentoring, reciprocal relationship formation, healthy adaptation to change relative to solitary living, aging, grandparents rearing grand children, and communal strengthening. The paradigm also offers action as an antidote to what family advocate Maisha Bennett (1991, p. 215) calls "poverty-induced stressors," the lack of viable relational, financial, and social supports so common among African American women. Thelma's paradigm also addresses what Epifania Akousa Amoo-Adare (2006, p. 351) refers to as the awareness of "critical literacy of space" relative to the urban black woman's demands to forge communality in conjunction with achieving social and economic self-sufficiency and traditional cohesion of the family in climates of challenge and change. This approach to inclusive woman-to-woman, self-sufficiency knowledge exchange also encompasses Galvan's (2006, p. 263) notion of "convivencia," which means that we gather to share and live among one another.

Conceptually, there is a clear need for the awareness and will of the elder woman to provide critical nurture and facilitation of self-sufficiency leadership to others and a carrying of one's burdens in the heat of the day (King and Ferguson, 2006, p. 166). The critical passing on of self-sufficiency leadership can provide people with a priceless and self-reinforcing sense of hope, competency, and mastery over their environment. Overall, the passing on of self-sufficiency-oriented leadership provides people with a sense of hope, competency, and mastery over the environment that is priceless and self-reinforcing.

NOTES

1. The Women's Mystery School leaders are those women of preliterate and tribal societies who possessed knowledge of the sacred feminine and who used ritual as a means to access this font of spiritual power. These leaders or priestesses were consulted for the purposes of helping women through cycles of birth, the passage from childhood to womanhood, marriage and maturity, aging and death. They carried with them advanced knowledge concerning the cycles of the moon, ritual manifestation, animal husbandry, herbalism, reincarnation, and healing. Through the ages and across cultures (Eastern, Western native American, and Caribbean) these women leaders have preserved a sense of communality, tradition, health, wholeness, and connection to the numinous and divine.

2. From Kahlil Gibran, *The Prophet*, chapter 4, "Children."

3. *Sevaa*, translated from Sanskrit, means "worship" and "devotion to service." It also refers to giving service and the dharma or responsibility and duty to serve. Vaman Shivram Apte (2006), online Practical Sanskrit-English Dictionary.

4. "I Don't Want Nobody to Give Me Nothing (Open Up the Door, I'll Get It Myself)" (1969), is one of the socially conscious songs James Brown released as a part of his larger social activism during the 1960s and 1970s.

REFERENCES

Amoo-Adare, E. A. (2006). Critical spatial literacy: A womanist positionality and the spatio temporal construction of black family life. In L. Phillips (Ed.), *The womanist reader* (pp. 347–58). New York: Routledge.

Apte, V. S. (2006) *Online Practical English-Sanskrit Dictionary*. www.practicalenglish-sanskritdictionary.com.

Bailey, A. (1924) Discipleship in the New Age. *Mediation on the Mount, 11,* 175.

Belenky, M. F., Clinchy, B. M, Goldberger, N. R., & Tarule, J. M. (1986). *Women's ways of knowing: The development of self, voice and mind*. New York: Basic.

Bennet, M. B. (1991). Afro-American women, poverty, and mental health: A social essay. *Women and Health. 12* (3–4), 213–38.

Bennis, W. (1994). *On becoming a leader.* Reading, MA: Perseus.

Betsch Cole, J., Guy-Sheftall, B. (2003). *Gender talk: The struggle for women's equality in African American community life.* New York: Ballentine.

Chessler, P. (1972). *Women and madness.* Garden City, NY: Doubleday.

Chodron, P. (2005) *No time to loose: A timely guide to the way of the Bodhisattva.* Boston: Shambhala.

Estes, C. P. (1992). *Women who run with the wolves: Myths and stories of the wild woman archetype.* New York: Ballantine.

Freire, P. (1980). *Pedagogy of the oppressed.* New York: Free.

Galvan, R. T. (2006). Portraits of Mujeres Desjuiciadas; Womanist pedagogies of the everyday, the mundane, and the ordinary. In L. Phillips (Ed.), *Womanist reader* (pp. 248–50). New York: Routlege.

Gannon, J. P. (1989). *Soul survivors.* New York: Simon and Schuster.

Gibran, K. (1938). *The prophet.* New York: Knopf.

Gilligan, C. (1982). *In a different voice: Women's conceptions of self and morality.* Cambridge, MA: Harvard University Press.

hooks, b. (1994a). *Teaching to transgress: Education as the practice of freedom.* New York: Routledge.

hooks, b. (1994b) Black woman artist becoming. In Patricia Bell-Scott, (Ed.), *Life notes: Personal writing by contemporary black women* (pp. 151–59).

Hughes, L. (1922; 1995). Mother to son. In Arnold Rampersad and David Roessell (Eds.), *The Collected Works of Langston Hughes.* New York: Columbia University Press.

Hurston, Z. N. (1938). *Tell my horse.* New York: Lippincott and Crowell.

Johnson, M. (2004). *Working while black* (pp. 99–103). Chicago: Hill.

King, T. C., & Ferguson, S. A. (2006). Carrying our burden in the heat of the day: Mid-life self-sacrifice within the family circle among black professional women. *Women & Therapy. 18* (2), 148–69.

Ladner, J. (1971). *Tomorrow's tomorrow: The black woman.* New York: Doubleday.

Lundberg, S., & Rose, E. (2000). Parenthood and the earnings of married men and women. *Labor Economics, 7*, 689–710.

McIntosh, P. (2001). White privilege and male privilege: Unpacking the invisible knapsack. In Paula Rothensberg (Ed.), *Race, class, and gender in the United States, an integrated study* (pp. 165–69). New York: St. Martins.

Nadasen, P. (2002). Expanding the boundaries of the women's movement: Black feminism and the struggles for welfare rights. *Feminist Studies, 28* (2), 271–301.

Newsome, Y. D., & DoDoo, F. N. (2002). Reversal of fortune: Explaining the decline in black women's earnings. *Gender & Society, 16* (4), 444–64.

Nobles, W. W. (1976). African philosophy: Foundations for a black psychology. In R. L. Jones (Ed.), *Black Psychology* (pp. 18–32). New York: Harper and Row.

Payne, R. K. (1998). *A framework for understanding poverty*. Baytown, TX: RFT.

Schaef, A. W. (1991). *Co-dependence: Misunderstood-mistreated*. New York: Harper.

Valentis, M., DeVane, A., & Weinstein, A. (1994). Female rage: Unlocking its secrets, claiming its power. New York: Carol Southern Books.

Walker, R. (2001). Couple victims of predatory lending. *Call & Post*, Cleveland Edition, *85* (52), 1.

Walsh, M. R. (1987). *The psychology of women: Ongoing debates*. New Haven: Yale University Press.

9

I Remember Mama

The Legacy of a Drylongso *and* Ajabu *Leader*

RHUNETTE C. DIGGS

1
I remember mama in her prime, washing clothes on the scrub board
            reminiscing out loud about us children as babies.
2
Catching us in bed without a bath, spanking our dirty feet, or waking
us abruptly with a stinging switch if the dishes weren't washed.
I see her chiding;
And wrinkling her forehead as she prepares a plaited switch.[1]
3
I imagine her with her sisters, being the ladies of the house—taking care of their daddy—
having it hard, but looking back and accepting, "that's just the way it was."
4
I understand better why she's not the best cook, having no mother to teach her,
just lard and flour to deal with,

doing the best she could with what she had—no mother.
5
I want to keep the image I have of her in her prime.
No longer spry, but just as humorous.
her voice, though aged, sounds no different to me.
6
—often viewed as solemn or mean looking—
She likes to laugh
me too.
7
I regret that she cannot remain as my thoughts see her.
but, regret gives way to thankfulness.
For, I remember her smiling with pride as she says
"all nine of mine graduated from high school!" (Awwww, Mama).
8
And I'm thankful for these memories of Mama—
seeing her smiling face now in this always moment.
9
Oh, Mama, I love you!

By 1989 when I wrote this tribute poem, "I Remember Mama," I had been married for thirteen years, was the mother of three children, and had returned to graduate school. Needless to say, I had had a few experiences. The overall goal of the poem [2] is to capture a moment in which I felt the strong presence of my mother through time and distance and to remember her at her strongest and best. The poem illustrates aspects of my mother's life history. Along with subsequent interactions with my mother, face-to-face interviews, and relevant scholarly sources, I use the poem to construct a composite picture of my mother's leadership: her modeling behavior, her interactions with her family, and her talk—all in the home—shows the family site to be an important context for leadership. The questions guiding this endeavor include, What understanding of my mother's leadership characteristics emerge from the poetic text, my interactions with her, and from the interview data? and How does this understanding reflect what we know about black female leadership?

Remembering is important for this chapter. Daniel Schacter (1996) notes, "What we already know shapes what we select and encode.... Our memory systems are built so that we are likely to remember what is most important to us" (pp. 45–46). The poem captures my memories of actual repeated patterns of interactions with my mother or of intense family events. Other memories that emerged during the research I conducted on leadership from the perspective of *"drylongso"* (Diggs and Miller, 1999). *Drylongso* is the African American term for "ordinary" or "everyday" to describe leadership that contrasts with the traditional notion of heroic, mythical, male leadership. It is the term used by anthropologist John L. Gwaltney (1980/1993) in his study of ordinary black people's ideas of living in America. I believe my mother, a black woman, represents an everyday, *drylongso*, invisible leader.

However, by her children's evaluations, she would be considered an *ajabu*, a Swahili term that means "extraordinary." My mother's *ajabu* characterization is located in her demonstration of love, patience, and perseverance toward her children in the face of a difficult marital relationship that ultimately led to the dissolution of her marriage to my father. Her acceptance of her life—to show love, patience, perseverance—as woman's "reasonable service" has masked viewing her role as a source of knowledge about leaders. Yet ordinary people working and making direct physical contact with others, whether in family settings, in small groups, or in large organizations are actually extraordinary and make better models for understanding leadership than the image of a leader, created largely by the media, who has minimal contact with or effect upon others or on society at large. We need to recognize the real difference between these two leadership models and break the silence.

My mother would not describe herself as a leader, just as I, who have taught, wifed, mothered, mentored, authored, presented, and performed academic and community responsibilities have never claimed that I led. I eschewed the term *leader*. The absence of 'leader' from my mother's everyday language and my inability to apply the term to myself are rooted in African American history. The patriarchal and enslavement history of blacks explains, to some degree, why black women have not embraced a concept that has been largely defined by an oppressive culture. And yet, as we recognize the accomplishments of our ancestors and ourselves, we must choose terms accurate in our own view to describe our actions and aspirations.

HOMEPLACE LEADERSHIP AS EQUATED TO *DRYLONGSO*

Drylongso leadership emerged from a recognition that limiting leadership to the few, visible, heroic images of black leaders, predominantly male, is inadequate (e.g., DeHoney, 1997; Marable, 1998; Porter, 1999; Wyatt, 1988). The author's experiences with secondary organizations in the black community also supported the importance of recognizing *drylongso* leadership (Diggs, 2001; Diggs and Miller, 1999). Everyday leaders address a myriad of concerns that abound in the black community, and I contend that local concerns require more, rather than fewer, leaders who are home- and community-level visible. The need for a visible home and community leadership presence is more pressing than the more society-level visible leadership we find in such events as the Million Man March and Million Woman March. Along this line, the feminist research by Liisa Horelli and Kirsti Vepsä (1994) presents a theory of everyday life in their discussion of women and housing that reflects my use of the concept as well. Everyday life as a theoretical concept brings into focus the meaning of the 'natural' and invisible activities women perform that are often defined by the dominant culture as trivial. Instead, *Everydayness* and *ordinariness* are terms that hide drama and magic, conflicts and change. Indeed, all social or cultural transformation is a process rooted in everyday life.

INTERPRETING MY MOTHER'S LEADERSHIP

Leadership can be defined as the display of verbal and nonverbal communication for the purpose of achieving group goals. An emphasis is placed on one's ability to affect another (or influence) through their words, gestures, and behavior (e.g., Adams and Galanes, 2009, chap. 10). Existing research on leadership indicates that women are influential and work very hard and are influential within groups, but they avoid using the term leader; instead they choose a term such as *facilitator* because of the stigma associated with 'leader.' However, scholars of gender behavior research and of "women's ways of knowing" literature (e.g., Belenky, Bond, and Weinstock, 1991; Goldberger, Tarule, Clinchy, and Belenky, 1996; Nelson, 1988) note that female leaders value group interaction that is more collaborative and less authoritarian; they use noncompetitive, egalitarian techniques for problem solving and decision making, and they foster emotional expression and collegiality.

Black feminist writers (sometimes called "womanist") and black cultural critics encourage us to examine the lives of black women to further contextualize the knowledge that may benefit our situations as black women. As Delores Williams asserts, "Womanism allows women to claim their roots in black history, religion, and culture" (Floyd-Thomas, 2006; Williams, 1989, p. 179). Other authors (Collins 1990a, 1990b; Walker, 1983; hooks, 1994; and James, 1997) offer a view of black women leaders as spiritual, God-conscious, nonelite, fearless, risk-taking, nurturing, fiery, hard working, expressive, and unselfish.

Because we find women performing many of their leadership tasks in what is viewed as a home place, an "accepted place," we often ignore the lessons and interactions that we learn in the family and that we practice elsewhere. bell-hooks (1994) describes the homeplace as follows: "In our young minds houses belonged to women, were their special domain, not as property, but as places where all that truly mattered in life took place—the warmth and comfort of shelter, the feeding of bodies, the nurturing of souls. There we learned dignity, integrity of being; there we learned to have faith. The folks who made this life possible, who were our primary guides and teachers, were black women" (p. 448).

Much social science research has been devoted to the ways in which our values, behaviors, and psychosocial concepts such as self-esteem and identity are influenced by our socialization. There are also cultural transmission theories that study what and how we learn socially and how we pass on this knowledge. Some scholars have studied intergenerational transmission (Gilligan, 1982; Maccoby and Martin, 1983; Rotheram-Borus, Dopkins, Sabate, and Lightfoot, 1996). Others address cultural transmission from a natural selection perspective (Heinrich and Gil-White, 2001). Still others address cultural transmission from a genetic and social learning perspective (McCourt, Bouchard Jr.,

Lykken, Tellegen, and Keyes, 1999). My poem, "I Remember Mama," explores the influence of a mother's performance on the family and a daughter's response to a mother's teaching about leadership.

In addition to these theories, I use an evolving, developmental, and interactional (E-D-I) perspective to examine the role of mothers in developing leadership. In an E-D-I perspective, I posit that I am always becoming and that my point of interpretation is tied to the moment where I am currently in my growth, development, and knowledge about a particular subject matter (Diggs, 1996; Murphy, and Ellis, 1996). Each day of life and every new interaction presents opportunities for expansion of the interpretation ("every round goes higher and higher"). As an example, my perspective on my mother will reflect my age and the knowledge I have gained to that time about what is important for a leader in the context of home and beyond. In this approach, I can also look at the past and compare it with new experiences and with future expectations (Nussbaum, 1989).

The face-to-face, interpersonal encounters with my mother and with those she has reared provide an additional rich source for my analysis. The family context is the premiere location where the repeated interactions among members result in a range of messages to emulate, question, or ignore. Employing the E-D-I concept helps identify and contextualize notions of leader and leadership.

"I REMEMBER MAMA" EVOKES STABILITY, HARDNESS/*HALAIDO*, AND GOODWILL

From this point on, I use the term *mother* interchangeably with *mama*. Mama is Ophelia Williams Curry, born in 1921 to a sharecropper family in Baker County, Georgia. Mama was the oldest of three sisters and two brothers. She married my father in the 1940s. In the 1960s, Grandfather became too old and ill to live alone, and he came to live with us.

The characteristics of leadership that are projected in the poem, "I Remember Mama" reveal characteristics that I label as "stability," "hardness" (or *halaido*), and "goodwill" are crucial. These characteristics emerge from Mama's communication—her words and actions—her expressiveness. Words and actions were not mutually exclusive because

Mama's expressions and actions flow into and out of one another. As I enumerate the characteristics of her talk, gestures, and behavior, you will begin to see the pattern that I have named. I have italicized words and phrases from the poem that are actual words spoken by Mama and others who were interviewed.

Stability

Everyday, Mama was physically present to meet the everyday needs of the family. I think more than anything, her presence prompts this memory of Mama in the poem: In my mind's eye, I see her *in her prime. . . . I can see her*. I could see her, smell her, feel her, hear her voice, and experience her moods (calm, fussy, and fitful). She was energetically present. I cannot recall Mama ever being too far away from her home during my childhood. Even when she worked outside of the home, we knew we could locate her quickly if necessary. Her presence was evident in the tasks she performed (like cooking) and in the punishments that we received if we were lax in our duties. In the second stanza of the poem, I remember the punishments. These were delivered deftly and predictably. Presently, I can remember the punishments fondly and without bitterness, which suggests that I now view her tactics more tolerably and see how they were beneficial.

Not only was she physically present, but Mama was also emotionally present: *I see her chiding; I think of her wrinkled forehead. She likes to laugh; I remember her smiling with pride.* All of these details reflect Mama knowing her children; she was aware of our personalities and capabilities. *She told us about ourselves through her stories: she reminisced out loud about us children as babies.* Her communication let us know that we were in Mama's heart and that she knew our origin and background. She answered the questions that curious children ask. I even noticed how she responded to her grandchildren (my children). This physical and emotional presence let us know that Mama was on our side. She was available to protect, punish, chastise, and praise (*all nine of mine graduated from high school*). The stability created by her presence provided a safe, peaceful, and clean space to nurture children to adulthood. Mama's presence was integral to this nurturing and to the messages that she communicated to her children.

My favorite times were when Mama talked about her past. She inevitably got to a story about fighting a boy from school and her ability to take care of herself. Further, she let us know that she had no fear of living or dying. "Ain' scared," she would say. When she tells these childhood stories, I see her face aglow; I consider her role as mother and provider. I think of my mama as a tree—planted—unshakable—a survivor.

Hardness/Halaido

Halaido is a term from the anthropological work of Sheila Feld and Bambi Schieffelin (1981). They indicate that *halaido* is a pervasive Kaluli notion that has three cultural meanings: physical growth, maturation in socialization, and the ability to use hard words or the fully developed capacity for language" (p. 351). I employ the concept of 'hardness' (or *halaido*) to Mama's physical, emotional, and internal strength. Mama's physical hardness is visible in her work at home and beyond. She placed great value on physical as well as moral cleanliness, and she expected us to respond to her values: *spanking our dirty feet; waking us up abruptly . . . if the dishes weren't washed.* In the poem, Mama's hardness is put in terms of her physical stamina: *taking care of their daddy—having it hard.*

During my childhood years, Mama not only was home during the day making preparations for us, caring for the home, and taking care of her ailing father (her first shift),[3] but when we returned home from school at about 4:30 in the afternoon, she went to her salaried job (her second shift). While she was gone, she left the older siblings "in charge," and when she arrived back home at 1:00 or 2:00 in the morning, she examined the home to see if her instructions had been followed and the values of cleanliness and obedience had been upheld (third shift). If she found that all was not as it should be, she took action whether that meant waking us up to take a bath, or to wash dishes, or to feel *a stinging switch*. It seems that Mama had a clear idea of her family role, where it began and ended. She worked hard, but she was not going to "kill herself" for these children she had borne. We were assigned daily tasks. We knew what Mama did, and we knew what we children were to do. That distinction was clear even if we did not always observe it. But I remember her behavior as a wife, mother, and laborer, and I understand that she was a woman who "wouldn't take no mess."

My observation about *Having it hard but looking back and accepting, "that's just the way it was"* reflects emotional hardness. Growing up, Mama was assigned more than the usual chores children complain about. My mother had to take full charge of the organization and management of the home because her biological mother died when she was a girl. In the poem, Grandmother's death seems to be stated as a fact: *no mother* occurs twice in the fourth stanza. I remember that Mama's talk about her mother seemed devoid of explicit sadness. Perhaps her response is explained by the level of responsibility she had to assume very young.

In a 1999 telephone conversation with my mother, she revealed details about how her responsibility began. I asked Mama to tell me about her mother (my grandmother):

> I think about Ma a lot. She use to go to the field where Pa was, to carry Pa his breakfast. She'd leave on the stove for me to cook and set out how many things to put in and how much wood to put in the stove. I 'seed' about the food while she go out to the field. I'd look at her as long as I could see her, I'd look. She 'tole' me stay in the back yard and not the front. I did just what she tole me, stayed where it was cool. I didn't never forget what she tole me. I mind her. That food would be done by the time she got home. She knowed how to tell me, and I would do it.

Mama said that she was about eight years old at the time. She was immersed in household duties because of necessity (*she use to go to the field where pa was*) and a mother's sensibilities (*she knowed how to tell me*). The adults had to leave home to provide material goods for the sustenance of the family and to care for each other (*to carry his breakfast*). It made sense to teach a child who was physically and intellectually able and willing how to help.

Grandmother died when Mama was about ten years old. After her death, mama lived with her maternal grandmother for a few years, then returned home to care for my grandfather and her two younger sisters. During my childhood and young adult years, I never saw my mother cry or heard a sad tone when she talked about her life. The absence of a mother would be difficult for a young child, yet this absence seemed to create the opportunity for my mother and her sisters to step into a position of *being the ladies of the house*. I saw this designation in operation when my mother gave us the rationale for *why she's not the best cook*. However, the poem challenges one to be all one can be even with missing people (*no mother*) and inadequate resources (*just lard and flour*). My mother's strength of character is evident by her taking responsibility for cooking and caretaking at such a young age, and she demonstrates it again as an adult wife and mother by working through all her difficulties with pride, confidence, and by submerging pain (an interview with mother, July 2000, revealed that she had experienced pain). "I see her every night, my mother—look like she was on the water, and I said that's my mother. I dreamed I could see her. A lot of times I couldn't sleep. I'd wake up crying. Yep, yep. It was every night too—then she stopped." The experience of being a child-adult too soon, a *lady of the house*, included pain that went undetected or was forgotten or if remembered was submerged. The best one can do is accept and be healthy; *that's just the way it was*. The need to accept is a hard lesson, but it was a lesson of the time, and it was a lesson in survival. Mama and many of her peers seem gifted in conveying an acceptance of death as a part of the whole life cycle. Perhaps this emotional toughness enabled her to maintain focus on the present without becoming too engulfed in past losses and regrets, or future fears.

In a figurative sense, Mama kept her mental space and physical space clean, and she drew some clear boundaries about what she accepted or rejected as her responsibilities as a wife and mother, and laborer. My mother was a "tough" (hard), "no nonsense" person. For example, she was tough enough to deal with my dad's "running around" and tough enough to call the police when he "tried to put his hand on her." Also, there is a saying that "cleanliness is next to Godliness." Mama seemed to keep an uncluttered mental space to make personal and spiritual decisions and to reject a "dirty" life of cheating and mistreatment of her children. For my mother, there was no contradiction between striving for an outward display of cleanliness and leading a "clean," uncorrupted interior life characterized by an ethic of telling the truth, being rule-abiding, and being firm but fair. Even though Mama knew how to deal with the dirtiness of the world, she also was able to carve out a role that focused on family and right behavior.

Mother exhibited strength through her daily routines of working in her home, mothering her children, meting out punishment, caring for others, and dealing with a "rolling stone" spouse. Her inner strength was evident in that she did not speak about troubles but often accepted them as "that's just the way it is." Living with her and observing her personal faith and testimony, I know she looked to her faith in God and not to people (or gossip) to deal with her circumstances, hopes, dreams, and fears. Thus, hardness flows into her goodwill.

Goodwill

Mama's hardness fostered her goodwill toward her family: *I love her dearly and I want to keep the image I have of her in her prime.* Goodwill is valuing of self and others, living ethically, and pursuing a purpose that uplifts. "I Remember Mama" reveals a mother who instilled an ethic of responsibility in her household (*with a stinging switch if the dishes weren't washed*). She also exhibited recognition of her children's achievements: *all nine of mine graduated.* My youthful experiences of helping others in school, helping in the church, and helping my senior neighbors were primarily prompted and supported by my mother and the community. Mama saw the value of education, showing respect for God's work, and helping those in need.

Without formal training, Mama persisted in the pursuit of what she believed was right. She did not thwart our ambition but insisted that we could become whatever we wanted. I believe that Mama's strength in one area served her well in others. For example, Mama was a member of the lumber mill union that fought for better wages and working conditions, a parallel to her efforts at home to instill her values of fairness and right action. I can remember when my youngest sister, Mela, interned at our hometown local newspaper in southwest Georgia, during her sophomore year in college. My sister reported that she felt the management did not want her there, but Mama would not let her give up. I asked my sister to tell me her memory of that situation.

"The boss said that I wasn't doing a good job. I felt bad and sad. I wanted to quit. Mom said that you're not going to quit. If they don't want you there, they'll have to fire you. I stayed until the term was over and they never said anything again about it. The message for me was 'don't quit.' I think the experience helped my confidence. I was able to stand and not let emotions overtake me. Mom's voice has helped me through the years. She instilled in me that staying power." Just because they did not want my sister on the internship was not sufficient. Mama emphasized that my sister had a right to work there. She didn't go to the newspaper or make a scene; she worked her magic behind the scene. It seems that Mama must have known we were capable of managing the situation if we were bold enough to enter into it.

Mama was considered nice, peaceable, friendly, hardworking, caring, but she fought and cussed when she had to. For my mother, the use of the term *racism* was a foreign concept. She would most likely say, "What's that?" and was not cowed. For sure, she displayed an understanding of her surroundings, but she displayed goodwill.

Mama was considered enjoyable to be around because of her easy laughter and her ethic of fairness. She was not typically critical or a difficult personality, and she insisted on "knowing" all her children. For a Westernized adult, being "known" is not comforting. Yet she was a practical woman who would praise you when you deserved it and condemn you when you offered her good reasons to do so. Her ways now make good sense to me, and it has been an important life skill to learn how to "rightly" judge situations: *I'm thankful for these memories of Mama.*

Mama's stability, hardness, and goodwill suggest leadership characteristics that are evident in effective contemporary leaders. Those who engage in communication and participate in the work of a group are highly valued as potential leaders (e.g., Adams and Galanes, 2009; Boyatzis, Johnston, and McKee, 2008). Other characteristics of black female leaders are also mirrored by Mama's behavior: having faith, being a problem-solver, working hard, being persistent and fair, and valuing the group as a whole (e.g., hooks, 2009; hooks, 1994; Williams, 1989).

Important aspects of the Afrocentric perspective include understanding self, having a sense of self-worth, and holding racial pride. This perspective depends upon an understanding of the African American history of slavery, institutional racism, and inequality of power while at the same time envisioning a future and working toward goals of liberation and harmony. Patricia Hill Collins (1990a), a theorist of black feminism, notes that even as "standpoints of oppressed groups [like African American women] are discredited and suppressed by the more powerful ... such standpoints can stimulate oppressed groups to resist their domination" (p. 301).

REPRODUCING THE *DRYLONGSO* AND *AJABU* LEADER

In a family setting, members grow and develop under the leadership of the parents. Because a family is a complex system in which members of different ages, genders, and personalities express a range of needs, it is an ideal context to study leadership. The family offers a practice space to learn about one-self and others and to engage in repeated interactions that encourage competence and risk-taking. It is a place where one may express fears and contemplate defeats. From this "homeplace," we can take what we have learned and try it out both intentionally and intuitively in other arenas.

In my family, Mama's leadership has been quite intentional in the particular area of discipline: *spanking our dirty feet; waking us abruptly*. In my own parenting, however, the spankings formed a pattern that I chose to resist. As a child, I believed that I received too many spankings (and who doesn't?), so I decided very early that I would do more talking and explaining and less spanking. Initially, from an E-D-I perspective, I just wanted to correct what I considered spanking "overkill," but what I learned later about child development and parent-child communication seemed to validate my notion that talking is a more informed way to handle situations than spanking. As I matured, I realized that I must have exaggerated the amount of punishment I actually received because my memories—and my body—wouldn't support the idea that I got a spanking for everything. Nevertheless, the spankings I received were still intense enough that I wanted to diminish the experience for my children.

In evolving toward higher consciousness about the appropriate discipline for my children, I revisited the question of how my education and my culture have influenced my behavior. By "consciousness" I mean an awareness of myself both individually and culturally as well as an awareness of the perspective I hold and the role I take in the world. Elizabeth Kasl and Dean Elias (2000) state that "consciousness evolves through successive orders of structure that emerge in response to demands of a changing environment" (p. 231). "Unconscious" describes the unreflective, taken-for-grantedness of our lives and being; we are unconscious if we have not yet engaged in serious pursuit of how we came to be who we are. From my child perspective, it seemed that any error was punishable. As a parent, I rationalized that frequent spanking without conversations about problem solving or in the absence of the child's voice created an oppressive relationship. I wanted to avoid that in favor of a more focused and caring response to misbehavior. Through explanation and dialogue, we admit that we have good and bad days and that people make mistakes but emphasize that we must continue to pursue certain ideals. Such an approach fosters maturity and growth and the development of consciousness.

An Afrocentric framework places Afrocentric values such as spirituality, respect, and belonging at the center (Asante, 2007; Asante, 1988; Myers, 1993) and emphasizes the use of theory and action to gain liberation and to foster well-being and harmonious relationships. When there is a distortion of values or an absence of consciousness about ourselves, leadership can help us to relearn what is important. I presently use spanking my children as a last resort (unless the child is old enough to know better and has a history of repeated infractions).[4] This approach strays from my mother's child-rearing model of "spank first, talk never," but I am comfortable with my choice and recognize that I'm trying to raise different children in a different household for a different world. I am released from some of the constraints that were placed on my mother because of this different context and because I am different in my level of education and in my thinking about my children's place in the world. I have had to extend and innovate in this changed world.

This issue of discipline is illustrative of the way that one's perspective changes over time. As a child, I did not like my mama's spanking or stinging switches, but I was operating with limited understanding. To ask someone in situ if they like a person's leadership is mistaken; the evolving, developmental, and interactional elements are lost when we assume an informed judgment can be made at the moment. Only later can a person make a judgment that takes in the complexity of the situation. However, even as a child, I did like the fact that I had a mama who was stable; she was hard in some ways, but she characteristically showed goodwill. Now, my eldest daughter's responses to my decisions about discipline remind me of my own responses to my mother's choices. I believed I could do better than my mother, and I did in some ways. I realized that I needed to make different value choices in order to be successful in my life. This has been true for me; it will be for my daughter. Change is inevitable. I have pride in my accomplishments, but as I have evolved (to know better and think better), I realize that my mother had pride in hers, and my daughter, also, will have pride in her accomplishments. Mama's ways supported my accomplishment by providing a safe space where she took care of our needs and showed interest in us. It is obvious that I identify with Mama (*I'm like that too*) just as my eldest daughter identifies with me. She says, "Mom, you're smart; you work hard. What should I do? This is what I'm doing; what do you think?"

Age changes us externally, but internally we retain a core self-identity: *I want to keep the image of her in her prime. No longer spry, she's just as humorous.* I saw this in Mama; she was certain about what she had experienced even though, at the latter stage of her life, her language and thinking had diminished and she could not clearly convey her strength or hardness as in days gone by. A product of her mothering, I work to uphold her dignity, and I continue valuing her voice as I remember her as a leader: stable, hard, and of goodwill. I hope her children and their future children never lose the memory of Mama.

I view this work as a precious opportunity because I am alive to tell about this *drylongso* and *ajabu* leader. I know that because of Mama, I am a leader and a producer of future leaders. I had the following exchange with Mama in 2001 when she was eighty-one years old.

> Me: Mama, who do you think is a leader?
> Mama: What about you? You a teacher.
> Me: What about you?
> Mama: Aw naw, you.

Me: Why not you?
Mama: I can do things, a lot of things and know things, but I'll say you, 'cause you a teacher.
Me: But you were my first teacher.
Mama: I'm still that.

Mama's response elevates others rather than herself, and this "elevating of community is a form of women's leadership commonly found throughout the African Diaspora" (Belenky, Bond, and Weinstock, 1991, p. 160). Mama's response reflects her pride in speaking the truth as she sees it and believes it for good reasons. She recognizes achievement and offers praise. Yes, Mama was still proud of her children at the end of her life in 2002. This encouragement and recognition from a mother has worked in a subtle way to keep blacks healthy in a world that offers few other sources for good health. Finch (2001 lecture)[5] describes a black family model from an African orientation that places spirit rather than body as the prime focus. I believe that Mama offered my sisters and brothers and everyone in her circle of influence something of her spirit in each encounter. What a legacy!

Presently, my thoughts on my mother's leadership and mine are still evolving. However, I end with my daughter's perspective at the age of nine years old. At that moment in her evolution, development, and interaction (EDI) she found her mother's ways quite delightful:

> What is a mother without a daughter?
> What is a daughter without a mother?
> They're both very special.
> God made them like no other.
> Mother is someone who always cares.
> A daughter is someone who is always there.
> A mother is like God; she's always watching over you.
> A daughter loves you no matter what you do.
> Mothers, mothers, daughters, daughters
> Help each other when things go wrong.
> Daughters, daughters, mothers, mothers
> Their bond will always stay strong.
> —Alisha Malené Diggs[6]

NOTES

1. A switch is a flexible twig taken from a tree for physical punishment, typically administered by an adult to a child's body. Terms used to describe include *spanking* and *whooping*.

2. Aptheker (1989) discusses the reading of texts about women's lives and offered how poetry may be used to help us "learn from the shape, texture, the rhythm of the telling" (p. 29). Authors King and colleagues build on the work of Arlie Hochschild as they address the multiple hidden or invisible jobs of women in academia. First and second shifts represent the ostensible hours of paid job and home duties respectively. Third shift is introduced as a metaphor to convey the additional difficult and invisible tasks that black women view as necessary to promoting an organization that is functional and just. I find the analysis useful to suggest that the unique circumstances of women primarily have historically exhibited the third-shift phenomenon as a way of life. Specifically for this chapter, the third shift for our African mothers in America has been borne out via their multiple tasks among home, plantation, or wage labor.

4. Spanking is reserved for those twelve years of age and under, even though my nine year old requested that I dismiss spanking with her because she believed she did not require this mode of discipline.

5. "Black Family Model" lecture presented at the annual meeting of the National Black Family in America Conference.

6. This poem was written by my daughter, Alisha Malené Diggs, when she was nine.

7. Special thanks to James F. Black and Marilyn A. Johnson for their reviews of this article.

8. "Florida's First Negro Resort," *Ebony*, February 1948, pp. 23–26.

9. Dickens passed the board examinations in 1945, becoming the first female African American board-certified Ob/Gyn in Philadelphia. By 1956, Dr. Dickens became a member of the staff and faculty in the Department of Obstetrics and Gynecology of University of Pennsylvania's School of Medicine, becoming the first black woman to serve in this position.

10. I am grateful for Marilyn A. Johnson and Evangeline Tierney for their annual retreat work for African American women. The 2002 theme African American Daughters: Carriers of the Promise discusses the joy and pain of legacy work and the hope and disappointment of dreams.

REFERENCES

Adams, K., & Galanes, G. J. (2009). Applying leadership principles. In *Communicating in groups* (pp. 276–312). Boston: McGraw Hill.

Aptheker, B. (1989). Conditions for the work. *Tapestries of life: Women's work, women's consciousness, and the meaning of daily experience* (pp. 5–35). Amherst: University of Massachusetts Press.

Asante, M. K. (1988). *Afrocentricity.* Trenton, NJ: African World.

Asante, M. K. (2007). *The Afrocentric manifesto.* Malden, MA: Polity.

Belenky, M. F., Bond, L. A., & Weinstock, J. S. (1991). *A tradition that has no name: Nurturing the development of people, families, and communities.* New York: Basic.

Billingsley, A. (1968). *Black families in white America.* New York: Touchstone.

Boyatzis, R. E., Johnston, F., McKee, A. (2008). Igniting resonance: Creating effectiveness in teams, organizations, and communities. In *Becoming a resonant leader: Develop your emotional intelligence, renew your relationships, sustain your effectiveness* (pp. 175–214). Boston: Harvard Business School.

Chin, L., Lott, B., Rice, J. K., & Sanchez-Hucles, J. (2007). *Women and leadership: Transforming visions and diverse voices.* Malden, MA: Blackwell.

Collins, P. H. (1990a). The politics of black feminist thought. In P. H. Collins (Ed.), *Black feminist thought: Knowledge, consciousness, and the politics of empowerment* (pp. 3–18). New York: Routledge.

Collins, P. H. (1990b). The social construction of black feminist thought. In M. R. Malson, E. Mudimbe-Boyi, J. F. O'Barr, & M. Wyer (Eds.), *Black women in America: Social science perspective* (p. 325). Chicago: University of Chicago Press.

Comer, J. P., & Pouissant, A. F. (1992). *Raising black children.* New York: Plume.

DeHoney, J. (1997, May). Steps for achieving the extraordinary. *Emerge: Black America's Newsmagazine* (p. 7). Washington, DC: Black Entertainment Television.

Diggs, R. C. (1996, March). Communication and global self-esteem: An evolving-developmental-interactional perspective. Paper presented at the annual meeting of the National Black Family in America Conference, Louisville, Kentucky.

Diggs, R. C. (2001, November). All the lonely phony, drylongso, and ajabu people... met by love: A radical approach to research and to community. Panel presented at the Annual meeting of the National Communication Association, Atlanta, GA.

Diggs, R. C., & Miller, D. (1999, April). Communicative group-centered approach to everyday leadership: The case of *Ujima* Community Council. Paper presented at the Kentucky Association of Blacks in Higher Education, Louisville, Kentucky.

Feld, S., & Schieffelin, B. B. (1981). Hard word: A functional basis for Kaluli discourse. In D. Tannen (Ed.), *Analyzing discourse: Text and talk* (pp. 351–67). Washington, DC: Georgetown University Press.

Finch, C. S., III. Black Family Model. National Black Family in America Conference, University of Louisville. Louisville, Kentucky. March 12, 2001.

Floyd-Thomas, S. M. (2006). Mining the motherlode: Methods in womanist ethics. Cleveland, OH: Pilgrim.

Gilligan, C. (1982). *In a different voice: Psychological theory and women's development*. Cambridge, MA: Harvard University Press.

Goldberger, N. R., Tarule, J. M., Clinchy, B. M., & Belenky, M. F. (Eds.). (1996). *Knowledge, difference and power*. New York: Basic.

Gwaltney, J. L. (1993). *A Self-Portrait of black America*. New York: New. (Original work published 1980).

Heinrich, J., & Gil-White, F. J. (2001). The evolution of prestige—Freely conferred deference as a mechanism for enhancing the benefits of cultural transmission. *Evolution and Human Behavior, 22* (3), 165–96.

hooks, b. (1994). Homeplace: A site for resistance. In D. S. Madison (Ed.), *The woman that I am: The literature and culture of contemporary women of color* (pp. 448–54). New York: St. Martin's.

hooks, b. (2009). Returning to the wound. *Belonging* (pp. 174–83). NY: Routledge.

Horelli, L., & Vepsä, K. (1994). In search of supportive structures for everyday life. In I. Altman & A. Churchman (Eds.), *Women and the environment* (pp. 201–26). New York: Plenum.

James, J. (1997). Transcending the talented tenth: Black leaders and American intellectuals. New York: Routledge.

Kamusi Project. (2001, November 11). Creating new habits of mind in small groups. In J. W. Kasl & D. Elias [electronic reference forum]. www.yale.swahili.edu.

Kasl, E. & Elias, D. (2000). Creating new habits of mind in small groups. In J. W. Mezirow (Ed.), *Learning as transformation: Critical perspectives on a theory in progress* (pp. 229-252). San Francisco: Jossey-Bass.

King, T. C., Wright, L. B., Gibson, N., Johnson, L., Lee, V., Lovelace, B., Turner, S., & Wheeler, D. I. (2002). Andrea's third shift: The invisible work of African American women in higher education. In G. Anzaldua & A. Keating (Eds.), *The bridge called my back: Twenty years later—Enacting the visions of radical women of color*. New York: Routledge.

Maccoby, E. E., & Martin, J. A. (1983). Socialization in the context of the family: Parent-child interaction. In E. M. Heatherington (Ed.), *Handbook of child psychology* (pp. 1–101). New York: Wiley.

Marable. M. (1998). *Black leadership*. NY: Columbia University Press.

McCourt, K., Bouchard Jr., T. J., Lyken, D. T., Tellegen, A,, & Keyes, M. (1999). Authoritarianism revisited: Genetic and environmental influences examined in twins reared apart and together. *Personality and Individual Differences, 27,* 985–1014.

Murphy, N., & Ellis, G. F. R. (1996). *On the moral nature of the universe: Theology, cosmology, and ethics.* Minneapolis: Fortress.

Myers, L. J. (1993). *Understanding an Afrocentric worldview: Introduction to an optimal psychology* (2nd ed.). Dubuque, IA: Kendall/Hunt.

Nelson, M. W. (1988). Women's ways: Interactive patterns in predominantly female research teams. In B. Bates & A. Taylor (Eds.), *Women communicating: Studies of women's talk* (pp. 199–232). Norwood, NJ: Ablex.

Nussbaum, J. F. (Ed.). (1989). *Life-span communication: Normative processes.* Hillsdale, NJ: Erlbaum.

Parker, P. S. (2005). *Race, gender, and leadership.* Mahwah, NJ: Earlbaum.

Porter, J. L. (1999). "Lead on with Light": A phenomenology of leadership as seen in Gloria Naylor's Mama Day. In T. McDonald & T. Ford-Ahmed (Eds.), *Nature of a sistuh: Black women's lived experiences in contemporary culture* (pp. 267–78). Durham, NC: Carolina Academic.

Rotheram-Borus, M. J., Dopkins, S., Sabate, N., & Lightfoot, M. (1996). Personal and ethnic identity, values and self-esteem among black and Latino adolescent girls. In B. J. R. Leadbeater & N. Way (Eds.), *Urban girls: resisting stereotypes, creating identities* (pp. 35–52). New York: New York University Press.

Schacter, D. L. (1996). *Searching for memory: The brain, the mind, and the past.* New York: HarperCollins.

Walker, A. (1983). *In search of our mother's gardens: Womanist prose.* San Diego: Harcourt Brace and Javonivich.

Williams, D. S. (1989). Weaving divisions: New patterns in feminist spirituality. In J. Plaskow & C. Christ (Eds.). *Womanist theology: Black women's voices* (pp. 179–86). San Francisco: HarperCollins.

Wyatt, N. (1988). Shared leadership in the weavers guild. In B. Bate & A. Taylor (Eds.), *Women communicating: Studies of women's talk* (pp. 147–75). Norwood, NJ: Ablex.

10

"A Little Lower Than the Angels"

A Partial Legacy from My Mother and Mom-Mom Ione

SIMONA J. HILL

> **8:3** When I consider thy heavens, the work of thy fingers, the moon and the stars, which thou hast ordained;
> **8:4** What is man, that thou art mindful of him? and the son of man, that thou visitest him?
> **8:5** For thou hast made him a little lower than the angels, and hast crowned him with glory and honor.
> —Psalms 8 (KJV)

INTRODUCTION

THE IMAGINATION of my mind's eye and my cultural belief system emerge from the fact that I am two generations away from slavery. My great-great grandmother Fannie Mae Winston, who helped raise my mother during the Great Depression and the early years of the 1940s, was a former slave who lived to be 109 years of age. For my family to go from slavery to Ph.D. in such a short period of time is a remarkable feat of triumph, but one that is fraught with pain, anguish, and sometimes even guilt about those in my family who have not had (or wanted) the opportunities for higher education that I have pursued so vigorously.

When I consider the keen survival lessons passed from mother to daughter in my family, I think of my mother, Mildred C. Hill, and my godmother, Ione Barkley. I have always regarded these two women as powerhouses of industry and spiritual deliberation, never ones to accept "no" as the final answer. They fiercely leaned on the abundance of the universe for support when family and friends said that their goals were impossible. Mom-Mom Ione died when I was seven years old, more than thirty-five years ago now. Yet her legacy of community service, teaching coupled with activism, and endurance are the inheritance that I proudly consider my own as I negotiate my own boundaries and deal with my growing up indecision and anger. I now use the maturity I gained from these past experiences to deal effectively in a world of predominantly white colleges and universities.

My mother, Mildred, is alive and well and at eighty-two years of age, vibrant in mind, wisdom, and grace. She is a resource and a trusted sounding board for me. To be true to myself requires a balancing of the past with the present in order to remain hopeful about my future and the future of other black women in the academy (Crawford and Smith, 2005). Mildred and Ione have been the "angels" in my life who gave me a blueprint for "walking the walk and talking the talk" with my students and colleagues in higher education.

Writing about legacy for a woman of color is a difficult matter for me. Excavating what is my legacy is a complicated, on-going process because it occurs within the interlocking hierarchies of racism, white privilege, and mainstream oppression (Harnois, 2010; Parks, 2010; Scafe, 2009). bell hooks (1989) refers to this as the "special vantage point" for black women (14) when they take on an investigation of their legacy. Not only are black women "collectively at the bottom of the occupational ladder," but their overall social status is lower than that of any other group. Occupying such a position, we bear the brunt of sexist, racist, and classist oppression. At the same time, our group has not been socialized to assume the role of exploiter/oppressor in that there is no institutionalized "other" that we can systematically exploit or oppress (hooks 1984, p. 14).

The late Joseph Campbell spent a lifetime of scholarship devoted to understanding the role of myth in human life. Myth functions in various contexts, and some of its functions can be applied to the concept of 'legacy.' Campbell (1988) states: "There is a fourth function of myth, and this is the one that I think everyone must try today to relate to—and that is the pedagogical function of how to live a human lifetime under any circumstances. Myths can teach you that" (p. 5). Oftentimes familial legacy is connected with myth. This is true for me.

The beginning part of my narrative, which I cannot document, but nevertheless believe to be true since I have heard it so often during my childhood and adulthood, is this: when my mother was about thirteen or fourteen years of age or maybe a little older, she met Mrs. Eleanor Roosevelt and Mrs. Mary McLeod Bethune[1] at the Mayfair Hotel in Washington, D.C., when my godmother, Ione, took my mother to her first Democratic National Convention of women. I have had research librarians working on verifying this meeting, but we have not been able to substantiate this story through any historical records. However, it is a matter of fact that Mrs. Roosevelt and Mrs. Bethune commonly met on issues of government. According to my mother, she exchanged a smile, a glance, and then a hug with Mrs. Bethune in a receiving line. My mother's recollection is that "neither of the women (Mrs. Roosevelt nor Mrs. Bethune) was much to look at in terms of physical attributes, but both radiated an inner beauty I'll never forget."

In thinking about this chapter and reading about the life of Mary McLeod Bethune, I now realize that meeting Mrs. Bethune was indeed a momentous occasion in my mother's life—one that helped to define the way she thought about life choices, career decisions, and raising a daughter to maturity. Mythical perhaps, but the encounter was an important influence on her concept of 'self.' That brief meeting helped expand my mother's views of who she could be as a black woman living in American society. The fact that my godmother, Ione, was the one to take my young and impressionable mother to meet this great woman leader, black America's first lady, helped to solidify the importance of leadership through education for my mother.

Ione was active in the Democratic Party and worked closely with Congressman Earl Chudoff until he resigned and then for Representative Robert N. C. Nix Sr., Esquire. In 1958, the senior Nix was the first African American elected to Congress and he served as a representative until 1979. During the 1940s and 1950s, Nix's offices were located at Twenty-second and Diamond Streets in a North Philadelphia community where many black professionals lived. My mother always reminded me that professional people lived in the community because segregation and redlining prevented them from living anywhere else. Lawyers such as Nix, doctors such as Helen O. Dickens. M.D., dentists, nurses, and funeral directors were part of the foundation of the community. At that time, blacks were most commonly cloistered between Girard and Lehigh Avenues on the north and west and from Tenth Street to Twenty-Sixth Street going east to west. On Thirty-Third Street and beyond were large Jewish neighborhoods, and it was common for young adolescent girls such as my mother to walk from North Philadelphia through Fairmount Park and find after-school work "laying by the floor," that is, cleaning houses, scrubbing stoops and floors, and doing other manual labor for Jewish housewives.

Ione was a Democratic committeewoman for her district and used her political connections to help found and operate the Jeanne H. Barnes Memorial Center at Tenth and Boston Streets. The goals of the center were to feed children and run an after-school educational program. As long as the children went to school and did their homework, they received a hot meal of meat, two vegetables, a dessert, and all the milk they wanted to drink. The Barnes Center fed as many as seventy children each weekday. This was a benefit to the working-class and poor members of the community whose incomes often forced children to leave school and earn wages to supplement the salaries of their laborer, custodian, and domestic servant parents.

The center operated for more that twenty-five years under Ione's leadership. It closed permanently during the mid-1960s when gang violence and urban decay ravaged the community. But during her tenure, Mom-Mom Ione used whatever political clout she had to get jobs for the people in the neighborhood. People were often amazed by the power she wielded in the 1950s and 1960s when, according to my mother, she could "pick up the telephone and get jobs for folks." She helped William Galloway get his position as the first black person to drive a trolley for PTC (Philadelphia Transportation Company). She was influential in breaking the color line by gaining employment for sanitation workers. A job with the city's Sanitation Department was highly respected in the community because it meant a family would be provided with health benefits and union backing. Some of these workers are now entering retirement.

My mother describes Ione Barkley as a "highly respected, good, *good* woman." She was a girl scout for more than forty years and believed in the power of community groups. She helped found other organizations, too, such as Philadelphia Beautiful, which began gardening programs in the city. Upon reflection, I learned that women of color have a high tolerance for pain, anxiety, and coping with almost insurmountable difficulties. Since my godmother died in 1969 when I was only seven years of age, this part of her legacy did not become clear to me until much later when my mother became a caregiver for Ione's widowed husband. I learned, sometime in my adolescence, that the man was physically abusive to my godmother and would drink to the point of blackouts. Part of what jettisoned Ione into community work was the need to escape the invectives, disrespect, and beatings of an active alcoholic. What I learned from this is that abuse in any form is unacceptable, and this belief is one of my guiding principles.

What else did I learn from Mom-Mom Ione? What is her specific legacy to me? I believe that community service should be incorporated in my professional and personal life. I seek to function as a social change agent in areas of scholarship and career. I value organizations that are run by folks within the community. I understand the importance of networking—women get things done by both informal and formal associations. Ione taught me a "make politics work for you" credo. Because politics helps to provide the resources of a project, find jobs for people, or break the color lines in city government, it is appropriate sometimes to get funding for projects from sources that have historically been linked to oppressing one's cultural group.

My mother's family was part of the Great Migration of blacks from the South. Scholars generally agree that this was a time in United States history when northern industries looked southward to fill labor vacuums and found a large and poorly paid pool of black workers struggling for economic survival (see, e.g., Johnson and Campbell, and 1981; Hine and Thompson, 1999, Tolnay, 1997; Woodson (1918) 1969). Although my paternal grandmother, Grandma Fannie, remained on (she now owns some of the land) the Calvert plantation in Fluvanna County, Virginia, where she had been a slave, my mother's family moved to the suburbs of Philadelphia—first to Fort Washington and then to Ambler, Pennsylvania. While our family had a small, fairly sufficient farm in Ambler during the late 1930s, work was still hard to find for my maternal grandmother, Orbrey Lucille, the primary breadwinner in the family. There were times when the family lived up North, and the children had to be shipped back to Grandma Fannie's so that Orbrey could find better paying jobs as a cook, caterer, seamstress, laundress, or domestic. In fact, my mother started school at a one-room schoolhouse in Virginia before the family moved permanently to the North. It was a few years before Orbrey decided to move from the suburbs, bringing the children from "the country" to live nearer to relatives in the city, in North Philadelphia. By then, Orbrey was working at a fairly stable position: sewing children's clothes and coats for the WPA (Works Progress Administration). It was Ione, a neighbor and close friend to the family, who helped watch out for my mother and her three siblings while Orbrey was at work.

The World War II years hold many bittersweet memories for my mother. She remembers how children collected silver linings from cigarette packages and took them to corner stores in exchange for negligible amounts of money. My mother recalls that young girls were taught how to make slips and underwear out of flour sacks. Afterwards, when times got better, they could be made out of fifteen-cents-per-yard material.

Growing up in the city of Philadelphia before her marriage at age twenty to my father, my mother (following Ione Barkley's model of civic leadership) created some fairly good opportunities for herself and others. One that she is especially proud of was her work with a Mr. Fred A. Johnson in establishing the Columbia Branch of the YMCA. The original Y in this area consisted of three rooms on the second floor of an office building located at Broad Street and Columbia Avenue (now Cecil B. Moore Avenue). "We started it because we did not have a Y for black children, and we were excluded from all the other city Ys," my mother recalls. Some of the Y activities included canvassing for jobs, after-school activities for children, and, in the summer, taking children to the city pool at Eleventh Street and Susquehanna Avenue. My mother will tell anyone, "That's how I got to be a junior lifeguard!"

There is much in a name. Perhaps I should have made clear to the reader at the onset of this piece that the correct pronunciation of Mom-Mom's name is "I-OWN." As I see myself in both my mother, Mildred C. Hill, and Ione Barkley's lives, I must pose several questions about ownership. What is it that "I own" for my personal identity? What must I keep safe and treasure of their legacy to me? What must I disregard so that the boundaries between my past and present interface in meaningful ways?

I continue to see my mother as an exemplar of community service. It was impressed on me from childhood that we do not live in a vacuum. It is important to be a contributing member to the community in which one lives. I have a strong conviction that my volunteerism is vital to renewing myself, replenishing scarce resources in the community, and modeling service learning for my students, in my professional life especially, service learning enhances leadership development by placing students outside traditional classroom settings into the local community. This experiential learning model offers students the opportunity to use critical thinking skills, problem-solving techniques, and teamwork. Service learning is a collaborative experience between teachers and students that provides vital knowledge for the students' professional development and identification, as well as the development of important personal and social skills. I was taught: "Be good at what you do and believe in yourself." I confess that my interpretation of this advice has led to establishing perfectionist standards for myself. But I believed my mother wholeheartedly when she repeated a quote by Eleanor Roosevelt, that "no one can make you feel inferior without your consent."

And finally, collective unity—at all costs. This is the part of the legacy that my mother and I grapple with today and the part that affects my leadership development in both positive and negative ways. I see so much of myself in my mother that there is a need to draw distinct boundaries between us from time to time. There is also the need to create boundaries in my current work with the communities in which I am involved. The burden of drawing these boundaries seems to fall, most often, upon me. I find that legacy work compels me to create space to meditate, journal, regain perspectives, take care of my health and well-being, and grow in new directions. My mythmaking will be somewhat different from that of my foremothers, and my personal legacy will be altered by future circumstances. More important, in this process, I need to reassure my mother that she will not be "left behind" as those who leave the shackles of slavery often are. We are both fettered to the remnants of slavery's legacy and must find our own coping mechanisms. In this respect, we will remain mutually interdependent. Sometimes this is unspoken between us, but it exists as surely as the air we breathe. My commitment has come down to this: to appreciate our shared history, to bring her forward in all my success in this new century as long as life exists, and to create a legacy for the next generation of which she can be proud.

I do a great deal of this—bringing forward my mother's and Mom-Mom Ione's legacies in my professional work. For me teaching is a form of social activism. It allows me to empower others through critical thinking and deliberate attempts at consciousness-raising. Putting social justice theories into practice is important to me, as it has been for black women throughout our sojourn in the United States and globally (Hall, Garrett-Akinsaya, and Hucles, 2007; Normore, 2008; Williams, 2001; Zackodnik, 2007). Charmaine C. Williams (2001) wrote: "As an academic and an activist, I know that this knowledge [about experiences as a black woman] is essential to my appreciation of the superficial boundaries between the researcher and the researched, the activist and the disenfranchised . . . Expressing the emotions that accompany individual existence is an important part of writing against the marginalization of our experiences, connecting the personal to the social and the political, and challenging the smooth hegemonic discourse" (p. 95). The social scientist in me wants completion, but in conducting legacy work there is no such idea. Legacy work takes me to the next generation. Legacy to me means acknowledging both that which I cherish and that which must be overcome. I cherish the fact that I still exist in the academy in the midst of white privilege that wants to coopt me in such a way that I disappear into the fabric of social conformity. I must overcome the fears that still haunt me at times of somehow not belonging and of the outsider status that being a woman of color can sometimes confer (Hall, Garrett-Akinsaya, and Hucles, 2007; James et al., 2010; Kawahara, et al., 2007; Kidwell et al., 2007; Vasquez and Comas-Dias, 2007).

Barbara Omolade (1994) discusses the dilemma of the black woman scholar: "The Black woman griot-historian must wrestle herself free of the demons of the discipline of history which deny her. Eventually she must break the fetters of the academy and its shadow on black women's thought. She must retrace the steps of our people, allowing the capacity of her dreams and her struggle to guide her through the raw material and data of our history. She must embrace the men and women of the past who push their voices into her body and mind, ignoring time and death to do so" (p. 110). In order to develop my leadership role as a black woman, it is necessary for me to do legacy work. I need to recognize the bequests of significant, loving women in my history who are examples of how to be my highest self under the harshest circumstances. Leadership reflects my deepest sense of self (who I am and who I strive to be) that I want to share with the world. Realizing that I will probably never have the luxury of a low profile within predominantly White institutions, leadership provides me with opportunities to break free of the margins. The qualities of my two role models reflect my best self, free of any constraints.

The challenging part of this process for me is to relinquish thoughts of lack and limitation that are mired in the realities of racism, sexism, and classism. What I strive to understand is that success is not measured by outer manifestations, but by the knowing that I am doing the best that I can at any given moment. Far too many African American women and other women succumb to the "must do it all" pressure that robs us in fundamental ways of our ability to say "no" to others and "yes" to ourselves. "No" is a complete sentence that exists without qualifiers. The central task of my leadership work today is to bear the weight of legacy without being bound by it. It means examining issues of work, family, and other relationships in their complexity. By giving myself permission to say no and hold to that decision without guilt and remorse, I am opening my life to opportunities, including leadership roles that my mother and Mom-Mom Ione could only dream about and hope for me.

I recently heard historian Charles L. Blockson describe the Underground Railroad as the first civil rights movement in the United States. I like that notion because it demonstrates that the legacy of slavery laid a foundation for more freedom for all Americans. My personal "underground railroad" is to understand what is essential to my sense of freedom as a professional woman of color in a twenty-first-century global world. I must learn to "dream dreams that bear the mark of identity."

Ironically, writing about legacy work is not as freeing as I anticipated. Although it is key to boundary management, important to me personally, and a fixed part of my scholarship, I resist public disclosure of the process. It is a remnant of survival tactics for black women to keep silent until we are with those who understand the unspoken. To move my legacy work forward, I need to make appropriate disclosure without the cover of shadow and silence that lets the world know that I exist. It means being a model of leadership that my mothers were to me, but on a larger, institutional scale. Finally, it means finding myself in the midst of change, but solidly rooted in the historical ownership of who I am physically, spiritually, and emotionally.

Being oneself in the face of racist and sexist hostility and criticism is embedded in my roots. As Lili Kim has argued, "Trying to separate what is a result of racism and what is a result of sexism is an impossible, as well as ineffective, exercise." To continue in a leadership role—on my campus, within my home community, or within the academy—I cannot afford to deny the existence of oppressive forces. Most assuredly, Ione and Mildred did not deny these conditions in their lives. I choose to honor them and their legacy to me by a steady progression in the face of obstacles.

As Darlene Clark Hine (1999) declares: "Black women's history teaches us that, unless we fulfill our duty to family and community, there is no satisfaction and no possibility for peace. However, it also reveals that each individual's sense of self-worth must come from inside" (p. 308). If motherhood is indeed pedagogy as Woollett and Phoenix suggest (1996), then the task for black mothers is to identify and model productive ways for their daughters to survive and thrive. To be a "little lower than the angels" means that the best of heaven is only an instant away. This is my challenge and conviction: to remember and to trust that the multiple gifts of my foremothers' legacy and vision are true.

NOTES

1. Mary McLeod Bethune, educator and civic leader, founded the Daytona Educational and Industrial Institute for black girls. This school later became Bethune-Cookman College. Darlene Clark Hine (1994) describes Bethune as a pivotal figure of the twentieth century in black women's history for her central role in U.S. politics and government, black social uplift, and particularly the education of black girls and women. See *Hine Sight: Black Women and the Reconstruction of American History*, 1994.

REFERENCES

Campbell, J., with B. Moyers. (1988). Myth and the modern world. In B. S. Flowers (Ed.), *The Power of Myth.* (pp. 1–43). New York: Doubleday.

Crawford, K., & Smith, D. (2005). The we and the us: Mentoring African American women. *Journal of Black Studies, 36* (1), 52–67.

Flax, Jane. (1990). *Thinking fragments: Psychoanalysis, feminism and postmodernism in the contemporary west.* Berkeley: University of California Press.

Hall, R. L., Garrett-Akinsaya, B., & Hucles, M. (2007). Voices of black feminist leaders: Making spaces for ourselves. In J. L. Chin (Ed), *Women and leadership: Transforming visions and diverse voices* (pp. 281–96). Malden, MA: Blackwell.

Harnois, C. E. (2010). Race, gender, and the black women's standpoint. *Sociological Forum, 25* (1), 68–85.

Hine, D. C., & Thompson, K. (1999). *A shining thread of hope: The history of black women in America.* New York: Broadway.

hooks, bell. (1989). *Talking back: Thinking feminist, thinking black.* Boston: South End.

James, S. M., Foster, F. S., & Guy-Sheftall, B. (2009). *Still brave: The evolution of black women's studies.* New York: Feminist.

Johnson, D. M. & Campbell, R. R. (1981). *Black migration in America: A social demographic history.* Durham, NC: Duke University Press.

Kawahara, D. M., Esnil, E. M., & Hsu, J. (2007). Asian American women leaders: The intersection of race, gender, and leadership. In J. L. Chin (Ed.), *Women and leadership: Transforming visions and diverse voices* (pp. 297–313). Malden, MA: Blackwell.

Kidwell, C. S., Willis, D. F., Jones-Saumty, D., & Bigfoot, D. S. (2007). Feminist leadership among American Indian women. In J. L. Chin (Ed.), *Women and leadership: Transforming visions and diverse voices* (pp. 314–29). Malden, MA: Blackwell.

Kim, L. M. (2001). I was [so] busy fighting racism that I didn't even know I was being oppressed as a woman! Challenges, changes, and empowerment in teaching about women of color. *NWSA Journal 13* (2), 98–111.

Normore, A. H. (2008). A volume in educational leadership for social justice. Information Age.

Omolade, B. (1994). *The rising song of African American women*. New York: Routledge.

Parks, S. (2010). *Fierce Angels: The strong black woman in American life and culture*. New York: One World/Ballantine.

St. Jean, Y., & Feagin, J. R. (1999). *Double burden: Black women and everyday racism*. Armonk, NY: Sharpe.

Scafe, S. (2009). The Embracing I: Mothers and Daughters in Contemporary Black Women's Auto/biography. *Women: A Cultural Review, 20* (3), 287–98.

Tolnay, S. E. (1997). The great migration and changes in the northern black family, 1940 to 1990. *Social Forces 75*, 1213–38.

Vasquez, M., & Comas-Diaz, L. (2007). Feminist leadership among Latinas. In J. L. Chin (Ed.), *Women and leadership: Transforming visions and diverse voices* (pp. 264–80). Malden, MA: Blackwell.

Williams, C. C. (2001). The angry black woman scholar. *NWSA Journal, 13* (2), 87–97.

Woodson, C. G. (1918, 1969). *A century of Negro migration*. New York: Russell and Russell.

Woollett, A., & Phoenix, A. (1996). Motherhood as pedagogy: Developmental psychology and the accounts of mothers of young children. In C. Luke (Ed.), *Feminisms and pedagogies of everyday life* (pp. 80–102). Albany: State University of New York Press.

Zackodnik, T. (2007). *African American feminisms, 1828–1923*. New York: Routledge.

PART IV

Tensions along the Motherline—Translating Mother Templates to Daughter Actions

> Motherline stories are haunted by ghosts.... Women whose ties to life and family were disrupted by the wild tides of history—natural disasters, human cruelty—cast shadows on our souls ... But we can honor our stories, attend to our ghosts, remember our ancestors, tell their stories to our children and grandchildren.
> —Naomi Lowinsky, "Mother of Mothers, Daughter of Daughters: Reflections on the Motherline"

WHEN ANY GENERATION tries to tell another what life is and how to live it, tensions arise. The next four chapters illustrate some of these tensions and raise such questions as the following: How does the leadership template from mothers work for daughters who exist in a new time and place? How do daughters pull from their mothers a vision for their lives that both honors Motherline traditions and still allows daughters to make a life on their own terms? How do the expectations of the Motherline create difficulties for the daughters? And how do daughters deal with the tensions that arise between them and Motherline women?

The four women in this section write from the daughter's point of view. The first chapter, by Sonya Turner, outlines her mother's skills in setting her toward the horizon of success in the world. Turner explains how her mother diagnosed and sought to break the intergenerational and repetitive cycle of stagnancy and self-destruction within the family by providing Turner with unconditional support and encouragement. As Turner's mother supported every phase of her daughter's success, she increasingly broke through her own limits. Yet the inoculation Turner received was not without costs: extended family rejection, envy, fear of abandonment, and expressions of resentment, including the age-old accusation of acting white. In her telling of stagnation, she also reveals redemptive cycles of intergenerational healing and reconciliation. Turner, a licensed psychologist and an administrator in higher education, now applies her mother's medicine to help her clients examine their internal dialogue, changing their beliefs from the inside out so that they too can break free of stagnation.

The second daughter, Sandra Y. Govan, tells us of the tensions that arise when both mother and daughter have been gifted with strong personalities yet are so different in their personal styles that they clash when they interact. To Govan's good fortune her mother both encouraged Govan's independence, outspokenness, self-assertion and courage and also aimed to control disobedience, defiance, and rebelliousness. As a literary entrepreneur and a professor emeritus of literature in a southern university, Govan depends upon the centering she garnered from withstanding the heat of the strong mother. She has prepared others to withstand the tests of their own lives—beginning with the tests meted out by Govan in the safe space of her classroom. She urged her students to seize their own destiny and bring their best work, even when they were afraid to try.

Leah C. K. Lewis, the third daughter-writer, draws strength from her mother's quiet example and prophetic encouragement. As a minister and theological scholar, Lewis has worked to transcend the limitations and compromises of her mother and, indeed, of the Motherline generation. The task of translating from her mother's life to her own requires her to make peace with how she views her mother's life. She had to find a way to come to terms with her feelings about the assertive, courageous, resourceful mother figure who faced down the neighborhood bully and brought back her best friend's stolen bicycle with the mother who sacrificed much of herself to her husband's increasing economic and emotional dependence. In looking back, Lewis synthesizes her mother's lessons into a major theme that we create our own destinies, despite the prototypes that influence us. As a result, Lewis brings to her leadership in ministry an unapologetic, self-actualized self—a new template for women's leadership in a male-dominated sphere.

Finally, Lakesia D. Johnson tells us of the Amazonlike strengths her Motherline marshaled against the tripart oppression (of racism, sexism, classicism) that laced their lives and of the high costs they incurred in wearing the warrior mantle. In "OtherMothers, Amazons, and Strategies for Leadership in the Public and Private Spheres," Johnson shows us the complexities of her Motherline, which forced her to sort through the multiple, and at times conflicting, messages about women's leadership. Johnson learned to value each othermother's strengths and weaknesses, to critique each leadership model in its own context, ultimately selecting for herself those aspects congruent with her life and values. As a women's studies and literature scholar, who also has a law degree, Johnson helps her students to see the complex negotiations women make in the public and private spheres and guides them in assessing women's lives and leadership within a larger social and political context.

Life experience is a formidable teacher, and there is particular potency in all of the Motherline's experiences. On the one hand, daughters may honor a mother's vision, drive, and self-sacrifice and be able to use these as inspiration for developing a higher order vision of self-sufficiency and leadership. On the other hand, daughters can be outraged by the incongruities they see in their mother's lives. They register the dissonance between a mother's spoken vision for a brighter future and her inability to achieve health, wealth, ease, safety, love, or joy in her own existence. When daughters see that their mothers have not done themselves well in this life, they feel a rift out of which emerge fears, fears that the mother will die and leave too soon, that she has suffered so much that she will never find the strength to make changes or achieve her dreams, that the daughter can never repay the mother in ways that will undo any of the mother's pain, sacrifice, or soul hunger.

There is also tension if the mother is living vicariously through the successes of the daughter; then the daughter does not have room to veer off the charted path. When the mother has failed to model healthy boundary management within the family, the community, or work, the daughter finds herself mired in a mixture of appreciation and disapproval of her mother's example. In response to the gap she perceives between the imperfection of what is and the ideal of what should be, the daughter rails against the Motherline. Although this may appear to be an interpersonal dispute, it is actually a reflection of the daughter's dismay that such a gap exists and her lament over the threats from society against the Motherline, its values, and its teachings (Ferguson and King, 2008).

To gain the loyalty of daughters, the Motherline must assume mythic proportions. Yet to preserve the Motherline credibility, testimonies of victory must be counterbalanced by admissions of failure, of times when mothers succumb to the pit of vipers or to the dragons under the moat. In addition, daughters must be shown that the women of the Motherline can heal, can rebound, can even find value in adversity. Until daughters recognize this complex reality of the Motherline experience, the mother-daughter relationship will produce tensions. The daughter's fears of failure will stoke the fires of rage and separation. Her need to escape the raw vulnerability of succumbing to the feet of clay as witnessed in the mother will fuel her own missteps. The daughter may cleave so ardently to the pursuit of traits exactly opposite those of the mother that she will inadvertently create a new dragon that she must then spend much of her adult life slaying.

In summary, the leadership lessons here reveal that each woman must learn Motherline knowledge in the midst of complex emotional ties to their mothers and their mothers' personal histories. Beyond the mother-to-child adage, "Don't do as I do, do as I say," daughters must summon the courage and feral instincts to translate Motherline lessons for their own lives and times. Vital, clear leadership by daughters demands release from those aspects of Motherline tutelage that no longer serve. This may be the final lesson of the Motherline. It whispers, "The line is too taut." Or "The line has knots that need to be smoothed." Or simply, "Hold the line with care until it can be repaired."

REFERENCES

Ferguson, S. A., & King, T. C. (2008). Going down for the third time. In Amber Kinser (Ed.), *Mothering in the third wave* (pp. 166–86). Toronto, Canada: Demeter.

O'Reilly, A., and Abbey, S. (2000). *Mothers and daughters: Connection, empowerment, & transformation.* Lanham, MD: Rowman and Littlefield.

11

Mother's Transformative Medicine

An Inoculation against Intergenerational Stagnancy

Sonya M. Turner

As much as I wish to romanticize my African American family network, I do not immediately descend from a stock of progressive, accomplished, critically conscious women and men who served as a prototype for professional and community leadership. Undoubtedly, my grandparents' generation faced psychosocial struggles pertinent to their era, including institutional racism and Jim Crow edicts that were oppressive and constrictive of one's potential; however, even with the passage of time, these relatives and their progeny could not manage to engage in an evolution of thinking, feeling, and behaving that would inspire visionary thinking and bold leadership. Despite their unremitting capacity to withstand emotional and physical suffering precipitated by physically and emotionally abusive marriages, substance abuse, family betrayals, legal involvement, tragic deaths, and poverty, these family members actively brought to my attention generational patterns that I simply could not accept.

A vigilant and perceptive adolescent with an abundance of mother-wit, I was determined to chart a life course diametrically opposed to my extended family, with my mother serving as the catalyst for this change. A wounded healer and, therefore, a most masterful teacher during my formative years, my mother nurtured those characteristics necessary for me to deviate from the traditional life course of my kin. She applied a medicine that was groundbreaking, unprecedented. To me, her medicine was powerfully simplistic; to the family, it was perhaps impractical and inconceivable. Her medicine was nothing more than a vision for personal growth and achievement, a bold and novel reimagining of what life could be for me as an African American female if appropriately inspired and nurtured. It doubled as a salve to assuage her own psychic pain stemming from early years replete with discouragement and hardship and as a preventative to deter me from a similar life course.

MOTHER'S EARLY YEARS AND THE FUNDAMENTAL INGREDIENTS OF HER MEDICINE

Mother's parents, Georgia and Otis, were born and raised in Haddock, Georgia, and were married in late adolescence. They emigrated to Cleveland, Ohio, after their second child was born in 1946. Georgia was twenty-two; Otis was twenty-seven. Leaving behind a bleak existence laden with financial hardships, troubled family relationships, and unbearable Jim Crow laws, my grandparents made their new home with relatives who had earlier emigrated to the near east side of Cleveland. They settled into their own home once Otis found work as a laborer at a local copper foundry. My grandmother eventually obtained employment as a domestic in the home of a white family.

Mother was born one year later. She was the third eldest child among five siblings and the only female. Since both parents were employed outside the home, my mother bore the responsibility of feeding, clothing, and monitoring her rambunctious brothers. For the first eight years of her life, Mother witnessed her parents struggle in an unstable and dysfunctional marriage plagued by alcoholism and domestic violence. Getting drunk on whiskey, Otis spent more evenings away from home—drinking, gambling, and engaging in infidelities—than he spent with the family. When he did return home, there was tremendous tension, due to Otis' irritable mood and uncontrollable temper. He was known by family and friends for his drunken paranoia that would trigger physical abuse against his wife in the presence of his children. Other times, his children fell victim to his temper and alcohol binges. Curiously, although he spent days away from the family to engage in his drinking binges, he maintained patriarchal control over the household.

He maintained employment at the local foundry for nearly eight years, but he was eventually fired due to excessive tardiness, absences, and arriving to work inebriated. By the time Mother was eight years old, Otis had lost the ability and desire to commit to his wife and to parent his five young children, who, at that time, ranged in age from thirteen to two. He decided to leave the family home but continued to pay visits to his wife and children. Despite their separate residences, the abuse persisted and became so unbearable that Georgia's sisters provided him the money to board a Greyhound bus headed back to Georgia, where he lived until his death twenty-one years later. Rather than being distressed about her father deserting the family, Mother was filled with a sense of relief, for the frightening violence had finally ceased. However, her care-taking role expanded, since her mother worked various factory jobs even though, at times, she also relied on government assistance to help meet the family's financial needs.

Through a historical and psychological exploration, I have come to understand what precipitated my mother's transformative medicine and why she experienced a need to teach survival and self-sufficiency. Undoubtedly, Otis created a terribly depressive, vicious cycle for himself. Impacted by overt and covert racism, which materialized in poor education, unemployment, inadequate housing, and perhaps overall feelings of powerlessness, he likely experienced immense emasculation because of his inability to fulfill the role of husband and father as defined by the broader culture. I would surmise that he sought to self-medicate against a feeling of insurmountable disenfranchisement, powerlessness, and failure. Boyd (2007) asserts that social, political, and economical challenges inherent to the African American male experience create an overwhelming amount of stress and burden on the black male psyche. Overt and covert forms of discrimination likely caused my grandfather, as did so many men of his and subsequent generations, to search for alternative, and often destructive, forms of personal power in the home. Elaine Pinderhughes (2002) asserts that the demonstration of such misdirected power, along with the psychosocial stressors relative to racism, strain the African American marital system. In my grandfather's case, the psychic pain displaced onto his wife in a defensive maneuvering must have instilled feelings of powerlessness and helplessness in my grandmother, the available scapegoat, and in my mother, the innocent witness. Indeed, Otis did not have the social status to wrestle for power with his white colleagues or supervisors; therefore, he swindled power by physically dominating his wife.

My grandmother demonstrated role flexibility common to many African American mothers in her ability to be not only the caregiver, but the breadwinner of the family (Boyd-Franklin, 1998). Despite the reshaping of her maternal role to meet the needs of her children, my grandmother certainly experienced her share of disempowerment, given her ninth-grade education, limited employment skills, and poor, rural background. Therefore, her worldview and expectations for my mother reflected her limited educational and occupational opportunities and economic resources. Having little to no exposure in her daily living experiences, either as a young girl or an adult woman, to highly educated African Americans or African Americans serving in key leadership positions, she lacked appropriate models for success and achievement. Moreover, sheer mental stress and physical exhaustion resulting from the day-to-day demands inherent to the role flexibility she was compelled to demonstrate doubtlessly stifled her ability to dream of the possibilities for a different life for her daughter. Consequently, she did not instill in her daughter a value system that upheld higher education for the purposes of personal edification, financial independence, self-actualization, or professional accomplishment.

When Mother was twenty-three years old, she married my father, Jake, a thirty-year-old Alabama native who had relocated to Cleveland. My grandmother encouraged Mother to marry my father because he worked full-time as a laborer in a chemical plant and part-time as a taxi driver. Georgia believed he could offer financial security to which Mother previously had been unaccustomed; however, this security came at a costly emotional price.

Mother married a man whose psychological needs, unfortunately, triggered a replication of her emotional experience of her father. Dad seemed to fit the prototype of masculinity constructed by my mother's father, despite my father maintaining strong beliefs against alcohol (his own father was an alcoholic), and unlike Otis, he felt fully responsible for sustaining the family and meeting our physical needs. As institutional racism cycled through another generation of African American families, it is probable that my father struggled with the same powerlessness as his father-in-law. He too exhibited patriarchal domination, chauvinism, and an aggressive interpersonal style that were very much characteristic of Otis's style of relating to the family. In addition, Dad, like Granddad, was what Boyd-Franklin (1989) termed a "peripheral father" in that both men spent more time away from home than in the home and, consequently, did not participate much in the daily life of the family (Alperin, 2001). My father defined himself through his role as the family provider, the person within the family structure whose goal was to meet the myriad physical needs of the family; however, his strong sense of responsibility and duty resulted in his absence from home in the evenings, weekends, and most holidays. Despite his limited presence in the home, he, like Otis, maintained unilateral control over my mother, my siblings, and me.

During the early years of my parents' marriage, Mother was not employed outside the home, and she was wholly dependent both financially and emotionally on my father. She, like her children, had to request money from him and give an account of how that money would be spent. As a result, she suffered a lack of self-sufficiency and emotional safety in that her livelihood and security depended too strongly on the vicissitudes of my father's moods or decisions. Consequently, Mother experienced mounting dissonance in relation to the inequity, powerlessness, and infantilization she experienced in the marriage relationship.

Her dependency and lack of control motivated her to seek avenues for creating her own income. She opened our three-bedroom house to neighborhood children to start a babysitting venture, which became quite profitable over the five years it was in operation. Babysitting soon gave way to a position as a payroll operator within the state system, which greatly increased her sense of well-being and self-control.

I believe the parallel relationships Mother experienced with her father and her husband shaped her attitude toward female empowerment and thereby laid the groundwork for her medicine. In addition, the members of my mother's family gave her negative feedback that froze her in a pathological status quo within a family mired in emotional, behavioral, and legal problems. Family therapy pioneer Murray Bowen (1994) identified the multigenerational transmission process through which psychological dysfunctions are maintained in families across generations. Moreover, the social and political history of African Americans that increases the probability that this group faces conditions that produce such dysfunctions is also well documented (Bernal et al., 2003). For Mother's family network, this dysfunction was manifested in substance abuse, incarcerations, thefts, prostitution, infidelities, domestic violence, and other problematic behaviors. By witnessing the perpetual stagnancy and struggle that defined her family, my mother challenged herself to engage in unconventional forms of thinking and imagining in order to differentiate her self from and transcend the stressors associated with the legacy of institutional racism and misogynistic patriarchy. Thus, she laid the foundation for the type of woman she envisioned me to become.

MOTHER'S MEDICINE

Mother diagnosed the seemingly infectious disease manifested in each generation of the family and sought to break the repetitive cycle of self-destruction for me by administering a unique medicine that propelled me beyond the professional and personal fate of my maternal family. The initial dosage of this elixir took the form of a vision for change to disrupt the familial homeostasis. It then crystallized as a mental plan for my self-sufficiency, achievement, and self-preservation. Mother provided me daily supplements that consisted of boundless confidence in my intellectual skills and abilities. I am doubtful that the primary motivation behind my mother's vision was to create a professional and community leader. Her goal, instead, was to insulate me from the potential adversities associated with African American females in American society. As admirable and healthy as her medicine was, it nevertheless was accompanied by seemingly uncontrollable side effects.

My earliest memories of Mother applying her medicine begin when I was a timid youngster at Adlai Stevenson Elementary School. "Oh, I know *you* can do it!" was her signature response after I described to her a seemingly insurmountable scholastic challenge. Mother made winning the reading competition in second grade especially significant. What primarily motivated me to win that competition was not absorbing the adventurous tales I loved so much but the anticipation of my mother's pride and her special recognition of my accomplishment. After I won, she photographed me smiling radiantly while pointing to my hard-earned prize, an iron-on "Reading Champion" patch that was affixed to my white cotton blouse. Whether it was entering that reading contest, taking an examination in third grade to qualify for "major work" classes, or competing for a violin position in the all-city orchestra in sixth grade, my mother generously and evenly applied her medicine. She demonstrated confidence in my abilities, encouragement in my personal development, and a belief that I could aspire and achieve whatever I wished.

At the end of my ninth-grade year, I discovered that the potency of Mother's medicine magnified as she administered large doses to inoculate against the disease of covert racism. Not only did Mother instill a vision for change through achievement, but she boldly challenged those egregious obstacles that could potentially thwart my success. In doing so, she modeled for me actively addressing and challenging various forms of discrimination.

One week before my ninth-grade promotion ceremony, the junior high school guidance counselor, Mr. Hainsworth,[1] a charismatic white male, informed me that the B+ I earned in algebra prevented me from being included in the top 10 percent of the ninth-grade class. Needless to say, I was greatly disappointed and resentful. Once I apprised my mother of my class standing, she was quite disturbed and grew immediately suspicious of the process through which the top students were selected. The following day Mother contacted Mr. Hainsworth to request an appointment with him. Before meeting the guidance counselor, Mother enlisted the assistance and support of African American teachers who were well aware of my outstanding academic performance and could closely investigate the matter. We discovered that of the top 10 percent approximately 85 percent were white students, and the rest were African American, despite this particular public school enrolling, among other cultures, approximately 12 percent white students and 85 percent African American students.

Mother marched into Mr. Hainsworth's office with me by her side. She exuded power, assertiveness, and control, refusing to concede to his boyish charm. Indeed, she was outspoken, self-assured, and clear about her concerns and expectations. She went as far as to request to speak with the school's principal, Mr. Thomas, about the apparent disproportionate racial representation of the top 10 percent, as well as my teachers to understand why my grades were not sufficient to qualify me for the top 10 percent. After Mother requested to speak with Mr. Kendrick immediately, the guidance counselor directed us to the algebra teacher's classroom. Without mincing her words, Mother explained to Mr. Kendrick the dilemma involving my outstanding grades and the racial composition of the students comprising the top 10 percent. She requested to review his gradebook in an effort to examine my grades on exams, homework assignments, and class participation. Mr. Kendrick, appearing rather unprepared and dismayed by mother's presentation, gently stated, "No problem! I'll review Sonya's performance and recalculate her grade."

As a result of what happened in a matter of minutes in Mr. Kendrick's classroom, I was able to walk proudly across the auditorium stage, claiming my award for being among the top 10 percent of my class. My mother deliberately modeled for me the process of, first, questioning the underlying motivations of white authority figures, then, appropriately challenging potentially discriminatory practices, and finally, tapping into African American support networks that can exert their individual and collective power to effect change. Mother believed the key to being well-equipped to fight discrimination and racism would be educational advancement. It is my opinion that in her maternal, nurturing way she truly believed that if she could motivate me to seek professional accomplishment and status, I would be shielded or even insulated from overt and covert forms of racism. For this reason, Mother committed herself to networking with teachers, colleagues, church members, and anyone else who could lend support or provide a stepping stone to my personal development and academic advancement. When my interest in pursuing a career in medicine burgeoned in high school, Mother became my intermediary in actively gaining information from her coworker about medical school programs in the Midwest, prerequisites, and medical specialties. Mother could not advise me on careers in medicine, but she sought someone who was knowledgeable in this area and took it upon herself to help me learn more. Mother planned informational meetings for her coworker and me and also arranged telephone contacts with a medical school student who was acquainted with her coworker. She would humorously reflect on the energy she invested in this effort, as if she were the potential medical student.

During my senior year of college, I expressed to Mother an interest in pursuing a doctorate in clinical psychology, a relatively new and highly specialized degree. Initially, Mother was disturbed, concerned that achieving a Psy.D. would be professional suicide. However, by recognizing my intent on matriculating into a clinical psychology program and then familiarizing herself with the practicality and multiple uses of this degree, she offered whole-hearted support for my professional decision. Mother's confidence, encouragement, and active involvement also reinforced my diligence. Beginning in high school and continuing through graduate school, Mother acknowledged and rewarded my academic efforts with exciting vacations that she fully financed. We explored islands and countries—including the Caribbean, Hawaii, and Mexico—that her family members were not fortunate enough to have visited. The family labeled Mother and me "jet-setters" and would question, in a bewildered manner, why we would want to board an airplane and venture to such unimaginable destinations. My father would turn down my mother's invitations to travel but would aggressively challenge my mother when she decided to travel without him. When we took our first trip to Freeport, Bahamas, my father became verbally confrontational towards my mother just as we were preparing to leave for the airport. It is likely that he began to feel fearful about my mother's growing self-sufficiency. However, over the years it became easier for him to accept her gradual transformation. In fact, rather than becoming hostile at the idea of mother exhibiting personal freedom, he would actually initiate questions about where she and I would travel next and would be excited to see photographs and souvenirs obtained in our travels. Traveling not only increased her sense of agency, but expanded our knowledge of the world and other cultures. Furthermore, Mother's reward system provided intrinsic and extrinsic benefits that triggered continued motivation to do well.

MOTHER'S MEDICINE AND THE SIDE EFFECTS

Although my mother inspired me to transcend the educational and career levels set by our family members and to embrace the self-sufficiency and dignity derived from my academic and professional achievement, she did not anticipate that her transformative medicine could cause me to feel alienated from my extended family network. The more engaged in personal and academic growth I became, the more disconnected I felt from my relatives. I experienced an array of mixed feelings ranging from guilt, to anger, to disappointment in my inability to fit into their world and their inability to fully understand mine.

While it seemed that our value systems clashed, I sought to relate to my grandparents, uncles, and cousins in a respectful, humble manner, trying to avoid the easy labels they seemed to apply to any educated, middle-class African American: "snooty," "s'ditty." Or they would say, "She must think she's something!" As I developed a critical consciousness and engaged in painful analyses of my own internalized racism, I desired to wrestle my family free of what Thomas Parham, Joseph White, and Adisa Ajamu (1999) termed "mental enslavement" by which their life potential was held captive. However, I ran the risk of "acting better than" or deeming myself superior because I was fortunate enough to be well-educated. I absorbed the effects of their internalized racism perpetuated throughout the generational cycles. Whether it was due to my being told I spoke like a "white girl" or that I was destined to marry outside of my race because an African American male could not match my educational and professional standards, I experienced disconnection and dysphoria about the way they viewed themselves.

The scholarly literature talks about the psychosocial conditions that divide and conquer, including: class differences, the pressure to "be black enough," and various manifestations of internalized oppression that include the negative residuals of centuries of enslavement and its aftermath of institutionalized oppression (Frazier, 1965; Hill, 2005; Hine, 1994; Jones and Shorter-Gooden, 2003 ; Parham, White, and Ajamu, 1999). Parham, White, and Ajamu (1999) argue that some black intragroup, including intrafamilial, relationships are affected by the dynamics of mental enslavement. They explain that this form of internalized oppression is the psychological by-product of generations of racial oppression and assert, "The pathology of our people's condition is not simply in the chaining/shackling process that incarcerates our minds . . . [but the] dysfunctional associations in establishing cause-effect relationships among variables that shape our lives. As a consequence, instead of associating pain with enslavement, we now link pain with freedom, self-determination and liberation" (p. 45). In saying goodbye as I prepared to leave home to return to college after holiday breaks, my grandmother would state, "So, you're going back to school. You're putting old Grandma down." She associated my attending college for personal edification with a rejection of her. The nature of the internalized racism exhibited in my family suggested that African Americans were relegated to working-class or impoverished conditions engendered by our own ignorance, shiftlessness, and immaturity.

Mother also was the target of her family's damaging, self-denying thought processes, which gave way to cruel jealousy and "crabs in a barrel" mentality. As a young woman, Mother, unlike her cousins, refrained from drug and alcohol use, located gainful employment at a local hospital, and attended community college. Certain cousins refused to associate with her by not speaking to her or leaving the room during family visits. An older cousin, who was addicted to cocaine and demanding of money, cracked a glass pop bottle and wielded it against my mother while accusing her of "acting better" than the rest of the family. When mother decided to continue working on an associate's degree thirty years after graduating from high school, her mother questioned why she would waste her time in such an endeavor. When Mother then earned two associate's degrees, I was the only representative of the family to attend her graduation ceremony. I continue to marvel at the extent to which family members enable dysfunctional behavior through financial assistance, telephone calls, visits, attention, and so forth, whereas those, like myself or Mother, who try to advance themselves get little direct support.

Charisse Jones and Kumea Shorter-Gooden (2003) address the search for sister affiliation that ambitious, upwardly mobile African American women pursue in an effort to combat the physical and mental isolation common to women who make educational and professional strides. Throughout college and graduate school, my search for community landed me in circles of friendships with like-minded

African Americans who had experienced family struggles akin to mine. Reaching out to African American colleagues and other African American psychologists, networking at the grassroots level within the African American community, and cultivating friendships with critically conscious Afrocentric thinkers allow me to cope with the family estrangement. A more personal coping mechanism I use to preserve my ego strength is emotional cut-off wherein I erect psychological boundaries to protect myself from family dysfunction and the ensuing feelings of guilt, shame, and powerlessness. I closely monitor the engagement and disengagement process in order to manage the internal angst triggered from our life differences.

MOTHER'S MEDICINE AND ITS HEALING

Mother's vision for my personal and professional accomplishment was rooted in her denied aspirations and a desire to initiate change in the family dynamic. Her vision was instrumental in my efforts to become a well-rounded woman through a process of personal, professional, interpersonal, and spiritual growth. While it is unfortunate that I have experienced a need to disengage sporadically from my extended family system, I believe that my having to cope with their dysfunction facilitates my empathy toward clients who are in emotional pain and permits me to remain grounded so that I may relate better to individuals in my ethnic/racial community.

I administer doses of Mother's medicine in my professional endeavors as a clinical psychologist, whether it is treating African American clients or supervising African American graduate students. My goal with clients and students is to encourage them to envision personal or professional goals and to empower them to tap into their internal resources, which will allow them to effect necessary change and achieve their goal. Examining internal dialogue has been essential in helping these clients, and students recognize and obliterate old messages that serve as potential blocks to their progress and achievement.

In addition, Mother's medicine was applied on the numerous African American teenage mothers whom I mentored in the past. These young women and I shared similar family backgrounds with respect to the value placed on higher education or professional accomplishment. We also shared similar socioeconomic levels of the immediate and extended family. In attempting to inoculate them with Mother's transformative medicine, I encouraged academic achievement and provided career guidance that their family members could not or would not be able to provide. Challenging these young women to look beyond the apparent limitations of young motherhood or financial disadvantage was key to their empowerment. In some respect, this was a herculean task, given that these women had lived most of their young lives without any influential individuals inspiring them to create and pursue meaningful life goals. However, I realized it was essential for me to administer Mother's medicine to those in my community. I am the direct recipient of Mother's medicine, and through me, her medicine will indirectly heal the lives of many.

NOTES

1. Pseudonyms are used to refer to all individuals in this chapter, with the exception of family.

REFERENCES

Alperin, R. M. (2001). Barriers to intimacy. *Psychoanalytic Psychology, 18*, 137–56.

Bernal, G., Trimble, J. E., Burlew, A. K., Leong, F. T. L. (2003). Introduction: The psychological study of racial and ethnic minority psychology. In G. Bernal, J. E. Trimble, A. K. Burley, and F. T. L. Leong (Eds.), *Handbook of racial and ethnic minority psychology* (pp. 1–12). Thousand Oaks, CA: Sage.

Bowen, M. (1994). *Family therapy in clinical practice.* Northvale, NJ: Aronson.

Boyd, H. (2007). It's hard out here for a black man! *Black Scholar, 37* (3), 2–9.

Boyd-Franklin, N. (1989). *Black families in therapy: A multisystems approach.* New York: Guilford.

Frazier, E. F. (1965). *Black Bourgeosie.* New York: Free.

Hill, Shirley, A. (2005). Black intimacies: A gender perspective on families and relationships. Walnut Creek, CA: AltaMira.

Hine, D. C. (1994). Hine sight: Black women and the re-construction of American history. Bloomington: Indiana University Press.

hooks, b., & West, C. (1991). *Breaking bread: Insurgent black intellectual life.* Boston: South End.

Hopson, D. P., & Hopson, D. S. (2001). *Team-spirited parenting: Eight essential principles for parenting success.* New York: Wiley.

Jones, C., Shorter-Gooden, K. (2003). *Shifting: The double lives of black women in America.* New York: HarperCollins.

Parham, T. A., White, J. L., & Ajamu, A. (1999). The Struggle for identity congruence in African Americans. *The psychology of blacks: An African-centered perspective* (3rd ed.) (pp. 40–51). Upper Saddle River, NJ: Prentice Hall.

Pinderhughes, E. B. (2002). African American marriage in the 20th century. *Family Process, 41* (2), 269–83.

12

"Contending Forces" or Contrariant Strains in the Mother-Daughter Leadership Dynamic

Sandra Y. Govan

At some sixty plus years, were I of a more dramatically poetic turn of mind, I could borrow from that gospel song that speculates, "I look back and wonder how I got over." The truth, however, is that I know very well how I got over. I've known for some time, although I could not consciously admit it for years. The fact of the matter is that my mother carried me across. And despite the fact that she departed this vale more than twenty years ago, having crossed the River Jordan back in 1991, called home (as we say) to help St. Peter maintain order in the mansion (making sure new arrivals "clean their feet" as they pass through the Pearly Gates, greeting the new comers, and distributing to them the inevitable list of things to do), I am nonetheless convinced that my mama still takes time to speak to me. In this speaking, she gives me her love, comfort, and counsel, guiding my feet as I continue to run my race here below. I still hear her quite often, speaking her piece in my subconscious ear. She warns me still when I am driving too fast, "like a bat out of hell." Or she speaks to me when I find myself in a particularly adverse situation, telling me that I should "never let them see you sweat" and that I should "never let them get you down" because what I have learned, "they can't ever take away" from me.

My mother's deliberately vague use of the objective pronoun "them" or the subjective "they" always seemed indefinite when I was young. As I grew older, I learned to discern that my mother, renowned for the razor-edged sharpness of her tongue, could also speak with great subtlety when she chose. Further, I came to understand that her choice of personal pronouns was encoded to suggest the on-going struggle against racism without specifying precisely that "they," generally construed as white teachers, or white administrators, were (could be) the enemy.

"They can't keep you down, Sweetie," she would assert enigmatically whenever we discussed race issues, "unless they stay down with you," for "a man with his knee in your back must also stay down" in the kneeling position. Then she would add, in her left-handed manner of conveying hope for change, "He can't rise unless you do." And presumably, the country wanted to rise.

In my mother's expert, if wry, political opinion, few of Chicago's finest politicians, white or black, were effective leaders. Most of them she dismissed as "those rascals" who were "no good." Worse, in her view, they were all "sorry" and "ought to be shot" for whatever they did or said that was particularly insipid or stupid. Had my mother had her way, a bloodbath could easily have ensued, one that would have swept up all of Chicago's corrupt officials. She would have "lined them all up against that wall and shot every one of them."

With wit, wisdom, commonsense commentary and a tart assessment of "sorry fools," whom she could not abide (and with the additional aid of the flat side of a wooden ruler or the rounded ply-wood backside of a paddle-ball handle), my mother prepared me to be a survivor. She showed me how to live with grace, humor, courage, and compassion for others while strolling among lions, holding my own. She taught me independence for I absorbed the adage that "every tub must sit on its own bottom." She trained me well.

Mama's job as my first instructor was not an easy task. I was a trying child. The perspective of distance now permits me more sympathy for her situation. She was stuck, or blessed, with a handicapped, or "physically challenged," child in an era when very few accommodations were made for such children. Ironically, she created for herself additional challenges because she chose to mold (or in her words "train"), an independently minded child, one at times given to aberrant behavior. I was quite literally what many people—relatives, family friends, teachers, or church folks—deemed "difficult," initially because of physical constraints that I constantly rebelled against, but more critically because of the determined independent streak my mother, perhaps unwittingly, instilled.

During my infancy and through my earliest years, my mama frequently carried me. She had to. I could not walk because I was born with dislocated hips. Both legs were encased in hip-to-ankle casts during my very first years of life. As a consequence, my legs had almost no muscle tone or muscle strength, and I did not learn to walk until I was about four. Even then, though my sense of physical balance remained precarious, emotionally I was quite sound. Actually, several of the doctors who treated me never expected me to be able to walk at all. My mother, however, refused to accept the pronouncement of these experts and worked to prove them wrong. (In truth, Mama never had much faith in any medical or nutritional "so-called experts." She believed their opinions changed like the seasons or that time too often proved them wrong anyway. Mama's slogan was "everything in moderation" because "those experts don't know everything.") One day, at long last, the too-tight leg-scarring casts came off; then finally, the daily muscle massages Mama gave me, and the warm dishwater rubs my Grandma Bertha contributed for the home-grown physical therapy program, stopped. I could at last move under my own power. For a long while, however, I was afraid of open space. I kept at least one finger touching some stable secure surface as if I were some mobile miniature brown outgrowth, attached by my right forefinger to the walls, the kitchen chairs surrounding the kitchen table, the living room couch, the big chair across from the console TV, the TV itself, or the hallway banister as I made my way around the house. It was Mama who assured me that I could make it, that I could stand alone and walk across the living room without touching any surface, that I had to have confidence in myself and in my ability to stand on my own two feet. Of course, her advice was far more than literal, although I neither recognized nor internalized the metaphor until much later.

When I eventually learned to move well and function smoothly under my own power, I shamelessly took her advice to the max. How, I used to wonder, could any parent finally relent (after *years* of begging), buy a girl a bicycle, and then expect her just to "stay on the block" with it? There were worlds beyond our block best explored by bike. Staying on the block was not possible; or rather, because I was my mama's self-reliant (if hardheaded) child, it was not possible for me. At eight, having "borrowed" a friend's bike to learn upon, and following several rather brutal physical confrontations with every tree, every other lamppost, and most of the thornier bushes on our block, I ultimately mastered the art of steering and the intricacies of maintaining balance on a two-wheeler. Then, I was gone. Possessed of a penchant for exploring far away places, for "sailing off" upon Betsy, my five-speed black-and-gold Raleigh English racer, I cruised Chicago's various ethnic neighborhoods. I loved wandering through distinctly different territories. My friends and I would ride through places like Maple Park, a newly built black neighborhood abutting Morgan Park. At other times on slow summer days we'd cruise, or be chased, through the segregated and sometimes dangerous white neighborhoods that served as Morgan Park's boundaries, places such as Mt. Vernon or Beverly Hills or Sheldon Heights. Several slightly younger neighbor children often rode with me when I went exploring. Unfortunately, we occasionally lost our bearings. When that happened and we were way late returning home, I was sometimes accused of being a bad influence, of leading the other kids astray as we went adventuring. I aroused just a few irate neighborhood parents whose irritation sometimes caused me considerable discomfort at home when the police were called to search for the presumed lost and missing—though our pictures were not plastered on any milk cartons. To be sure, we might have been late coming back, but I made sure my crew always made it home safely.

It should also be noted here that my mother had raised no dummy. Mama warned us repeatedly of the potential for senseless violence existing in our world. "You always have to be on your guard," she'd say; "you don't know the latest trick they might try to pull or what they might do to you." So, the day that Joey's bike chain broke, when we were way beyond our territory and far from home, and Joey could not ride with us any further, I was prepared. I dutifully memorized the license number of the rather considerate Black man who put Joey and his bike into his car and claimed he would take him home. Although I'd been trained to be suspicious and to question the motives of unknown adults, I also had to comfort Joey. "If he kills you," I whispered to him, "I'll report him to the police because I got his license plate number."

I should like to be able to romanticize my past and paint a warm and affectionate pastoral picture of my mother and me during my childhood, indicating that we had no problems until I hit puberty. I used to laughingly suggest to friends that my mama had lost her mind the day I turned eleven and did not regain her senses until I hit twenty-two. But as I have regretfully given up the really big lies, the ones that used to save me when I was a child, I confess that such a portrait would be terribly false. From the time I could stand on my own two feet and move under my own precarious power, I gave my mama a "hell of a way to go." She admitted as much to her friends frequently. She was twenty-seven when I was born and thus an older and, therefore, a far more sensible, understanding, educated, and patient parent than many in our neighborhood. Because of her greater maturity, my brother and I escaped many of the more frequent whippings my cousins and peers received. But make no mistake about it, we got our fair share.

As a child I could try the patience of a saint, and my mother, although patient, was not a saint. I moved slow; I could be determined or obstinate, depending on perspective. I tended to drift into daydreams and thus not be psychologically present to hear or respond swiftly enough to specific requests or commands: "Yvonne, you will finish all your dinner, or you will sit at the table until you do." Or, "Yvonne, I said turn off that TV. Come upstairs to bed now!" Or, "Sweetie, get dressed now! Sweetie, the school bus is coming! Aren't you ready yet?!" Usually though, when I received whippings, it was generally not for the customary childhood crimes of flippant smart-mouth "back-talk" at home or even for the crime of "talking back" to other adults. Rather, we were permitted, even encouraged, to speak up for ourselves. Mama had proclaimed on more than one occasion, "Just because someone is an adult does not mean they're always right. You have the right to defend yourself."

Neighbors down the block, the Sunday School teachers at Beth Eden Baptist, Chicago's city bus drivers, and several teachers at various schools were generally surprised and sometimes appalled by the regularity with which I applied the "my mama said" maxim and corrected them whenever I thought they were wrong, vigorously defending myself against any perceived injustice. Most of these people had grown up with the "children are best seen but not heard" rule. That rule was never applied at our house, and thus, I often remained a complete mystery to them. When accused of a crime, innocent or not, I never simply sniffled or sulked; instead, I became highly verbal in constructing my defense, articulate and analytical in deconstructing their arguments, demanding the right to present my side of any grievance, claiming the right to be heard. These were my rights; my mama had said so.

No, it was seldom from general parental impatience or poor grades in school that my brother and I got spanked (usually, unless it was arithmetic, I got good grades). When we were whipped, it was generally for the crimes of overt disobedience or stubborn "hardheadedness." Two of Sarah D. Govan's more enduring nature images are without question forever etched on my soul. "Talking to you," she would say to me, shaking her head in moments of absolute disgust, "is like pouring water off a duck's back." As a first-generation urban child, born and bred on the South Side of Chicago where there were no ducks, it took me years to decode this often repeated, favorite barnyard metaphor. The second phrase was far more concrete: "Your head is as hard as this rock" or "this table" . . . or "this wall." Any rigid surface sufficed to get her point across.

To the end of her days, my mother maintained and regularly sharpened her ability to put her "point across." She had a wealth of experiences from which to draw in order to make a point on virtually any subject. Mama grew up the eldest child on a family farm in Louisiana with four brothers and a sister. She went off to Southern University in Baton Rouge before World War II; then, she taught home economics in Colfax, Louisiana. While teaching, she met and married the soldier who was to become my father while he was on maneuvers in Louisiana. Witnessing the poverty of my father's Arkansas family, then moving to Chicago when he returned from duty overseas where she worked first at the Chicago Public Library, and later in a Chicago high school cafeteria, gave my mother plenty of points to make, plenty of hard-won life lessons to offer.

Among Mama's favorite "points," one that she strove to impress upon me quite often, was that "you always do the best that you can do; never mind what anybody else does." Another often repeated saying used to scare me with its conceivable ramifications. In telephone conversations with her friends Mama would say, "I gave [him/her/whomever] a piece of my mind." For years my brother and I worried that Mama would suffer from diminished mental capacity when she grew older as she constantly "gave some clown" a piece of her mind. We lived in terror that she would give too much away and would thus be seriously ill later in life. Nevertheless, along with my bottle, I imbibed this implicit tactical coping strategy: when aggrieved, you don't simply suffer in silence; you speak your piece; you set the record straight. I took the lesson to heart in my own life, improving upon it by putting into writing every transgression, documenting each case. I absorbed the primary lesson well after hearing it in connection to every disagreement on her job or at home in conversation with her friends. She would complain about "some stupid trick" she thought my Dad had pulled or some dumb move by "some stupe" down at the Board—most likely a newly hired supervisor fresh on the job who presumed to dictate to my mama how she should manage her school lunchroom.

"Stupes," were those people who did not know their obligations or who knew but failed to exercise proper responsibility; they were right up there with the "sorry" individuals (especially "sorry Negroes") my mother could not abide. She had no use for stupes or for sorry people or for sorry workers or poor and sorry workmanship. She demanded excellence and accountability. She trained me to appreciate the value of same.

There are mothers (and fathers, too, I suppose) who shout, "Praise God!" with every other sentence. There are parents who vociferously "thank the Lord" for all their blessings or who encourage patience and endurance by stipulating that it's best to "wait on the Lord" to provide. My mother operated from a different philosophical context. While certainly a woman of strong faith, she neither wore that faith on her sleeve nor believed anyone should just "sit on their hands and wait on the Lord to provide." Hers was an activist faith. Sarah D. Govan believed that the Lord gave you a brain and expected you to use it. You were expected to "apply yourself" to whatever challenges you faced and to work for whatever you wanted. If one method did not work, you were expected to try another. You were expected to be able to "roll with the punches," to be able to change your plan as circumstances warranted. Once, in dismay that bordered upon disgust at a stance my father suddenly adopted, Mama announced, "He said he's not going to change—well, I'm going to change." And she did, radically, illustrating her tenacious resolve and determination. Her truth was, as we heard on more than one occasion, "the Lord helps those who help themselves."

Mining that same vein, Mama would also tell us regularly that you had to "pick up after yourself," and you had to "clean up your own mess" because "once you make your bed hard, you have to lie in it." You also had to be able to "fight your own battles" as nobody else was going to fight them for you. These aphoristic nuggets of truth crystallized into instructions on how to live in this world; they were her methods of teaching personal responsibility which, over time and with constant reiteration, decidedly influenced my development. Mama imparted to me such leadership skills as assessment, situational analysis, initiation of action, and acceptance of accountability without ever once using these buzz-words.

My mother's words, her aphorisms regarding how one should live life, how one is expected to behave at home or on the job, have most certainly stuck with me and remained principles I continued to use when teaching or speaking to students. Mama's maxim, "You don't let anybody tell you what you can't do" because "you can do whatever you set your mind to," is one I live by and one I revised for my students when we discussed their difficulties in their classes or with their own writing. When demanding my students pay careful deliberate attention to critical reading or to their own writing, I often gave them a variant of a Sarah Govan maxim. I'd say to them, "Just because you did not learn it in high school, because someone else perhaps did a poor job teaching when he or she accepted shoddy work, does not mean you can continue with less than your best. I expect you to rise to the challenge. I don't accept sorry work." Generally, the students rose to the challenge because they came to understand that my demanding that they rise was a good thing.

However, when I hear a phrase like "You ought to be shot" emerging from my mouth, it gives me pause. I sometimes find myself alternately appalled or amused by the frequency with which my mother's often pungent observations cross my tongue unbidden, seemingly automatic, and fully situational. If my Honey says or does something silly, I catch myself muttering, "You ought to be shot." It seems that despite my intense struggles to be my own woman, I have been marked. I am my mother's daughter after all. Yet over time, I have come to admit that this is not such a bad thing. My mother had a great deal to offer the world, and she taught and led by personal example. While most often authoritative or highly "directional," she also believed in *showing* you how to do something. She would tell you how she would do it ("Sweetie, I always wrap my meats this way before I freeze them") but then let you make your own mistakes or find your own methods. She constantly encouraged the development of your best efforts. She could be patient, when she chose—but not to a fault, not to the point where people were allowed to mistake her patience or generosity for weakness. Those making that mistake paid for it, for my mother did not allow people to walk on her.

When he left for college in 1965 and returned for his freshman year Thanksgiving break, my big brother, only eighteen months my senior, brought home to us a lesson from his introductory psychology class that he thought would explain the tension-filled family dynamic sometimes operating in our home. I had always been a genuine Daddy's girl; he had been a Mama's boy. He was her first born, and the proverbial apple of her eye. Acknowledging our relative status, we had, we thought, neatly divided our parents equally between us. But eight weeks at Drake University had given him new insight. "Mama," he announced at dinner, "you and Yvonne fight all the time because you all are so much alike." At those words, with Daddy's chuckling laughter filling the kitchen, Mama and I both "hit the ceiling" in mutual denial. But time, as I can now admit, certainly lends credence to my brother's observation. And while distinct differences remained that even a blind man could see (and certainly hear), much of my mother clearly resonates in me.

Interestingly, our once distinctive differences, though apparent, seem less crucial now. I, for instance, am not a tall, svelte, impeccably attired (even while wearing jeans), elegant Negro woman the color of spun honey in the classic mode. I am the "scaled back" version of the black American woman—slim, petite, pecan brown, typically more casually dressed and "cute" rather than elegant. Nor will I ever be the model of domestic efficiency or good housekeeping. Where my mother's home remained orderly, spotless, and generally well organized with a place for every thing and everything in its place, I typically live amidst splendid disarray and resounding clutter or "mess" as my Mama would say. In my study, the surfaces of three desks lie covered by miscellaneous stuff: books, folders, stacks of assorted papers, unopened mail. Some other distinct differences: my mother actually loved math and could work numbers like a champ; no two-dollar deviation in a checkbook balance ever eluded her. I, on the other hand, hate math; I still suffer basic math anxiety, and I am far more willing to settle for a reasonable "approximate" balance in the checkbook—within the one-hundred-dollar range works for me. My mother retained superb control of her dietary habits; she never encountered a truly acceptable fast-food hamburger, while I never passed a White Castle without desire. Aesthetically, perhaps because her walls were plaster and not drywall, Mama hung very few art pieces on her walls and none that were Afrocentric. By contrast, the walls of virtually every room in my house are covered in work by African American artists, reflecting an aesthetic sensibility shaped more by external influences than by the home front. Finally, Mama disdained the television, watching almost no TV, barring news reports and professional football games, especially the Chicago Bears. Me, I'm a basketball person and a *Star Trek* fan; I have unabashedly watched every iteration of Gene Roddenberry's classic from the original series through each successive sequel.

Given my Mama's hard-held belief that whatever she said to me "went in one ear and out the other," I now find it curious that such a blending of habits, quirks, traits, and expressions actually "took hold" and are so indelibly embedded. Our similarities are as distinctive as our differences. One gift Mama imparted to me is an appreciation of quality clothing; we both loved particular designers and particular fabrics. Mama favored Calvin Kline, Bill Blass, and Evan Picone; her fabrics were cotton, silk, linen, denim, and wool. Some synthetics or rayon blends were permitted but no cheap polyesters. Because of my body's unique design parameters—one hip sits higher than the other; one arm is shorter while the elbow retains a permanent crooked bent—I've discovered that the designers who best "disguise my defects" are Liz Claiborne, Dana Buchman, and Chaus. I, too, only wear cotton, silk, denim, linen, or lined wool. I can't put cheap polyester on the sensitive skin inherited from my Mama. In another area, my love of books is a trait instilled by my Mama. She got me started on Agatha Christie murder mysteries from the public library; we also shared the thrill of World War II action suspense dramas. And though I will watch *Star Trek* avidly, like Mama, I am a far more avid radio person and a radio news junkie. Mama's favorite Chicago stations were WGN and WBBM; as a Black teen, I, of course, listened to WVON. But as an adult, once out in the world and moving from city to city, I became a National Public Radio (NPR) listener and supporter.

Ironically, while Mama maintained that in her household there was a proper place for everything, she frequently also suffered from "safe place syndrome," or SPS. Drapes that she had searched the house long years for would one day miraculously reappear as curtains recut and rehung. Although she'd looked right at them daily, hanging in the hallway windows, she simply had not seen those curtains as her long missing drapes.

Sadly, I, too, am cursed by SPS. Vitally important documents, checks, vehicle stickers, insurance papers, and bills or announcements I usually put in a secure location that I cannot forget. Then, at the moment I truly need it, the document required will mysteriously vanish from my desk to reappear miraculously days, weeks, or months later, long after the immediate need for its presence has passed. Those who suffer the heartache of SPS know the frustration, anxiety, or panic it can cause as an entire office, or a whole house, must be torn apart (or cleaned up!) in a frantic search for missing money or insurance statements.

Our other similarities could be summarized in this way: a love of baking, especially Christmas banana breads and sweet potato pies; determination in keeping the dirty hands of small children off of our walls; a strong belief in taking care of our things, of keeping them secure until needed. Here, however, another slight distinction emerges; Mama preserved all manner of "nice things," from silver serving trays to crystal glassware to evening purses with the price tags still attached and obviously never used. I use *all* my stuff—including the many wonderful things she bequeathed to me. We both have (had) limited patience; within our means we both have been generous to church, family, and friends; we both have done a lot of "visiting" by telephone, conserving our energy and getting our rest. "Sweetie, you have to get your rest," is another of those echoes that reverberates internally when I push past my endurance envelope. We have both been highly "directional" people, dispensing orders and offering advice or explicit directions freely, often in an unconscious, yet naturally imperative voice: "You need to do this . . ."; "you should . . ."; or, "I think it would be best if you . . ."

If it is true, as Richard L. Daft posits in *Leadership Theory and Practice* (1999), that leadership is a social relationship of influence that occurs among leaders and followers for the purpose of pursuing a collective goal or shared purpose, then I would surmise that those shared traits that still influence my behavior and guided my conduct in my professional realm are the indelibly impressed "mediations" of spirit that I prize most. These ingrained "codes of conduct," to paraphrase from cultural critic Karla Holloway's 1995 book of that same title, are meditations that emerge from the cultural storehouse of black "mother wit," derived from my mother's personal stock. They remain with me. Mama believed not in the "power lunch" while on the job but the powerful meal that got you ready to meet the man.

"Never start the day without breakfast," she'd say, and I don't, for "breakfast is the most important meal of the day." The fact that I can be relied upon to contribute my view, to give my two cents worth, at meetings or workshops, at departmental retreats or major conferences, to "speak my piece," offering my take on a particular development, is of course directly attributable to my mother's home training. Mama would also, from time to time, advise "holding your piece." Although more problematic for my nature, I've finally learned to adopt her laying-back-in-the-cut strategy when necessary as well. I learned early to go for whatever I wanted, to make determined efforts to achieve the goals I set for myself because first, I am entitled to my dreams and goals, but more important, because I knew no one would look at anyone with just a "hand out for gimme." I also learned that change was not only possible but necessary and critical to continued development. In her essay, "Catching Sense," Suzanne Carothers describes the kinds of things that I learned from my mother as critical understandings (1990, p. 237). These critical understandings help us as black girls learn how to survive and learn how to negotiate race, class, and gender to leverage influence and leadership (Carothers, 1990).

Through my mother I gained the knowledge that power comes from within the individual. I learned that I did indeed possess the ability to stand upon my own two feet, that I could proceed to walk without leaning upon a crutch or keeping a finger still attached to a wall. I was permitted to march to my own drummer and trained to be self-reliant, while simultaneously taught that "networking" (a current term never used in our home), or the ability to develop a diverse and supportive friendship circle, was also a highly prized attribute. Being a team player (as in never having a curfew where I had to be the one taken home early) was good; knowing when and how to step up and assert self-control (as in not even trying to experiment with hard drugs) was even better. From the genes of both my parents I learned how to greet and treat people, how not ever to meet a stranger. Most of all, I learned while sandwiched between my Mama's knees at hair-pressing time that she raised a daughter, not a carpet; no one had the right to walk on me and clean their feet. I was taught to give any individuals who tried a piece of my mind—and I do as I was trained.

Each contrariant strain of my developmental process occurred in the context of the strong mother-strong daughter archetype that Pinkola Estes identifies in her multicultural theory of women's development (1992, p. 181). Through the years of " exploring and inhabit[ing] a connection that breaks and frays and heals" (Quashie, 2004, p. 68), my mother and I were fortunate to find the hidden treasure in the process of my straining against the strong mother and becoming the strong child. According to Quashie, Brand calls this treasure the "the wild creativity" of women who "go outside the boundaries marked for their gender and who embrace their own and each other's otherness" (2004, p. 68). As contrary or hardheaded as I might have been in my youth, my Mama's principles somehow seeped through and saturated the sometimes tense but always loving and interactive relationship that existed between us. My mama definitely made me the woman I have become.

REFERENCES

Carothers, S. (1990). Catching sense. In F. Ginsburg and A. L. Tsing (Eds.), *Uncertain terms: Negotiating gender in American culture* (pp. 232–45). Boston: Beacon.

Daft, R. L. (1999). *Leadership theory and practice.* Fortworth, TX: Dryden.

Estes, C. P. (1992). Finding one's pack, belonging as blessing. In *Women who run with the wolves: Myths and stories of the wild woman archetype* (pp. 166–98). New York: Ballantine.

Holloway, K. F. C. (1995). *Codes of conduct: Race, ethics and the color of our character.* New Brunswick, NJ: Rutgers University Press.

Quashie, K. E. (2004). Self(ful)ness and the politics of community. *Black women, identity, and cultural theory: (Un)becoming the subject* (pp. 42–77). New Brunswick, NJ: Rutgers University Press.

13

"Like Mother, Like Daughter"

Prophetic Principles from the Motherline—A Sermon

LEAH C. K. LEWIS

> Like mother, like daughter.
> —Ezekiel 16:44 (NRSV)

THE MANIFESTATIONS of the proverb quoted above are as many as the number of mothers and daughters past, present, and future. This phrase means something different to each of us. "Like mother, like daughter." Some of us cringe at the thought. Others of us beam with a sense of pride as we stand in the glow of our thoughts of our mothers. Some of us have been and are still being shaped, molded, and built up by our mothers. Sadly, others have been or are still being poked, prodded, and torn down by their mothers. "Like mother, like daughter" is akin to the adage, "The apple does not fall far from the tree." But the question that I put before you in this chapter is, Is the apple a pristine, succulent delicious red, or is it deceivingly beautiful, only to be bitter, mushily overripe, or even rotten to its core?

"Like mother, like daughter." This proverb in the Hebrew Bible was intended as a condemnation. Ezekiel the prophet, God's mouthpiece, uttered the axiom as condemnation of Jerusalem. Chapter 16 of Ezekiel is a chilling pericope. As Ralph W. Klein (1988) observes, "This chapter is not for the theologically squeamish" (p. 87). It illustrates a prostitute metaphor in a striking fashion. Jerusalem for the God of Ezekiel was an infidel, a harlot, and a "headstrong whore" (p. 88). In fact, Jerusalem was considered worse than a prostitute because she *paid* to be defiled. That is, she sought after and followed not her first love, YHWH ("Yahweh"), who treated her exceedingly well, but the gods of other peoples. In verse 44 well into the chapter, Jerusalem is told, "Like mother, like daughter." In other words, "Your mother was a whore, and so are you." Oh, that is harsh. What an indictment! But wait, just give me a minute, and we will turn this thing around.[1]

In the book of Ezekiel Jerusalem is stripped down in verse for all to read as God conveys Jerusalem's story to Ezekiel. This is in part what it means to be a prophet. God speaks not only *to* the prophet but *through* the prophet. So Ezekiel tells the story—one recorded for the ages. What we have here is Jerusalem's story . . . as told from another's perspective. Who shall tell your story? Who shall write your story? More important, how shall you live your story? Will you be hindered by your past, buoyed by it—that is merely kept afloat by it—or elevated by it? These questions form the crux of today's message.

Let me give my perspective upon "Like mother, like daughter" as it is informed by my relationship with my own mother and by my experiences of her far-reaching wisdom. Elisabeth Hayes and colleagues (2002) offer an understanding of the ways in which I gleaned knowledge from my mother's words and experiences. Her principles assist in discerning when and how to be "like mother" and when to write a new story that veers from my mother's life script. Some of my mother's lessons were spoken to me directly and consciously. Others were nonverbal and implied. As it is not possible to cover or even to know all that my mother taught me, I will focus on the following three points to display my mother's prophetic presence in my life and the way that she shaped my leadership development so that I became like my mother and yet at the same time more my distinctive self.

> Her first principle: Live your life—write your own story.
> Her second principle: Operate out of the integrity of your
>   heart (God willing yours is a good heart); take a stand for

what is right, regardless of the consequences and the perceptions of others.

Her third principle: Make no apologies for the goodness of God in your life; reject any unjust limitations on your liberty, your voice, or your blessings.

"Like mother, like daughter." Let me show you how the proverb may serve as an affirmation or a compliment. My mother was in many ways a prophet, and you will get glimpses of why I deem her so as we proceed. I take my model from her as I assume the posture of a bold, truth-telling preacher and a well-grounded being. "Like mother, like daughter." Indeed, mother's presence and her proclamations have had a reverberating impact on my life even unto this day, more than two decades after her death.

However, even though similarities exist between my mother and me, I am a distinct and independent woman. My mother fostered this characteristic. She cultivated a critical consciousness in me that would require me to write my own story. She affirmed my authority to deviate from her template. She was much like a mama bird—letting go of me, she ensured my transformation, making sure that I would fly high and free. Prophets, like mama birds, prompt transformation.

My mother, Thelma L. K. Lewis, mother of three, sister, friend, nurse, care giver and wife, was a paradigm of gentleness, sweetness, beauty, strength, and long suffering. She was the *über* constellation—the life force in what was our cohesive family unit. Raised in the South she was a woman of her word—her nay was nay—and indeed—her yea, yea. My mother was a pristine soul, beautiful and loving to her very core.

Early in my young life, however, events brought on a tragic turn for my mother and my family. At five years old, I witnessed my father's self-esteem and mental health crumble, triggered by a crushing blow to his index finger while working on an assembly line. I witnessed the downward spiral of my family's stability and the beginning of my mother's long-term hardship. From that time on she single-handedly supported the family for what would be the last twenty-four years of her life. Talk about being a trooper, she saw all three of her daughters through private school, college, and advanced degrees. She provided my father with a lovely home, ample food, transportation, clothing, and spending money. She coddled him as though she herself had given birth to him. And she did all this on the salary of a licensed practical nurse.

The slight disabling of my father's right hand and his subsequent all-encompassing mental illness pushed my mother into the role of sole breadwinner of her family. On one level my father defied the Holy Scripture that says, "When I was a child, I spoke like a child, I thought like a child, I reasoned like a child; when I became an adult, I put an end to childish ways."[2] Father ultimately failed to put away childish things. He took narcissism to an extraordinary depth. After all he did not lose the appendage; he did not even lose the use of his finger. He simply lost bragging rights about his prowess on the machine that had defeated him. He became my mother's fourth child. His prolonged irresponsibility and narcissism led to the deterioration of his mental health. My father paid a substantial price for violating our and God's expectations that he would care for his wife and family.

After the accident I never saw any indication that my father was grateful for my mother's care. I do not recall my father ever saying, "Thank you." I do not remember my father ever giving my mother a gift of any sort. He did, however, routinely take her to and from work. My mother, you see, did not drive. My father apparently had the faculty to realize that if she could not get to work, she could not provide for him and their children.

My mother once told me that just because her marriage had not been a joyous one did not mean that mine must also lack joy. She literally said that her story did not have to be mine. Especially on the subject of marriage, she said, there would be no decree of "Like mother, like daughter." With this powerful declaration, she strengthened and buttressed my spirit of independence. My mother made plain for me the opportunity to do as I had often done: create my own story. That is what a good mother does—she sets us free of the limitations of our lineage. The significance of this story: live your life; write your own story.

I am writing my own story. In this fourth decade of my life on this earth, I am still a single woman. I enjoy my life, my peace, and my freedom. Like everything, peace and freedom have a cost, but I am willing to pay it until the right kind of man comes along. I do not have the patience or long-suffering ability of my mother. I know quite well my limitations, and they have spared me certain types of heartache and brought on heartaches of another sort. I have loved but I have not found a suitable partner. My internal cost-benefit analysis would not allow me to continue an unfulfilling relationship. After all, I had seen that dynamic firsthand and I wanted no part of such a saga. I am writing my own story just as my mother encouraged.

I acknowledge that some of us cannot say such glowing things about our mothers. In such an instance, I am here to tell you that people need not look upon you and proclaim, "Like mother, like daughter." They need not, for you can indeed write your own story.

However, to write your own story you have to take it upon yourself to do it. To write your own story you must assert your God-given right to a proper and healthy interdependence—one rooted firmly in the self-knowledge and self-expression permitted by righteous independence. I ask you, Who are you? What are you? And whose are you? These are questions *you* must answer for yourselves. I encourage you to keep in mind those age-old sayings, "Know thy self"; and "To thine own self be true." My mother was the first to say these things to me. Another pertinent axiom is, "As a woman thinketh, so she is." Our thoughts and outlook shape our actions. Write your own story.

Clearly, other people's perspectives affect us—both positively and negatively. We feel the impact of other people as well as the influence of factors such as environment, circumstance, status. My mother's words to me on the subject of marriage illustrate the dichotomous nature of dialogue. Each person has a distinctive viewpoint, and the viewpoints exchanged during the dialogue may be contradictory. In the exchange, we each have the opportunity to accept or reject the other person's view. But beyond a simple exchange, there is an opportunity to "be changed," to let the other person's view shape our thinking just as we hope they remain open to being shaped by ours. This is the mutuality that Martin Buber (1958) speaks of in his I/Thou relationship. This is the reciprocity of "being in relation" with another. Personal growth and development are based on discovering and accepting from others what is enlightening, true, and good for our souls.

However, my mother taught me that I should choose to reject firmly and completely that which does not nourish my soul. She showed me that mutuality does not mean conformity. On this point, she gave me one of the pivotal lessons of my life—that I could reject any and all things that my instincts told me were damning, destructive, or diabolical.

A second prophetic direction was my mother's concerned courageous action and her willingness to take a stand. In this as in all things, my mother taught me to operate out of the "integrity of my heart."[3] She taught me to stand up for what is right and just. Rather than teaching by decree, my mother modeled this principle by her actions. For example, when I was about twelve years old, my oldest friend, Marvin, had his brand new bicycle stolen by the neighborhood thug, a strong and virile teenage boy who lived two doors down from us. Marvin came screaming and sobbing down the street to our house. Our little section of the block was stirred by his distress. Through the bushes in our backyard, my mother spied the hoodlum with Marvin's bike. She stormed through the bushes and literally stripped the thief of his ill-gotten gain. Needless to say, the bandit was startled and chagrinned. How dare a middle-aged woman, five feet tall, show him up before his cronies! He retorted by cursing my mother out and threatening to "pitch" her. It was quite a disconcerting experience for me as a child—witnessing a valiant, daring woman of small stature taking on the equivalent of the village bully. Frankly, it was surreal, but my mother made it real. This pivotal moment in my life stirred my naturally assertive qualities and showed me that there was little to fear, particularly when one is taking an ethical stand.

This too—this countercultural conduct—is a characteristic of a prophet.[4] Prophets often reject the conventional, particularly where the status quo is destructive or even diabolical. Prophets have the ability to perceive and speak on that which harms and hinders individuals, communities, and nations. Prophets urge right action. Prophets demand responsible action. Prophets call for just works. My mother was a prophet.

My mother's teachings continue to live in my current leadership, not just in remembrances of situations past, but in time present. Her third pivotal teaching that I will speak of now is this: "Reject any unjust limitations on your liberty, your voice, and your blessings."

Here is an example. Some time ago when I was seeking affiliation with a particular denomination, I encountered opposition and hypocrisy. The Reverend Dr. Theresa Fry Brown describes the ways that women in the ministry are blocked from inclusion and/or held back from ascending to places of power as the "brick ceiling."[5] After my initial meeting with the examining committee of ministers and lay persons, the liaison member misrepresented the committee's views to me. This person claimed to be helping my candidacy, but it appears that in fact she wanted to block my affiliation. Although I was taken "in-care" by the committee by a unanimous vote, she chose to report only that the committee found my "call story"—my call to Christian ministry—arrogant and offensive. Because I had stated that my call was connected to the catastrophic events of September 11, 2001, she reported that there was an impression among committee members that I was claiming 9/11 happened so that I could enroll in divinity school. Also, because I had mentioned having access to some of the ministerial giants of the day, some members deemed me an "ecclesiastical social climber."

The committee liaison apparently wanted to level me as if razing a building. However, she did not have my ministerial fate in her hands for, in fact, I had other options for affiliation. For me, a particular denomination is less important than service to God and God's creatures. My fate is ultimately in my hands and those of my Creator. I will not submit to the authority of a committee if such submission means compromising what my leadership is.

This is an instance in which I rejected the "limitations on my liberty, my voice, and my blessings." I will not apologize for the hard work that earned me both educational and corporate credentials. Nor will I apologize for the assertiveness that has always been my bent. "Like mother, like daughter," I break through the bushes of hypocritical behavior and look through the brush of unnecessary pecking orders. "Like mother, like daughter," I seek to reclaim territory unjustly taken, and I decry institutional bullying.

My ancestors have sacrificed too much for me to approach with head bowed or to pretend docility to satisfy the powers that be. My mother, my family, my friends, my mentors, and my teachers have invested too much for me to give away my power or to pretend a lower stature so that others can retain institutional superiority. As Mother advised, "Reject any unjust limitations on your liberty, your voice, and your blessings."

God has fashioned me into a creature of God's likening and invested me with God's purposes. I contend that my being and my life—just like your being and your life—are not the result of happenstance. Because of my faith, I can proclaim without reservation that our lives are the product of providence. How dare we violate God's sovereignty by placing greater trust in human agency—in humans who are given to envy, jealousy, hatred, and frailty? How dare we not recognize (as we learn in Psalm 75:6), that our promotion—temporal and eternal—comes from above?

In God's grand plan, Thelma L. K. Lewis was appointed and anointed to steward my development. She oversaw my growth from infancy to womanhood. She laid my earthly foundation, preparing me to live a fully actualized life. Her leadership supported the athletic prowess of my youth—I am a three-time national champion in karate. Her leadership propelled me into the legal professional—I practiced entertainment and international business law for seven years. She ensured that I would have the background needed for life on the public stage—I perform as an author, public speaker, and minister of the Gospel of Jesus Christ. Always, she was present as I stood out, out-distanced others, and rounded the corner in excelling. She prepared me for the attacks aimed at my brilliance. She prepared me to see through the flimflam. She nourished my soul.

When I graduated from college and left home for my first professional job, my mother gave me a little metal bicycle. Mother said that the bicycle signified that I was "going places." I am going places, and I am driving myself. Once again, by means of a symbol, she gave me prophetic direction. Perhaps she knew that I had been mesmerized by her fearless woman persona in retrieving the stolen bicycle. Or perhaps she did not connect the multiple messages her symbolic gift—the little metal bicycle—held for me. Either way, she encouraged me to be "Like mother, like daughter" as long as that would permit me to observe her three adages:

1. Live my life—write my own story. I now know that the story I write may need my interpretation for others to understand it, but "not my apology" for others to approve of it.
2. Take a stand for what I see as right and just regardless of the consequences. I now know that taking a countercultural

position will draw the wrath and misperceptions of others (Lucaites and Condit, 1990).
3. And reject any unjust limitations on my liberty, my voice, or my blessings. I now know that we need not give away our power, stifle or silence our voices, or apologize for the good within our lives.

Although my mother could not have known all the ways in which her teachings provided prophetic guidance for the issues I would face both in my coming of age and in my current life, she knew that I would need to be like her, she knew that I was going places, and she knew that I would need to be able to leave behind hindrances and encumbrances that might "steal my joy." So now, when you hear a person say, "Like mother, like daughter," remember my mother Thelma L. K. Lewis. Let her words be your reason to stand up and celebrate the prophetic wisdom that can shape us in our mothers' image! To God be all the glory! Amen.

NOTES

1. In *Mining the Motherlode: Methods in Womanist Ethics,* Stacy Floyd-Thomas provides insight into the type of womanist ethic that undergirds my hermeneutics.

2. 1 Corinthians 13:11 (NRSV).

3. See Genesis 20:6 (NRSV).

4. Vernon K. Robbins, *Exploring the Texture of Texts: A Guide to Socio-Rhetorical Interpretations,* pp. 86–88.

5. Theresa L. Fry-Brown, assistant professor of homiletics at Emory University's Candler School of Theology and an African Methodist Episcopal (AME) clergywoman, explicates the trials and tribulations encountered by African American women who are audacious enough to answer the call to ordained ministry.

REFERENCES

Brown, T. L. F. (2008). *Can a sistah get a little help? Encouragement for black women in ministry.* Cleveland, OH: Pilgrim.
Buber, M. (1958). *I and thou* (2nd ed.). New York: Scribner.

Floyd-Thomas, S. M. (2006). *Mining the motherlode: Methods in womanist ethics.* Cleveland, OH: Pilgrim.

Hayes, E., Flannery, D. D., with Brooks, A. K., Tisdell, E. J., & Hugo, J. M. (2002). *Women as Learners.* San Francisco, CA: Jossey-Bass/Wiley.

Klein, R. W. (1988). *Ezekiel: The Prophet and his message.* Columbia: University of South Carolina Press.

Lucaites, J. L., and Condit, C. M. (1990). Reconstructing: Culturetypal and counter-cultural rhetorics in the martyred black vision. *Communication Monographs, 57* (1), 5–24 Mar 1990. Eric #: EJ405045.

Robbins, V. K. (1996). *Exploring the texture of texts: A Guide to socio-rhetorical interpretation.* Harrisburg, PA: Trinity Press International.

14

Othermothers, Amazons, and Strategies for Leadership in the Public and Private Spheres

Lakesia D. Johnson

WHILE MY MOTHER is the single most important female figure in my life, there were "othermothers" who participated in and contributed to my understanding of black womanhood and what that means for me as an individual and as a member of the black community. My othermothers provided the infrastructure and labor that supported my development and my mother's ability to work several jobs to make ends meet. My experience is probably quite common, given that African American communities often contain "women-centered networks of community-based child care" (Collins, 1990, p. 120). Some of the lessons that I learned from my othermothers were incongruent with values my mother wished to impart to me, but nonetheless, they inform the way I approach a variety of life issues. Reflecting on my past experiences with them, as well as on my present understanding of their lives today, gives me a greater understanding and appreciation of myself. More important, it provides a method of identifying, naming, and analyzing the skills and leadership strategies that influence my work today.

Grannie, Aunt G., Aunt K., and Momma all had prescribed roles in our extended family arrangement, some of which persist today. To me they were Amazonian women, who, like their ancient counterparts, created a complex network of roles and strategies. This network connected them to each other while simultaneously making it easier for them to choose autonomous lives, free from dependence on men. This does not mean that relationships with members of the opposite sex were not valued. The emphasis was on not being "dependent." Claiming the term *Amazon* to describe my family of origin is in some ways problematic, especially if one considers historical images and societal discourses that have cast black women as emasculating matriarchs. Michele Wallace explains that two distinct black female archetypes emerged from the experience of slavery—the Black Lady and the Amazon: "The great majority of women were somewhere in between. That is, they desired the ease, comfort, and respectability in the eyes of the white world that being a Black Lady to some extent provided; at the same time they realized the immediate necessity of preserving many of their Amazonian qualities" (1978, pp. 154–55). Despite efforts to suppress and deemphasize the role of Amazons within the African American community, it is clear that their survival skills and strategies are with us today. Given the independence and strength of the women in my family and the creative methods they used to survive, I consider it complimentary to associate them with the Amazonian archetype.

The following stories of particular personalities and individual experiences illustrate aspects or skills associated with leadership. My mother and othermothers are far more complex than these short portraits can describe, but they illuminate specific aspects of leadership that I will explore in order to better understand the subtle messages about leadership that were passed on to me. As I watched these women interact with each other and the outside world, it became obvious to me that they used a variety of coping strategies to deal with their unique challenges.

GRANNIE AND AUNTIE G.:
STRATEGIES OF LEADERSHIP IN THE PRIVATE SPHERE

> And another thing [my mother] used to say to me is, "Keep your mouth shut and do what you want to. You don't have

to talk so much; just keep your mouth shut and go ahead and do what you're going to do."
—Mary Crutchfield Thompson, from Jewell,
The Black Woman's Gumbo Ya-Ya

Grannie

Grannie was resourceful and always planned for the worst. She always made sure that I was looking for the next possible threat of danger. Dirty old men, nasty little boys, and pickpockets were all possible threats to a young girl growing up in the neighborhood. Grannie had a third-grade education and had been raised by her mother, Grandma Kirby. Grannie's mother was an ordained, sanctified minister, an unusual phenomenon for a woman in the early 1900s. Her father was absent, staying on an American Indian reservation for months at a time.

Grannie worked as a domestic for many years and knew how to make ends meet in spite of not having much. Apparently, my grandfather was mean and very cheap. When she wasn't working as a domestic, Grannie had to count on the allowance that he gave her for household expenses. He never gave extra, so Grannie saved a little from each allotment to make sure that she could buy new dresses, shoes, or dance lessons for my mother and her sisters. In fact, it was clear that Grannie always made do with what she had. For example, Grannie never learned to drive. Despite this she never had a problem getting where she needed to go. When she didn't want to deal with asking my grandfather to take her places, she walked and rode buses all over Chicago. I remember Grannie dragging us on what seemed like a million different stops and transfers to get downtown to see the Christmas decorations or a matinee. Simply put, Grannie accepted her circumstances and never complained.

Leadership required a certain level of autonomy, which my grandmother did not readily associate with the institution of marriage. According to my mother, Grannie regularly told her five daughters that there wasn't anything that a man could do for them that they couldn't do for themselves. She didn't care much for marriage and refused to attend the weddings of her daughters. I heard her say on several occasions that she "didn't have any use for son–in–laws." In fact she didn't have much to say about her daughters' husbands, except for the occasional wisecrack about some amusing characteristic. She insisted that all of her daughters learn to drive so as to avoid being dependent on a man to get them from place to place. Reliance on one's own resources and not depending on others became a prominent message that I received from Grannie.

Aunt G.

Aunt G. was fierce. As kids we were terrified of the consequences of disobeying her. Aunt G. controlled the domestic sphere. She cooked the meals, delegated the chores, cared for my grandparents and made sure that "kids with hard heads had soft behinds." She was the fix-it lady, completing repairs around the house and the rental property owned by my grandparents. She also hated girls—or at least the emotional ones. She referred to them as "screaming Mimi/s" and took every opportunity to identify and squash that tendency in me. Outward expressions of emotion, especially fear and weakness, were not an option for Aunt G. The only exception was anger. The legend goes that Aunt G. boxed Papa when she was a teenager because she decided that she was not going to take another beating from him. They fought until her face was covered with blood and Grannie had wedged her body between the two. Aunt G. never shed a tear, and she never got another beating.

As a result of my interactions with Aunt G., I learned to associate leadership with aggression. That is, the person who could do the most harm earned the title of leader. This is not surprising because Aunt G. was the primary disciplinarian in my life. A possible beating from Aunt G. was enough to keep anyone in submission. This is not that different from how our patriarchal society views leadership. The country with the biggest guns or the most nuclear weapons becomes the leader. As a child, my perception of my aunt was limited by my feelings of powerlessness against her harsh form of discipline. When I discussed the abusive aspects of my Aunt's form of discipline with my mother, I learned that Momma's ability to exercise leadership over her children was limited by her reliance on Aunt G. to provide the domestic environment so that she could work to provide for us. She told me that she didn't agree with Aunt G.'s methods, but she wouldn't challenge her because she needed her to watch us. Momma was also afraid.

As an adult, I can look back on my relationship with Aunt G. and more clearly evaluate the model of leadership that her life represented. I ask myself whether she was harder on me than on the male children in order to prepare me for battle, as Amazonian cultures were believed to have done with their young girls. Accounts of Amazonian cultures allege that these women removed "one breast in childhood so as to be able to pull back their bows unimpeded and so that the energy went into their bow-pulling arm" (Wilde, 2000, pp. 3–4). Was my sensitive nature and willingness to express emotions openly seen by Aunt G. as an obstacle to my survival?

Within the domestic sphere, Aunt G. maintained her authority through aggression, especially in relationship to the children and to my grandfather, particularly after Aunt G. and my grandmother became the caregivers for my grandfather, who became blind and confined to a wheelchair. Only Grannie's authority limited Aunt G.'s ultimate status as leader. Outside the confines of our extended family and community, Grannie and Aunt G. were invisible. This is common for many African American women who are leaders in their families and the community, but who are voiceless and powerless in society at large. However, this does not diminish the ways that their lives represent a model of leadership that challenged patriarchal control and domination. When faced with control and domination at the hands of Papa, both Grannie and Aunt G. used strategies of resistance. My aunt relied on direct physical confrontation to resist the oppressive environment that she lived in as a child. My grandmother relied on a nonconfrontational approach and creatively reallocated resources to deal with my grandfather's penny-pinching. She carved out a space where she could pursue her goals within the boundaries of their relationship. Both of these were forms of strategic confrontation that involved determining a position, assessing/evaluating risks, and selecting a plan that would maximize benefits and minimize risks.

AUNT K. AND MOMMA: STRATEGIES OF LEADERSHIP IN THE PUBLIC SPHERE

> It is our duty to fight for our freedom. It is our duty to win. We must love each other and support each other. We have nothing to lose but our chains.
> —Assata Shakur, from Jewell, *The Black Woman's Gumbo Ya-Ya*

Aunt K.

Aunt K was proud. When Aunt K. came to town we were always excited because, unlike the rest of the adults in our lives, she believed that children should be seen and heard. She also always volunteered to take us shopping, to the amusement park, or on some other adventure beyond the confines of our small, isolated world in the inner city. She introduced us to ancient African and African American history. Aunt K. gave her children African names and even wore her hair natural when it wasn't fashionable. In our family that was a bold and courageous act. Papa ruled with an iron fist, and no female in his house was going to have "nappy" hair. Momma tried it unsuccessfully, but only Aunt K. succeeded using words.

I remember the day that Grannie pulled out the infamous letter that Aunt K. had written my grandparents about her decision to wear a natural hairstyle. Aunt G. still has this letter. How could she lead the black student group on campus if her physical appearance did not explicitly convey a love of blackness? At that time among student activists, looking like the oppressor was synonymous with being a traitor to the race. Aunt K. was the first woman to serve as president of the black student organization at her school. For my aunt, and most African Americans actively engaged in the fight for equality and justice during the 1960s and 70s, the ability to lead effectively was tied to one's ability to give some external illustration of being "down for the struggle." For my aunt, how she wore her hair was the symbolic expression of her commitment to leading the other students. Embracing African traditions and African American adaptations of those traditions was another way of illustrating her commitment. Just as her letter to our family was a calculated risk, Aunt K.'s model of leadership as a student activist made use of taking calculated risks to protest injustice. Taking those risks in the public sphere was in many ways easier than challenging existing paradigms in our family.

When Aunt K's story was shared with me as a child, it primarily functioned as an illustration of the process by which expression of racial identity and pride was negotiated in our family. Later, during the late 1980s this story would be reframed as an example of black women's leadership. Professor Bracey from the University of Massachusetts was teaching a course on black women at Smith College, where I was an undergraduate. Since my concentration in my Afro-American studies minor was on black women, I was very excited about the course. We used texts by Paula Giddings, Bettina Aptheker, and other scholars who studied the black female experience. In addition to highlighting the experiences of renowned African American women in history, he often referred to the experiences of ordinary black women from his personal and professional life. On one occasion, he told the class about a skinny freshman who was the first black woman to head the black student organization at Northwestern University and how she had stood up to the administration during one of the black student protests. After rejecting an offer of minority scholarships for the protesters, she informed the administration that "slavery was over and that they could not be bought." As Bracey's story progressed, I realized that he was talking about Aunt K.! Needless to say this engendered a tremendous sense of pride. The juxtaposition of the stories of Ida B. Wells, Sojourner Truth, Mary Church Terrell, and Fannie Lou Hammer with Aunt K's story helped me to see black female leadership as both ordinary and extraordinary. This being the case, leadership was no longer something to be aspired to; it was simply an inheritance to be claimed.

Momma

Momma was ambitious. She was not interested in pursuing traditional academic success but understood that education was a means to an end. Because she wasn't a good student, when she became pregnant as a teen, my grandmother informed her that her days of going to school were over. She got a job, married my father, and, per Grannie's orders, served as our family's link to the outside world. She assumed the parental role for my cousins when arranging for medical, educational, and other services provided outside the home. Even when Aunt G. and Aunt M. were able to make the visits to the doctor's office or to school, Momma served as spokesperson. She also took care of filling out applications and other important documents for the family. It still amazes me that she had time to do all of this, while working full-time and raising my brother and me.

After divorcing my father, Momma decided to break free from Grannie's control and her reliance on the family for support. Education was the method by which she would pursue this dream. She decided to get her GED and go to college. Grannie was not supportive. With the exception of Aunt K., the family believed that there was no way that she would succeed. After passing her GED exam, Momma enrolled in college courses and eventually landed a scholarship to a university in Minnesota. Grannie said that she couldn't make it on her own. It is true that Momma only completed one year of school and eventually returned to Chicago, but she did not give up. She was hired by the federal government, worked her way up in the agency, and when I was twelve moved us to Brockton, Massachusetts.

Despite being confined by the rigid role that was imposed on her by Grannie, Momma used it as an opportunity to learn a great deal about negotiating in the public sphere. The leadership skills that she developed as spokesperson and advocate for our extended family served her well. On many occasions, particularly in our schools, I watched my mother speak out against policies and practices that she believed were limiting the opportunities of her children. As a teenager, I remember following Momma down the hallway to the headmaster's office to complain about my guidance counselor. She was always doing research, and she had discovered information about our school's early graduation policy and about a scholarship for which she thought I was qualified. Momma was angry because she felt that my guidance counselor was not doing her job and had failed to notify me of several opportunities for honors students, despite the fact that I was a 4.0 student. She was convinced that white children with 4.0 averages received regular information about these types of opportunities. Because each building had a designated counseling office, all the students went to the one in their building. The head master refused to assign another counselor. I don't remember much about the conversation after this, except that by the end, Momma was out of her seat yelling at the head master, and she forbade me to see the counselor again. A few days later, I was the only student in the blue building assigned to a counselor in the yellow building.

Momma and Aunt K. demonstrated strategies of leadership built on the acquisition of knowledge, a firm commitment to social justice, and the promotion of active protest. Either through reading books or personal experience, or some combination of the two, both women used knowledge to serve as the basis of their mode of leadership. Aunt K. used her knowledge of our African past. Momma used her understanding of the system. Both comprehended the ways that institutional structures and bureaucracies were designed to exclude African Americans.

LEARNING, DEVELOPING, AND APPLYING STRATEGIES OF LEADERSHIP

> The relationship between an African-American mother and her adolescent daughter carries with it a challenge: from the mother's point of view, she feels a responsibility to encourage great maturity at a relatively fast rate; thus the saying, "raising daughters but loving sons" is at the core of her attention.
> —Mary C. Lewis, from Jewell,
> *The Black Woman's Gumbo Ya-Ya*

How have the strategies employed by my mother and othermothers impacted my views and practices of leadership? To what extent are aggression, strategic confrontation, creative resource reallocation, knowledge of institutional structures, and a commitment to social justice present in my daily work and life?

My earliest recollection of being a leader involved mentoring and babysitting my younger brother. During one of the few occasions when we were living as a nuclear family, my mother charged me with the responsibility of looking after my younger brother. I was six, and Peewee was four. We were latch-key kids, and Momma had a detailed ritual for us to follow upon her departing for work. I was to lock and chain the door after Momma left and watch cartoons with my brother until it was time to leave for school. After turning off the television and helping my brother into his coat, I unlocked the door. After securing the door and tightly grasping my brother's hand, I guided him several blocks to the neighborhood elementary school. Once he was safely in his homeroom, I was off to class. Later, I would meet him outside his classroom and escort him home. Once inside, I'd stand on a chair to secure the lock, turn on the television, and give him the snack that Momma had prepared earlier. Once settled, I dialed Momma at work to let her know that we had made it home safely. Later upon hearing my mother's knock, I unlocked the door and was relieved of my duties.

In the context of my role as "surrogate mother," aggression as a strategy of leadership was not allowed. Despite my mother's belief in discipline, I was never allowed to hit my brother. My position as the oldest meant that I should be able to rise above any actions employed by my brother to provoke me. This served as a countermessage about aggression that balanced the ideas that I had gleaned from observing Aunt G.'s style of parenting. However, in both contexts control over one's emotions was framed as an important part of assuming a leadership role. I find it interesting that the groundswell of theory and research on emotional intelligence occurring throughout the past two decades corresponds to what I was ultimately taught to do. Daisy Grewal and Peter Salovey organize the knowledge on emotional intelligence into four areas. The fourth consists of the ability to manage one's emotions both internally and in the context of interpersonal relationships (2006, p. 107). This area of emotional intelligence is the one that is most commonly considered when discussing emotional intelligence theory because it has many implications for understanding how we navigate complex human situations. Little did I know that this was to be a part of my tutelage from the Amazonian traditions of my mothers.

As I child, I remember feeling a huge sense of personal responsibility, and I took my role very seriously. My ability to complete my task successfully was crucial. Removed from our extended family network, who else could do it? The theme of personal responsibility would follow me into my adult life and significantly influences how I approach my work today. I hold tightly to the projects that I am charged with, in the same way that I held my brother's hand as I walked him to school.

Either implicitly or explicitly, my mother always imparted to me the importance of finishing what you start and the importance of taking one's responsibilities seriously. Absorbing these maxims, as well as watching Momma's and Aunt K's efforts to attain equality and justice for black people cultivated a similar commitment in me.

When I was an administrator charged with working on issues of discrimination, harassment, and affirmative action, the lessons that I learned from Aunt K. and Momma about negotiating the public sphere were very important. Through their stories and through my direct observation, I learned that challenging authority in the pursuit of justice was a desirable goal. Indeed, choosing to oppose injustice is not optional; the issue is which strategy to use. A crucial aspect of this process involves learning about institutions, interrogating their policies and practices, and then being willing to point out injustice.

In institutional spaces where one is marginalized, yet "called" by both title and moral imperative to serve as a monitor of institutional compliance with legal civil rights regulations, it is not unusual to occupy the position of the "outsider within." Negotiating the space of "outsider" has been a central theme in the work of women of color in the legal field. In "Of Gentlemen and Role Models," Lani Guinier explains that "as a black woman civil rights attorney with insider privileges and outsider consciousness, I moved along the perimeter of cultural norms (roots, community, race, gender) and cultivated status (mainstream professional role) as an explorer and translator of these different identities" (Guinier, 2003, p. 75). Many African American women in leadership positions experience a multiple consciousness that requires them to evaluate their particular identities and roles within organizational structures, while simultaneously mediating between various groups and constituencies. This has been documented by scholars who confirm that black women are "often caught in the struggles between the boss and subordinates, blacks and whites, men and women, between units in the organization, and between the organization and the community in which it is located. Sometimes they are unclear who or what they are representing and find themselves trying to manage certain organizational boundaries without adequate authority and hence without appropriate backing and support" (Dumas, 1980, pp. 207–08).

Strategic confrontation is an invaluable resource in this context. Recalling the experiences of Grannie and remembering how she used silence and inventiveness to meet her goals within the confines of her marriage helps me today. Her method of leadership focused on the bottom line: gathering resources for herself and her daughters without directly confronting my grandfather's withholding of needed resources. Within the context of my professional life, I've learned to choose my battles carefully. In some cases, finding a particular resolution to a specific problem facing an individual is better strategically than trying to address systemic problems that apply to the whole organizational structure. This strategy constitutes a "delicate balancing act," described by Debra Meyerson and Maureen Scully, of earning enough legitimacy and belonging to ultimately use one's insider leverage to work with others toward changing the system (2003, p. 266).

On those occasions when it is necessary to fight for institutional change within an organization, it is sometimes valuable to call on the spirit of Momma. This spirit encompasses the strength, tenacity, and courage to fight for change until the battle is won. When I can't summon the spirit to help me deal with a challenging situation, it is good to know that Momma is just a phone call away. My mother, "the shade tree lawyer," battles with the phone company, insurance carriers, sales clerks, educational institutions, and anyone who she believes is trying to "pull a fast one." Some might view this as simply being argumentative. I view it as good advocacy for oneself and for those who can't fight. After observing her over the years, I've come to the realization that I probably learned more about critical analysis, negotiation, and advocacy from my mother than I did during my years in law school.

CONCLUSION

Recounting the legacy of leadership passed on to me by these warrior women has helped me to truly appreciate the sacrifices associated with leadership. Observing the emotional, spiritual, and physical warrior wounds sustained by my mother and othermothers while "battling" through life reminds me of the costs and benefits of leadership. This process of remembering, reflecting, and reframing the experiences of my mother and other mothers in terms of my own leadership development suggests a template for others to identify and analyze their own legacies of leadership. Momma, Aunt K., Aunt G., and Grannie all faced life challenges using a variety of strategies, all of which were passed on to me. Self-reliance, strategic nonconfrontation, and creative resource reallocation served my grandmother well as she negotiated the tension between her belief in independence and existing mores that privileged male authority over female authority in the household. These strategies helped her to survive and to provide for her children. Direct confrontation and aggression helped Aunt G. escape her father's beatings. Momma and Aunt K. successfully navigated institutional structures designed to exclude African Americans, while simultaneously challenging existing values and expectations within our family.

The women in my family have given me the will to stand with others and battle oppression. While their strategies of leadership are sometimes in conflict, they all reinforce solidarity and a clarity of values that resonate with the way Alice Walker speaks of her sister-friendship with June Jordan. Walker (2006, p. 4)[1] writes: "[A]ny argument arising between us would be silenced as we turned our combined energy to scrutinize an oncoming foe" because we are on the same side, "the side of the poor, the economically, spiritually and politically oppressed, "the wretched of the earth." My othermothers have given me a view of the world and the work that I am called to do in it. Reflecting on and celebrating their accomplishments has allowed me to truly appreciate the powerful legacy of leadership that I have inherited.

NOTES

1. Excerpted from Alice Walker's *We are the ones we have been waiting for: Inner light in a time of darkness*, first published by New Press, November 1, 2006. Reprinted by permission of Wendy Weil Agency, Inc. ©2006 by Alice Walker.

REFERENCES

Collins, P. H. (1990). *Black feminist thought: Knowledge, consciousness, and the politics of empowerment*. Boston: Unwin Hyman.

Dumas, R. G. (1980). The dilemmas of black females in leadership. In L. F. Rodgers-Rose (Ed.), *The black woman* (pp. 203–15). Newbury Park: Sage.

Grewal, D., Salovey, P. (2006). Benefits of emotional intelligence. In M. Csikszentmihalyi and I. S. Csikszentmihalyi (Eds.), *A life worth living: Contributions to positive psychology* (pp. 104–19). New York: Oxford University Press.

Guinier, L. (2003). Of gentlemen and role models. In A. K. Wing (Ed.), *Critical race feminism: A reader* (pp. 106–13). New York: New York University Press.

Jewell, Terri L. (1993). The black woman's gumbo ya-ya: Quotations by black women. Freedom: Crossing.

Meyerson, D. E., Scully, M. A. (2003). Tempered radicalism: Changing the workplace from within. In R. Ely, E. G. Foldy, M. Scully (Eds.), and the Center for Gender in Organizations, Simmons School of Management. *Reader in gender work and organizations* (pp. 266–71). Malden, MA: Blackwell.

Wallace, M. (1978, 1999). *Black macho and the myth of the superwoman*. London: Verso.

Walker, A. (2006). Introduction. In *We are the ones we have been waiting for: Inner light in a time of darkness*. New Press.

Wilde, L. W. (2000). *On the trail of the women warriors: The amazons in myth and history* (1st ed.). New York: St. Martin's.

Conclusions

Becoming the Motherline—Leadership for a New Generation

> "As you move toward your future look back and you will see your future has a past . . . because the FUTURE HAS A PAST."
>
> —J. California Cooper, *The Future Has a Past*

THE NEED TO HAVE SOME baseline understanding of how and what constitutes black women's leadership is crucial when one considers the current crises of leadership in society (Wren, 1995). Moreover, we commonly hear from within and without black communities the opinion that there is a void of black leadership in the wake of Martin Luther King Jr. and Malcolm X. We contest this claim and view the call for an iconic leadership figure as symptomatic of a failure to see and recognize all of the forms of leadership in everyday life. We commonly see the face of leadership in our clients, our students, our colleagues, and, yes, our mothers. Yet the current crises of black community life that call for us to understand black women's leadership are critically clear when one considers the state of black life in America. Andrew Billingsley (1992) articulates this American crisis when he writes that "while all African American families are not in a crisis state, many who do suffer inordinately are not so much in a crisis as they are engulfed by a set of crisis conditions most of which emanate from the society itself" (p. 22). The crisis conditions Billingsley speaks of are now traversing boundaries and becoming pervasive features within American life as a whole—though still inordinately affecting blacks and other groups in the margins (Beauboeuf-LaFontant, 2002, 2006, p. 280; Dym, Hutson, and Napier, 2005; Rich, 2007; Harris, 2009). Overall, contests of power between power holders and those pushing for social change call for current-day leaders to be at the ready. Black women are well positioned to respond to this call for leadership, yet society must also be able to recognize the leadership and leadership development models black women bring.

In order to do this, we need to know more about how black women lead and what our models of leadership and leadership development are. The stories in this text can help black women build a clear model of the leadership development elements common among us and can help us to recognize our leadership accomplishments even when our approaches do not fit the existing publicized models.

The scholarly discourse surrounding African American women's leadership has traditionally fallen under the rubrics of community activism; historical, biographical, and autobiographical accounts of the formation and evolution of black women leaders and the accomplishments of black women's associations; entrepreneurial activities; and public-sector organizations; as well as accounts of black women's leadership presence and challenges in corporate America (Gordon, 2003, p. 55; Parker, 2007, p. 130; Harris, 2009; Rich, 2007, p. 160; Jean-Marie, Sherman, and Williams, 2009 pp. 562–63). Therein, we find accounts and references to the life and times of this group's leading women, their characteristic leadership methods and strategies, and the consequences and impediments to their leadership. Yet relatively little is known about *how* African American women have managed to thrive, cultivate, and pass on patterns of strong and purposive leadership across intergenerational and communal mother-daughter lines in their own words.

As a response to the previous ways black women's leadership has been framed, *Tracing the Motherline* examines the cultural transmission of leadership skills and capacities from African American mothers to daughters. We further the framing of black women's leadership by speaking of its development as a deliberate method of socialization and as cultural rites of passage—regularly occurring within the context of extended mother-daughter relationships. In this way we heighten the significance of these relationships and place them within the context of leadership studies and adult development.

This examination of the stories "outta our own mouths" provides a range of resonating themes that we have synthesized to formulate a general model. From the stories contributors to this anthology shared, an emergent model of leadership development begins to take shape that scholars can further explore and that practitioners in clinical, social services and leadership studies fields can use as the backdrop to their work with African American women and other populations for which this model may apply. Combing through the stories in this book, we see the authors' attainment of leadership skills as intersecting Erik Erikson's (1968) model of psychosocial development and William Perry's (1970) stages of ethical development. Using our contributor's voices as an experiential starting point, we find that they have revealed a lattice of micro- and macrolevel developmental opportunities. Our synthesis of what their stories teach us results in the following formulation that the building of leadership progresses developmentally through four stages:

1. Basic Habilitation includes the simple yet profound acts of parental instruction on the rituals and regime of personal care. These include the following: socialization and knowledge building in the areas of habilitation, personal hygiene, and grooming; self-governance which offers the child a sense of place, heritage, and ethnic pride; and human relations skills, manners, codes of conduct, and civility. Berg (2002 pp. 45–47) and Higgenbotham (1992) discuss mothering and the teaching of domesticity as a type of race work. Together these works are grounded in the politics of respectability that equates "normalcy with conformity" to white middle-class modes of gender roles linked to codes of dress, sexual conduct, and public etiquette.
2. Communal Affiliation and Helping Skills Development stem from the Africentric notion of "cooperative work," which is giving service to help the tribe, family, or group. American families assign children age-appropriate chores to help cultivate the child's emergent work ethic and internalization of

cooperative behaviors. The options for learning can take place across the spheres of extended family, friendship circles, church, service guilds, civic, community and fraternal organizations, and school-based service-learning opportunities through both observation and participatory learning.

3. Work Ethic Cultivation/Vocational Maturity Formation is the the continua of parent and adult role modeling and instruction through the late oedipal, latency, and adolescent stages of development. Here parents teach their offspring the how to's of work at age-appropriate levels. Parental and elder-nurture during this phase includes the teaching of work skills, practice, praise, and affirmation and the introduction of progressive sets of skills to increase mastery. This stage also includes the reinforcement of skill performance and competence attainment, via validation, coaching, and personal or social rewards.

4. Organizational Citizenship is the fostering of social independence and functional interdependence. Here the ultimate goal of fostering organizational citizenship is to arm the growing child with a work ethic, skills in cooperation and the social benefits of joining in, and giving and receiving support while carrying projects to fruition individually and within team configurations. The building of these skills is tantamount to what Gordon (2002, p. 55) calls the mechanisms for gaining "full citizenship."

While we see the previous stages as a progression, we realize there are ongoing aspects of the developmental work that occur at each stage. New experiences in one's life can require returning one's attention to issues, to the addition of new competencies, or to the refinement of abilities already acquired.

Two additional components parallel and are integrated throughout the previous four components of leadership:

5. Social Justice Consciousness, which involves age-appropriate guidance for critical thinking about issues of ethics and social justice. This stage includes assisting and steering the child to engage in perspective taking, to recognize multiple

worldviews, and to consider the competing interests and contextual factors shaping individual and group motivations. It also includes supporting and encouraging progressive maturation with respect to agency and the ability to take a stand and hold to one's convictions as it pertains to visions and goals of equity and justice. The African American female child's early exposure to the inequities and injustices that intrude into the life experiences of African Americans and African American girls in particular guides the timing of tutelage in this area.

6. Capacities for Resistance involves building an identity that can resist the politics of oppression. This competency base includes helping children build bicultural and polycultural abilities so that they can move between cultural contexts with awareness and a sense of personal empowerment; it also involves helping the child begin to build strategies of resistance at the personal, group, and cultural levels to face the politics of subordination in society in ways that support their inter- and intrapersonal well-being and honor social and cultural systems of other groups. This psychological and relational well-being includes positive orientations to interacting with other women across differences of race, class, gender, sexual identity, and dis/ability. The acceptance of self and other, particularly the capacity to give and receive love and willingness to support other women is, in itself, a form of resistance within patriarchal society.

According to Parker (2007) this capacity likens the leading African American woman to a border crossing guard who is apt at breaking the silences of inequities and crossing the multiple boundaries of family, work, home, the streets, gangs and gang violence, and other challenges.

These latter two capacities refer to bringing an oppositional agenda—that of dismantling oppression and promoting social justice—to any context we participate in. Just as our earlier leadership development components intersect the work of Erikson and Perry, these latter two stages intersect the racial identity development paradigm arising from the seminal work of William Cross (1991) and from the paradigm of double consciousness beginning with W. E. B. DuBois (1903).

A major distinction, documented across multiple disciplines in the examination of African American mother-daughter relationships, includes the development of a kind of moral compass and capacities to interrogate the ethical implications of real life events or of social and political systems. When the Motherline combines teaching daughters to engage in ethical analysis with teaching them approaches to preserve and restore self-hood, mothers and othermothers are helping to ensure that the daughter is not overwhelmed by the knowledge of oppression. Rather the daughter is inculcated with a philosophical view that "if they can not love and resist at the same time, they will probably not survive" (Lorde, 1984a, p. 74) and that "in order for the oppressed to be able to wage the struggle for their liberation, they must perceive the reality of oppression not as a closed world from which there is no exit, but as a limiting situation which they can transform" (Freire, 1989, p. 34).

UNVEILING THE MOTHERLINE

For more than two decades scholars have already identified and directed our attention to the cultural and political nature of black mothering (Barkley Brown, 1991; bell hooks, 1994; Berry, 2004; Ferguson and King, 2008; Henry, 1998; Hill Collins, 1990; Omolade, 1994), yet at the same time its leadership implications have remained veiled from view. The daughters who wrote for this text show us the complex negotiations of Motherline women who engaged in a both/and epistemology (Hill Collins, 2000), that is, a way of teaching their daughters to "[get] along in a world shaped by men," while not "betraying their daughters's potential" but rather enhancing and cultivating it.

Our unveiling of the Motherline occurs in this spirit of seeking new ways of knowing the Motherline and its import that put black women at the center. Yet unveiling this dynamic system of knowledge transmission requires more than acknowledgment that the transmission process exists but methods of revelation to unpack its delivery modes and meanings. Scholarship about how to decenter the ways of knowing emphasized by the white academy began to flourish in the 1990s. Elsa Barkley Brown writes in her essay "Mothering the Mind" (1991) that she almost entitled the essay "How My Mother Taught Me to Be a Historian in Spite of My Academic Training" (p. 75). She goes on to explain that this training had "been designed to teach me how to interpret an Africentric community in terms of a Eurocentric worldview" (p. 75). Kathryn B. Ward uses the title "Lifting as We Climb: How Scholarship by and about Women of Color Has Shaped My Life as a White Feminist" (1992). She uses personal narrative to share the transformative power of the scholarship, teaching, and activism of women of color in the academy on her own work in these same areas. In doing so, she emphasizes the need to put women of color's experiences at the center of analysis in order to know and understand such experiences on the terms of the group themselves.

Our method of unveiling the Motherline sought to put black women at the center by inviting black women, themselves, to do the telling and by using the mother or othermother relationship with daughters as the primary unit of analysis, rather than locating leadership development within a series of life events, achievements, or concrete outcomes. As the women contributors in this collection tell us their stories, their memories cut into stark relief a persistent theme: that their mothers handed daughters an agenda to engage in social change. In our contributors' renderings, we find it noteworthy that they frame their current professional work in terms of its sociopolitical implications whether this work focuses on the individual, a particular context, or the society. In the same vein, Joseph (2006, p. 113) notes that the black feminist is able to politicize all areas of life as vital and worthy of radical political action and "a cause for concern" in improving the quality of community life. We find it compelling that the mothers our contributors describe conveyed a message of social and political resistance to these daughters that survived the intrusion of family, community, or societal tensions that might have ruptured its intact delivery.

Even as we acknowledge the profound characteristics of the Motherline, we want to guard against romanticizing it. We are aware that some might claim that commonalities in Motherline transmission evident in these writings indicate the kinds of common experiences one might find among any group of women who, themselves, share a profession and professional or social ties. Making too much of the commonalities among the fourteen women writers for this text could result in essentializing black women's lives, by creating a monolithic mythology that our lives are "essentially the same" and "othering" any black woman who has not had the kinds of experiences the women share in these pages. In contrast, making too little of the commonalities among the women in this text risks nullifying their experiences on the grounds of overgeneralization, thus invalidating their voices and meaning making.

While we see the Motherline as intentionally dispensing the six elements of our leadership development framework, we realize no woman's experience of it is perfect. Any woman will have experienced issues, omissions, or flaws in what she received; others may have received mixed or distorted messages that require them to seek resolution or reappraisal. We also know that life events may rupture what a girl or woman received, and personal propensities may make the knowledge indecipherable or unclaimed for immediate integration and use. We understand that women rise to leadership due to a culmination of many factors, none of which can be definitively delineated, and that women perform as leaders who lack experiences with mothers and othermothers such as those we describe here. Beginning with the particularity of black women's lives, we want to document the significance of the Motherline leadership development. And in doing so we hope to honor and embrace the many mothers across race, ethnicity, and culture who do this work with both daughters and sons, as well as the ways fathers provide such teaching, tutelage, and care. All of these sites of leadership are worthy of study. Our documentation of Motherline leadership development relies on memory and story. Yet memory is not truth. In her creative nonfiction work *Reading Lolita in Tehran* (2003), Azar Nafisi makes a claim about truth that we, too would like to apply to our work. As an author's note prior to the beginning of her story, she writes: "The facts in this story are true in so far as any memory is ever truthful" (p. iv).[1] Similarly our goal in this anthology was not to establish truth; rather it was to give you, our readers, entre to black women's ways of seeing and telling the Motherline leadership transmission process and how they now apply these lessons in their lives.

For many of the women contributors to this anthology, and for adults generally, one's workplace and professional career stream become main sites for evidencing leadership. Whether the women in our text call it "representational politics" (Lee), "jumping at de sun"

(Trotman), "thick-skinned leadership" (Gibson), "Ìdílé" (Dozier-Henry), "fixing her eyes on the prize" (Flake), "communal leadership" (King), "wearing struttin' shoes" (Massey-Dozier), "self-sufficiency leadership" (Ferguson), "*drylongso* and *ajabu* leadership" (Diggs), "community service and civic leadership" (Hill), "transformative medicine" (Turner), "excellence and accountability [leadership]" (Govan), "operating out of the integrity of your heart" (Lewis), "strategies for leadership in the public and private spheres" (Johnson), they all speak in numerous ways about how the Motherline prepared them to engage in leadership that promotes justice and negotiates the contradictions inherent in living out such leadership within a society that marginalizes them. Somehow, they ply knowledge from the Motherline as they move through the transitions of early-to-mid-to-latter career and encounter a host of opportune and serendipitous events that create a launch pad for emanence, ascendance, and contribution.

LEADERSHIP FOR A NEW GENERATION

The propagation of black women leaders is a predominant function of mothers, othermothers, allomother networks, and community elders. Distilling the time-honored elements of matrilineal leadership knowledge offers insights into how women of the African Diaspora have wielded power. Further, it promotes understanding of how leadership knowledge and skills are replicated across generations for the purpose of forging resistance to patriarchal authority while funding individual, intergenerational, unitary, communal, and occupational leadership.

Although the propagation of leadership ability in women and girls today is of urgent import, the opportunities to benefit from the Motherline are strained. Summarily this pre- and postmillennial period has been characterized by a movement away from collectivism and pan-Africanism to individualism and urban acculturation. The valuing of urban roots over our history of rural and agrarian roots has led to a form of resegregation as well as destabilization of black communities in ways that rob them of the wide range of productive African American adults capable of contributing to the development of children, family, and community life. The younger generation's overvaluing of modernity and urbanity also results in devaluing anything that seems "countrified" or reminiscent of the harsh life of the past, and this trend has blunted the influence and uptake of Motherline wisdom. These limits to the viability of African American community severely undermine the cultural collective's power to intervene in the grip of such lethal forces as poverty, ill health, violence, early mortality, disproportional representation in child welfare, juvenile and criminal justice sectors, and substance abuse. These negative social forces have also contributed to African American communities' underrepresentation in the world opportunity structures.

On the community front, the Motherline contends with a plethora of problems as it combats threats from within and without. Within, the community is succumbing to the psychological effects of alienation, family, social and cultural disconnection and dissociation, and a wounding of instincts. Further disruption of the community's quality of life is coming from intergenerational poverty, the devastating effects of alcoholism and other drug use, the lack of educational access, under achievement, community disinvestment, predatory lending and home piracy, and other acts of financial devastation that disrupt home ownership and land acquisition as a mechanism for the intergenerational transfer of wealth. On the family front, the Motherline must come directly to the aid of children so that their minds, hearts, and intellects are not starved. The rearing of the young will need to return to a process of rites of passage and motherhood training backed by an intentional and collectivist, village-oriented approach to child nurture, supported by allomothering. On the relational front, the Motherline must tend to its intimate relationships with men and women, its platonic relationships, and friendship circles so that there is order within those dyads and small-group relations that are closest to our hearts (McDonald, 2007; Gilligan, 2009; Vaz, 2006). According to bell hooks, "living as we do in a white supremacist capitalist patriarchal context, that can best exploit us when we lack firm ground in self-identity, choosing wellness is an act of political resistance" (1994). Accomplishing these feats of cultural and social survival requires crafting a collective Motherline agenda for the twenty-first century and beyond that translates what we need to do now from what we have done in our collective past. The women authors in our text spoke of how they translated what their respective Motherlines offered them then worked it into the present and continue to work it into the future. In this way we become the Motherline.

HEALING THE MOTHERLINE

Although the needs for Motherline leadership development are great, the characteristics of twenty-first-century institutional, communal, and personal life impede linking children to the Motherline. While historically the Motherline has remained viable, it is now threatened on two fronts: (1) rejection by the current daughter line and (2) the sheer limits to the arm span of women ready to dispense motherwork (Hill Collins, 1990, 2000). In our assessment of what needs to be done collectively, we must ask the following questions: Do girls and young women today still see and interact with us in numbers that reflect to them our presence and attention? Do the norms of family and community prevent our intervention in destructive family cycles without legal liability for "butting in where we have no right"? Do we still have the reach of access to them that we used to have in schools and youth centers, community centers, churches and mosques, and most important, neighborhoods?

The structural breaches that put Motherline relations out of reach for so many of today's women and girls make it necessary for us to be vigilant in analyzing where to begin the repair. There are broad swaths of information that girls and women of today have not had access to, and we cannot make assumptions about what girls have been exposed to and whether they value their previous exposure to Motherline knowledge. However, in our clinical experiences and everyday lives, we continue to find that the women we come into contact with express a hunger and craving for Motherline relationships, attention, and tutelage.

The relationships the women discussed in *Black Womanist Leadership: Tracing the Motherline* are not lost to us, however. Girls and women today still express a deep desire for meaningful relationships with us, in spite of ambivalence, resentments, rage, or mistrust toward us that such deep needs—particularly when those needs have gone unmet—may generate. And we, too, need the relationships with the generations of daughters among us today that allow us the generativity and fullness of connection we had with our Motherline. This mutual need exists at the deepest levels of our being and is a strong foundation from which to launch our agenda for current Motherline vitality. The strength and power of what we have the potential to bring to them lies in the irrevocable knowledge that we hold a particular leadership paradigm in our consciousness and in the certainty that we know what was passed on to us and how.

Interestingly, many women of our own generation have allowed the Motherline to go slack and to lose some of the potency and confidence of delivery—akin to what Andrea O'Reilly reports as its "funk and ancient properties" (p. 19). Under the ruse of economic gain, corporate success, educational opportunities, and access to material comforts there has been a falling off of adherence to the proverbial Africentric adage that "it takes a whole village to raise a child." The individualism of American society that dictates norms for nuclear family life and the popular culture's promotion of permissive parenting perspectives have also undermined Motherline relations. As a result of both the diminished sense of the communal village and new modes of parenting, we find such things as mothers who are afraid to give advice or intervene in wayward thinking and behavior of their own children because they fear it will stymie their child/ren's sense of agency and creativity, their ability to hold their own with adult authority figures, or their sense of being a full-fledged member of the family decision-making body.

With othermothers, we find them more hesitant to engage in the range of Motherline work so apparent in our authors' lives because this may be interpreted as butting in where they don't belong, criticizing the biological mother or parents, damaging or harming the children's sense of self by making them feel the need for improvement or otherwise undermining their self-esteem and sense of equality with all others. Overall, the new normative structures of society that compete with those handed down within-group among blacks have impeded bringing the tutelage of each of the four stages of Motherline leadership development we previously summarized.

Finally, we find in our current work with women and girls that the current idealization of multicultural progress in society has made mothers or othermothers refrain from guiding the current generation in explicit ways that help to build an identity that can resist the politics of oppression. We have observed many more of the current generation lacking in the bicultural and polycultural resilience needed for living well and engaging in the leadership of social change despite the politics of subjugation and neocolonization they encounter in daily life. In particular, we see the youth of today, stymied, baffled, and decentered by their run-ins with both overt and covert "isms" in this postaffirmative action, and as some would say, "postracial" era. We have also observed our students and younger clients ill-prepared to remain strategic in their pursuit of the tangible goals of equity and justice in their organizational settings and local community activist efforts when confronted by the wiles of modern day racism. Our observations signal to us that the Motherline knowledge that prepared prior generations for such levels of subtle and overt assault have been diminished by pervasive myths of progress that overstate the current status of race, class, gender relations. Healing the Motherline means that we need to solidify our commitment to the motherwork it accomplishes. Our *Black Womanist Leadership: Tracing the Motherline* narratives are a part of this healing journey in a very particular sense. By naming and claiming the elements of Motherline leadership development, we crystallize its contributions and marshal its properties for mass application against the social trends that threaten to dilute them and against the global Europeanization that would dissolve them.

To the extent that black women progress through the questions of personal Motherline leadership in their own lives, and broader questions of African American women's leadership, they will begin to bring the particulars of their leadership and that of those who taught them into focus. No matter the site of service, family, communal, or occupational, they will be more equipped to carry their leadership identities in the heat of the day. They will be more prepared to meet the heat of public scrutiny and will be encouraged by the knowledge that theirs is among the multiple narratives of leadership in the world. In the process of recognizing their place at the table of leadership, women of African descent will be more able to refine the transmission process for use with current generations. Jean-Marie, Williams, and Sherman (2009) suggest that the African American woman's brand of culturally competent knowledge of inclusion, crises response, action, and transformation is integral to the mobilization and management of today's diverse public- and private-sector organizations. As a result, we will be more able to step up to fulfill the Motherline needs of today and become the line of cultural survival and leadership knowledge to our daughters and to our sons.

Finally, we began this work by speaking of the importance of Motherline stories as a contribution to black women's studies, adult development theory, and leadership studies. We have created a space for our readers to hear from black women's "own mouths" what we feel was given to us along the Motherline. It is also our hope that through this gathering of women across the pages of this book, you have begun to connect to the stories of your own leadership development and the Motherlines of your own ancestry. Our ability to see ourselves in each others' experiences while neither coopting another's experience as our own nor placing the other's experience outside the realm of our human capacity to understand is a necessary part of living in a dynamic pluralist society.

There is something else we stand to gain from these authors' accounts of their Motherline experiences. According to Jean Baker Miller, "We have all been laboring under only one implicit model of human nature and of human development. Much richer models are possible. Glimpses of them have always been struggling to emerge ... in some of the hopes and dreams of all of us" (p. 26). With this writing, black women share the hopes and dreams the Motherline placed in them and the leadership that came about because of these developmental source points in their lives. Here and now, we reach across the kitchen table and invite you to celebrate with us the models of knowledge we have received in such spaces and the kind of talk that brings this knowledge to us. We hope we have begun a dialogue that helps you to consider or reconsider the models of leadership development you have had access to, particularly those you encountered in women-centered sites of connection and empowerment. We hope you leave the table satisfied and full and, in the tradition of black women, with a little something to take home with you.

NOTES

1. This quote appears on the fourth, unnumbered page in the book *Reading Lolita in Tehran*, by Azar Nafisi, prior to the table of contents. It is designated here as p. iv, so as not to confuse it with the other numbered pages.

REFERENCES

Barkley Brown, E. (1991). Mothers of the mind. In P. Bell-Scott, B. Guy-Sheftall, J. Jones Royster, J. Sims-Wood, M., DeCosta-Willis, & L. P. Fultz (Eds.), *Double stitch: Black women write about mothers and daughters* (pp. 74–93). New York: Harper Perennial.

Beaboeuf-Lafontant, T. (2002; 2006). Womanist experience of caring: Understanding the pedagogy of exemplary black women teachers. In Layli Phillips (Ed.), (2006) *The womanist reader* (pp. 280–95). New York: Routledge.

Berg, A. (2002). *Mothering the race: Narratives on reproduction 1890–1930.* (pp. 45–47). Champagne: University of Illinois Press.

Berry, C. (2004). *Rise up singing: Black women writers on motherhood.* New York: Harlem Moon.

Billingsley, A. (1992). *Climbing Jacob's ladder.* New York: Simon and Schuster.

Collins, P. H. (1989). The social construction of black feminist thought. *Signs: Journal of Women in Culture and Society, 14* (4), 745–73.

Collins, P. H. (1990). Black women and motherhood. In *Black feminist thought: Knowledge, consciousness, and the politics of empowerment* (pp. 171–99). New York: Routledge.

Cooper, J. C. (2000). *The future has a past.* New York: Random House.

Cross, W. E. (1991). *Shades of black: Diversity in African-American identity.* Philadelphia: Temple University Press.

Debold, E., Wilson, M., & Malave, I. (1993). Introduction. In *Mother daughter revolution: From good girls to great women.* Reading, MA: Addison-Wesley.

Dubois, W. E. B. (1903). *The souls of black folk: Essays and sketches.* Chicago: McClurg.

Dym, B., Hutson, H., & Napier, B. (2005). *Leadership in non-profit organizations* (p. 76). Thousand Oaks, CA: Sage.

Erikson, E. H. (1968). *Identity, youth and crisis.* New York: Norton.

Ferguson, S. A., & King, T. C. (2008). Going down for the third time. In Amber Kinser (Ed.), *Mothering in the Third Wave* (pp. 166–86). Toronto, Canada: Demeter.

Freire, P. (1989). *Pedagogy of the oppressed* (pp. 27–56). New York: Continuum.

Gilligan, C., & Richards, D. A. J. (2009). *The deepening darkness: Patriarchy, resistance, and democracy's future.* New York: Cambridge University Press.

Gordon, E. L. (2002). A Layin' on of hands: Black women's community work. In Ollie Johnson and Karen L. Sanford (Eds.), *Black political organizations in the post-cvil rights era.*

Harris, D. (2009). *Black feminist politics: From Kennedy to Clinton.* New York: McMillan.

Henry, A. (1998). *Taking back control: African Canadian women teachers' lives and practice.* Albany: State University of New York Press.

Higgenbotham, E. B. (1992, Winter). African American women's history and the meta-language of race. *Signs, 17,* 251–74.

hooks, bell (1994). *Teaching to transgress: Education as the practice of freedom.* New York: Routledge.

Jean-Marie, G., Williams, V. A., & Sherman, S. L (2009, October). Black women's leadership experiences: Examining the intersectionalities of race and gender. *Developing Human Resources, 11* (5) October. 562–81.

Joseph, P. E. (2006). The Black Power movement: Rethinking the civil rights-Black Power era (p. 113). New York: Routledge.

Lorde, A. (1984a). Age, race, class, and sex: Women redefining difference. In *Sister outsider: Essays & speeches.* Trumansburg, NY: Crossing.

Lorde, A. (1984b). Man child: A black lesbian feminist's response. *Sister outsider: Essays & speeches* (pp. 72–80). Trumansburg, NY: Crossing.

McDonald, K. B. (2007). *Embracing sisterhood: Class, identity, and contemporary black women.* New York: Rowman & Littlefield.

Miller, J. B. (1991). The development of women's sense of self. In J. V. Jordan, A. G. Kaplan, J. B. Miller, Irene. P. Stiver, & Janet. L. Surrey (Eds.), *Women's growth in connection: Writings from the Stone Center.* New York: Guilford.

Nafisi, A. (2003). *Reading Lolita in Tehran.* New York: Random House.

Omolade, B. (1994). *The rising song of African American women.* New York: Routledge.

O'Reilly, A. 2004. A politics of the heart: Toni Morrison's theory of motherhood as a site of power and motherwork as concerned with the empowerment of children. In *Toni Morrison and motherhood: A Politics of the heart* (pp. 1–46). Albany: State University of New York Press.

Parker, P. S. (2007). Race, gender, and leadership: (En)countering discourses that devalue African American women as leaders. In C. R. Daileader, R. E. Johnson, A. Shabazz, (Eds.), *Women and others: Perspectives on race, gender and empire* (pp. 32). New York: Macmillan.

Perry, W. G. (1970). *Forms of intellectual and ethical development in the college years.* New York: Holt, Rinehart, & Winston.

Rich, W. C. (2007). *African American perspectives on political science.* Philadelphia: Temple University Press.

Richardson, L. (1994). Writing: A method of inquiry. In N. K. Denzin and Yvonna S. Lincoln (Eds.), *Handbook of qualitative research.*

Vaz, K. M. (2006). Womanist archetypal psychology: A model of counseling of black women and couples based on Yoruba mythology. In L. Phillips (Ed.), *Womanist Reader* (pp. 233–46). New York: Routledge.

Ward, K. B. (1992). Lifting as we climb: How scholarship by and about women of color has shaped my life as a white feminist. Working Paper 13. Memphis, TN: Center for Research on Women, Memphis State University.

Wren, J. T. (1995). *The leader's companion: Insights on leadership through the ages.* New York: Free.

Contributors

RHUNETTE C. DIGGS, Ph.D., is an adjunct instructor at Columbus State Community College in the Department of Communication. She has taught at several U.S. four-year institutions and at a college in Ethiopia. Rhunette is also a cofounder and associate director of PRE-VAIL-RESPECT, an entrepreneurial education and training organization. Her research agenda spans the arenas of intercultural, spiritual, and family communication. She is coauthor of a book entitled *Communication, Race, and Family: Exploring Black, White, and Biracial Families* and author of numerous scholarly edited book chapters and articles. Daily, she focuses her energies toward helping individuals, families, communities, organizations, and institutions achieve their full potential.

JUDY MASSEY-DOZIER, Ph.D., is an associate professor in English and African American studies chair at Lake Forest College, where she has taught African American literature and black studies for thirteen years. She has also taught at Loyola University Chicago and Columbia College Chicago. Judy is a former advertising writer who also writes fiction. Presently she is at work on a manuscript focused on black women leaders.

OARE' DOZIER-HENRY, Ed.D., is a full professor in the Department of Educational Leadership and Human Services at Florida A&M University. Previously she served as a public school principal, precollege program administrator, and adult educator. Her recent publications address the need for self-care and spiritual well-being and the exclusion of African cosmology from the great thought systems of the world. She has committed her life to the healing and restoration of African identity and sensibilities.

S. ALEASE FERGUSON, Ph.D., LPCC, is a therapist and the director of Family Services for the Cleveland Urban Minority Alcoholism and Drug Abuse Outreach Program. She teaches psychology on the faculties of the University of Phoenix and Notre Dame College of Ohio. Over the course of her career, she has served as a social services program administrator, evaluation researcher, organizational change consultant, and curriculum designer. Her research and practitioner efforts focus on cultural diversity, relational psychology, African American women's mental health concerns, and resistances to social oppression. In her leisure, she is dedicated to the crafts of grandmothering, gardening, playwriting, and community activism.

CEARA FLAKE, J.D., is a practicing attorney and the principal of Expert Writing Solutions, LLC, a Washington, D.C.-based legal research and writing firm. Ceara's comprehensive legal background includes service in the judiciary and in private practice. Her private practice work in both Washington, D.C., and the Virgin Islands is rendered on behalf of individuals and corporations to ensure equal justice and fair play in business and matters of civil justice. Ceara also maintains an active presence in community development.

NANCY GIBSON is a senior associate director of admissions at Denison University, where she spearheads the Denison University campuswide multicultural recruitment effort. Throughout her career in higher education, she has conducted a variety of presentations on diversity and recruiting students of color at the local, regional, and national levels. Nancy also works as a consultant in the area of multicultural recruitment for various colleges in the Midwest and has served on the executive board of the Ohio Association for College Admissions Counselors.

SANDRA Y. GOVAN, Ph.D., a Chicago native, is a founding member and historian of the Wintergreen Women Writers Collective. She is Professor Emerita from the English Department at UNC Charlotte.

Across Dr. Govan's distinguished twenty-five-year teaching career, she also served as both the coordinator and director of the Ronald E. McNair Post-baccalaureate Achievement Program. A scholar (and a poet) focusing on the Harlem Renaissance and black writers in speculative fiction, Sandra has produced major articles on Langston Hughes, Gwendolyn Bennett, Octavia E. Butler, and Samuel R. Delany. Her works have appeared in numerous publications. In 2009, Govan established "Best Text: Write It Right," a consulting firm that helps community members hone their writing skills.

SIMONA J. HILL, Ph.D., became the first African American woman in 2009 to attain full professor status at Susquehanna University since its founding in 1858. As vice-president of the Mid-Atlantic Women's Studies Association, she works to further the areas of feminist pedagogy, cultural ideology, and "wanksta" feminism. Her research interests span diversity, higher education, community organizations, black feminist studies, and the challenges of incorporating the experience of social difference into the fabric of educational models. Her recent contributions include *Teaching Feminist Activism, Entremundos/among Worlds: New Perspectives on Gloria Anzaldúa,* and *Privilege and Prejudice: Twenty Years with the Invisible Knapsack.* She is coauthor of *Hip Hop and Inequality: Searching for the "Real" Slim Shady,* (Cambria Press).

LAKESIA D. JOHNSON, J.D., Ph.D., is assistant professor of English and gender, women's, and sexuality studies at Grinnell College. She has also held administrative and teaching positions at Denison University and the Ohio State University. Her areas of specialization include visual and narrative culture, black women's studies, sexuality studies, critical race theory, and feminist legal theory.

TONI C. KING, Ph.D., is an associate provost at Denison University where she taught black studies and Women's studies for twelve years. She has also taught at the State University of New York at Binghamton and at Norfolk State University. Her research explores relationships as a generative site for personal growth, recovery from institutionalized oppression, and personal/collective empowerment. Toni specializes in designing and conducting workshops, seminars, and leadership retreats geared toward supporting women who seek to *both* thrive *and* transform society from within their organizations, families, and communities.

VALERIE LEE, Ph.D., is professor and former chair of the Department of English at the Ohio State University, where she also served as chair of the Department of Women's Studies. Currently, Lee is interim vice provost of minority affairs and chief diversity officer at Ohio State. She has published in the areas of African American literature, folklore, American literature, feminist theory, and multicultural pedagogy. The author of *Invisible Man's Literary Heritage: Benito Cereno and Moby Dick; Granny Midwives and Black Women Writers: Double-Dutched Readings;* and *The Prentice Hall Anthology of African American Women's Literature,* she also coedits the book series Black Performance and Cultural Criticism (Ohio State University Press).

LEAH C. K. LEWIS, J.D., M.Div., is an associate minister at Olivet Institutional Baptist Church in Cleveland, Ohio. She has preached throughout the Midwest and the Northeast, including the "Space for Grace" at Riverside Church in New York City. She is published in *The African American Pulpit* and *The African American Lectionary.* Reverend Lewis also holds the distinction of being one of two individuals to serve two consecutive terms as a Magee Fellow at Yale University's Dwight Hall Center for Public Service and Social Justice. As a law student, she acted as managing editor of the *Howard Law Journal* (1994–1995). Leah is also the author of a children's picture book titled *Little Lumpy's Book of Blessings.*

FRANCES K. TROTMAN, Ph. D., is a professor of psychology and psychological counseling at Monmouth University and has been a practicing psychologist in New Jersey for more than thirty years. Dr. Trotman is a fellow of the American Psychological Association. She has written books, articles and other publications in the areas of individual and group psychotherapy with African American women. In 2009, Frances was awarded the Association of Women in Psychology's Feminist Pioneer in the Psychology of Women's Award for her more than one hundred publications and presentations on the psychology of women since the 1970's.

CONTRIBUTORS

SONYA TURNER, Psy.D., is the director of Health and Counseling Services at Denison University. She is a licensed clinical psychologist. Sonya's professional interests include depression, anxiety, cultural diversity, eating disorders, sexual trauma and recovery, bereavement, and stress management. Sonya holds a special interest in women's issues groups. Sonya cofacilitates In the Company of Sisters, a support group that addresses issues affecting women of color. She provides outreach programs and workshops to faculty, staff, students, and neighboring communities.

GARY WILLIAMS is a former attorney at law who resides in Cleveland, Ohio. His distinctive works are known for their physicality, emotional connection, and transcendent ethos. Works by the author have been commissioned for special projects, shown in numerous exhibitions, and awarded honors in juried competitions. Using pastels and water colors, as well as motifs of African cloth, he imbues his work with a tactile essence. The cover art for this book reflects the vivid immanence that characterizes his portraiture. Additional work may be seen at www.nubiandreamarts.com.

Index

Abbey, Sharon, 26, 178
adages and old folks' sayings, 11, 109, 129, 130, 214
Adams, Katherine and Gloria J. Galanes, 146, 154
affirmation, xix, 77, 92, 93, 109, 234
"Affirmation of the disciple" (Bailey), 136, 139
Africana, 9, 18
African American
    families, 38, 39, 183
        communal crises of. *See* Billingsley
    maternal rearing styles and philosophy, 28, 31, 32, 39, 40
    women, 15
African Philosophy, 69, 81, 98, 106, 141
aggression, 15, 220, 221, 225, 226, 229
"a line of cutting women," 16, 18, 20
"Ain't I a Leader," 5
Ain't I A Woman (Richardson, Taylor, and Whittier), 17, 42, 43
Ajabu leader, leadership, 111, 143, 145, 155, 157, 239
Ajamu, Adisa, intra-familial family relationships as affected by the history of slavery, 188, 192

Akan, 72. *See also* ìdílé, Matrifocal Societies, Yorùbá
Alcoholism
    domestic violence, 180
    drugs, 240
    Minority Alcohol and Drug Abuse Outreach Program, 250
Alperin, Richard M., 183
    barriers to intimacy, 191
"a line of cutting women," 16, 18, 20
allomothers, xii, xiii, xiv, xvi, 12, 16, 17
All the Women are White, All the Blacks Are Men, But Some of Us Are Brave (Hull et al.), 13, 19, 43
Altman, Neil, 27, 39, 40, 41, 161
Amazon, viii, 177, 218, 219, 223–226
    a description of family of origin, viii, 177, 218, 219, 221, 223, 225, 226
    archetype, 226
Amoo-Adare, Epifania Akousa, 230, 239. *See also* critical spatial literacy
Amos and Andy, 75, 80
Anansi the Spider, 94, 96, 101, 102, 103, 104
And Still I Rise (Angelou), 36, 41, 78, 80

Andolsen, Barabara Hilkert, 27, 39, 41
Ani, M., 80
Angelou, Maya, xi, 35, 36, 41, 72, 78, 80
And Still I Rise, 41, 78, 80
Animal Dreams (Kingsolver), xvi, xvii
antiracism as an ethical norm, 41. *See also* Laura S. Brown
Anzaldua, Gloria, 27
  borderlands/La Frontera, 26
  Making Face, Making Soul, 126, 128
  privilege and prejudice, 251
  This bridge called my back, 43, 104, 106
  Write on the insides of trees, 17
Anzaldua, G. and A. Keating, *This Bridge We Call Home*, xvi
Appiah Kwame Anthony
  Africana, the Encyclopedia, 9, 18
  See Henry Louis Gates
Apte, Vama Shivram, 139
Aptheker, Bettina, 3, 18, 159, 160, 223
  women's stories, 3
Arie, India, 121, 122
Asante, Molefi K. *See* Linda Myers
  Afrocentricity, Afrocentric idea, 80, 160
  Afrocentricity and feminism, 18. *See* Braun-Williams
  Relationship Agility, 76
Avery, Shug
  The Color Purple, and women taking charge of their sexuality, 120
Azar, Nafisi
  claims about truth, 238
  Reading Lolita in Tehran, 244

baby boomers, 72
back talk, 197

Bailey, Alice, *Affirmation of the Disciple*, 136, 139
basic habilitation, 233
Baker, Ella, 98, 105
  "The Fundi," 98
Barkley Brown, Elsa, mothering the mind, 236
Barkley, Ione, 167–172
Barnes, Jean H. Memorial Center, Philadelphia, 188
Barnett, Ida Wells, xi, 126
Barnes-Wright, Lenora, xvi
Basie, Count, 74
Beauboeuf-Lafontant, Tamara, 18, 232
becoming the motherline, viii, 14, 231
"being in the world," 10, 74
Belenky, Bond, Lynne A. and Jacqueline Weinstock, tradition that has no name, xii, xvi, 105, 147, 158, 160
Belenky, Mary Field, and Blythe McVicker Clinchy, Nancy Rule Goldberger, Jill Mattuck Tarule
  silence, 147
  ways of knowing, constructed knowledge, xv, 93, 98, 105, 139, 161
Belenky, Mary Field, and Nelson, 147
Bell, Ella Louise Edmondson, and S. Nkomo, 18
  Our Separate Ways, 14
Bell, Lydia Sardonia Morris, Valerie Lee's "Ma Bell," 45
Bell Scott, Patricia, and B. Guy Sheftall, 25, 112
  All the Women are White, 13
  black women writing, 18
  Double Stitch, 44
Bennett, Maisha, poverty induced stressors, 138
Bennett, Michael and Dickerson, Vanessa, *Recovering the Black Female Body*, 53–55

INDEX

Bennis, Warren, *On Becoming A Leader*, synesthesia, 141
Berg, Allison, and Higginbotham, 233
  mothering the race, 245
Bernal, Guillermo, Trimble, T.E. and Berlew, A. K., 27, 41, 184, 191
Berry, Cecelie, 236
  Rise Up Singing: Black Women Writers on Motherhood, 245
Bethune, Mary McLeod, 22, 165, 173
Bicycle
  as freedom, and not just "stay[ing] on the block," 196
  as a symbol of "going places," 212, 214
  stolen, 176, 212
Billingsley, Andrew, African American communal crisis, 231, 245
black child-white parents, 58, 59
black families in therapy, 191. *See* Boyd-Franklin
Black families in White America, 160
black family structure, 59
black feminism, 9, 10, 13, 19, 140, 177
  laying the foundation, 9
  pillars of black feminism, 10
black hair, 31, 45, 46, 47–53, 60, 68, 97, 114, 121, 205, 221, 222
Blacking, John, 34
  growing old gracefully, 41
Blues women, 113, 116, 118, 121
body politics, 51
Bogardus, Edwin, 18
  the seven epochs of racism, 19
bossiness as a trait of the burgeoning child leader, 121
border Crossing guard, Parker, Patricia, 235
Bowen, Murray, multi-generational transmission in process, 184
Boyatzis, Richard et al., 154, 160
Boyd, H., 181, 191
  difficulties for Black men in society, 181, 191
Boyd-Franklin, Nancy, 182
  peripheral father, 183
Braun-Williams, Carmen, 18. *See* Afrocentricity and feminism
Breath, Eyes and Memory (Danticat), 99, 105
Brer rabbit ingenuity and outwitting the oppressor, 15
Bridge leadership, 101. *See also* Belinda Robnett
Brown, James, 74, 138, 139
  songs, social activism, 139
Brown, Laura S., 41
Buber, Martin, "I thou," 211
building a basin of receptivity, reflection and action, 132
Bundles, Alelia, *On Her Own Ground: The Life and Times of Madame C.J. Walker*, 11, 18
Burns, James, McGregor, transactional and transformational leadership, 102, 103, 106
Bush, Wynona Barrett, xx, 88
Byrd, Ayana D. and Lori Tharps, *Hair Story: Untangling the Roots of Black Hair in America*, 54

Campbell, Joseph, 164, 165, 173
Campbell, R. Ricardo, 173
caretakers of spirituality, 38
Carey, P.M., 39, 41
Carothers, Suzanne, "Catching Sense," 205, 206
Carruthers, Jacob H., *Intellectual Warfare*, 81
Cattell, Maria G., 34, 42
Chemers, Martin M., pragmatism and organization as integral to leadership, 63, 66
Chicago Public Library, 198
Chin, Jean Lau, et al., *Women and Leadership*, 42

INDEX

Chodron, Pema, on praxis, 129, 140
Chop wood, carry water, 124
Chudoff, Earl (Congressman), 165
Church, Mary Terrell, 12, 13, 20, 223
circuits of power (Women's), 76
civic Leadership, 168, 239
Civil Rights Act 1964, xiv
Clarke, Septima, 13
cleanliness is next to godliness, 152
Clegg, Stewart R., 76, 81
Cole, Johnetta Betsch, xi
  on racism, 2. *See also* Guy-Sheftall, Beverly
Cole, Natalie, xi
Collins et al., *Double Stitch*, 44, 112, 245
Collins, Patricia Hill, 9, 13
  bearers of tradition, 72
  black feminist thought, 18, 19, 24, 26, 39, 42, 105, 155, 160, 229, 245
  fighting words, 81
  motherhood, motherwork, 18, 81, 109, 245
Comas-Dias, Lillian and Melba Vasquez, 171
comfortable in their bodies, 117
communal affiliation, 233
communal leadership, vii, xv, 68, 87, 98, 89, 239
Condit, Celeste M., 15, 16. *See* Lucaites, John L.
Cone, James, 89, 105
  radical creativity, 102
Convivencia, 138
Cooper, J. California, *The Future has a Past*, 231
Corinthians, 1st 13:11, 215
Crawford, Margo Natalie, 53
Cross, William, E., 235
critical literacy of space, 138
cultural and racial projections, 6

Curry, Ophelia Williams, 148. *See also* Rhunette C. Diggs

Daft, Richard L., leadership, leadership theory and practice, 204, 206
Danticat, Edwidge
  Breath Eyes and Memory, 99, 105
  matrilineal storytelling tradition, 99
Dash, Julie, women can do anything, 37
Davis, Angela Y., 13
Debold, Elizabeth, and Malave, Idelisse, 245
DeHoney, Joanne, steps for achieving the extraordinary, 146, 160
delicate balancing act, 228
Denton, Otissey Barrett, v, 1, 88. *See also* Toni C. King
Dessa Rose, neo-slave narrative, 47, 53, 55
dialectics, 94
Dickens, Helen, O., M.D., 159, 166
Diggs, Rhunette, C., 110, 111, 143–146, 148, 150, 158
Diggs, Rhunette C. and Miller, 145, 146, 160
Dill, Bonnie Thornton, 13, 42
Diop, Cheikh Anta, 76, 81
disciplining children, 6, 74, 155, 157, 159, 220, 226
dissonance, cognitive, 32, 177, 183
Dixon, Vemon J., world views and research methodologies, 76, 81
domestic violence, 127, 137, 138, 180, 184
"Don't Waste Your Breath" (King), 68, 87, 97, 98
Double Stitch: Black Women Write About Mothers and Daughters, 44, 112, 245
Douglas, Kelly Brown, 13
Dozier, Judy Massey, "I Earns My

INDEX

Struttin' Shoes": Blues Women and Leadership viii, 110, 249
Dozier, Mildred Wilson, 71, 72, 74, 75, 111, 164, 169, 172
Dozier-Henry, Ìdílé: the Power of Mother in the Leadership Tradition, vii, 67, 68, 71, 72, 74, 76, 78, 80, 82, 239, 249
driving as autonomy, 214
Drylongso, every day leadership vs. epic and heroic leadership, viii, 111, 143, 145, 146, 155, 157, 160, 239
Dubois, W.E.B.
  double consciousness, 25, 257
  The Souls of Black Folk, 3, 235
Du Cille, Ann, 52, 54
Dumas, Rhetaugh Graves, the dilemmas of black female leadership, 227, 230
Dym, Barry, Harry Hutson, Roger Napier, 232, 245

"Each one teach one," 11
eccentric bodies, 45. *See* Carla Peterson
ecclesiastical social climber, 213
Edelman, Hope, *Motherless daughters: the legacy of loss*, 1, 19
E-D-I, evolving, developmental and interactional perspectives, 148, 155
Eltis, David, 94, The rise of African Slavery, 81
Erikson, Erik, psychosocial development, 233, 235
Erotic, The, 140. *See also* Audre Lorde
  in touch with, 140
  as creative power, 113
  source of, 93
  uses of, 107, 122, 113
Espin, Olivia M, 49, 61
  on knowing you are unknown, 42

Estes, Clarissa Pinkola, 105, 140
  break the spell of maiden innocence, 129
  finding one's pack, 206
  nurture the spirit child, the union of opposites, 93
  strong mother, strong daughter, 205
  warnings and red flags for the maiden girl, 129
  wild self, stories and myths, 89
  women who run with the wolves, self preservation, 19
ethical development, 233, 246. *See also* William Perry
Evans-Winters, Venus, *Teaching Black Girls Resilience*, 88, 105
"Every round goes higher, higher," from "We are Climbing Jacobs's Ladder," 148
"Every tub must stand on its own bottom," viii, 110, 123, 130, 138
Ezekiel, verse 16:44, 208, 216, 217

facilitator, versus leaders, 146
family communications, 227. *See also* Rhunette Diggs
Feld, Sheila, and Schefflen, Bambi, 150, 160. *See* halaido
female only leadership, 24
Fennell, Hope-Arlene, 81
  Feminine Faces of Leadership, 81
Ferguson, Sheila Alease, xii, xx
  Thelma's Self-Sufficiency Paradigm: Every Tub Must Stand on Its Own Bottom, 101–120
Ferguson, S. Alease and Toni C. King, 178, 236, 245
Fitzgerald, Ella, 117
Flake, Ceara, vii, 67, 68, 250
  flexible and adaptive social roles, 39
  "Hard to Define," 107

Floyd-Thomas, Stacy, women claiming history, religion and culture, 89, 105, 147, 161, 215, 216
foundational selfhood, vii, 24, 57, 64, 65
Foundations of Mother-Daughter Tutelage, vii, 14, 67, 69
Fox, Dennis, Prilleltensky, Isaac, and Austin, Stephanie, 27, 42
Franklin, John Hope, 81
Franklin, V. P., 81
Frazier, E. Franklin, 188
  black bourgeosie, 191
Freire, Paulo
  pedagogy of the oppressed, 140, 245
  on praxis 129, 140, 245
  transformation, 236
Fry Brown, Theresa (Reverend), 212

Galanes, Gloria J., 159. *See also* Adams, Katherine and Gloria J. Galanes
Gallagher, Abisola H., 31–33, 44. *See* Trotman
Galvan, Ruth Trinidad, 127, 128, 138, 140
Garvey, Amy Jacques, 12
Gates, Henry Louis, 9
Gbadesin, Segun, 81
  African Philosophy, 69, 81, 98, 106, 141
  Traditional Yorùbá philosophy, 81
generative leader, 103
Genesis 20:6, 215
Genovese, Eugene, D., 118, 122
geophysical dispersion, 4
Gibran, Kahlil, 134, 139, 140
Gibson, Althea, xi
Gibson, Nancy, vii, 24, 25, 57, 250
Giddings, Paula, 13, 17, 19, 75, 81, 95, 105, 223

Gilkes, Cheryl Townsend, 6, 13, 19
Gilligan, Carol Rogers, *In a Different Voice*, 161, 140
Gilligan, Carol Rogers, A. G. and Tolman, D.L
  Women, Girls and Psychotherapy, xvi, xvii, 66
Gilligan, Carol R. and Jean Baker Miller, 94
Gilligan, Carol and Richards, D.A., patriarchy, 245
Goldberger, Nancy Rule, Clinchy, Blythe McVicker, Tarule, Jill M., 105, 139, 147, 161
Golden Age, 74
Gordon, Erika L., 245
Govan, Sandra Y., viii
  Contending forces and Contrariant Strains in the mother daughter relationship, 193–206
Govan, Sarah, D. 193–206, 198–199. *See* Sandra Y. Govan
Grandma Kirby, 219. *See also* Lakesia Johnson
grandmothering, as a paradoxical function, 28
Great Black Mother, 12
Great Migration, 167
Great Queens of Africa, 12
Greene, Beverly, 14, 19, 42
Greene, Beverly and Janice Sanchez, diversity and advancing womanist psychology, 42
Greenleaf Center for Servant Leadership, 78
Greenleaf, Robert, 77
  Center for Servant Leadership, 78, 82
  Theory of servant leadership, 77, 78, 81, 82
Grewal, Daisy and Salovey, Peter, 226, 230

Benefits of emotional intelligence, 226
Grimke, Angelina Weld, 12
Grimke, Charlotte Forten, 12
griot, 99
Guinier, Lani
   "of gentlemen and role models," 230
   Insider privilege, outsider consciousness, 227
Guy-Sheftall, Beverly, 2, 112
Guy Sheftall, B. and Jones Royster, 245
   Life Notes, 140

habilitation, 233
halaido, stability and hardiness, 148, 150
Hall, Ruth L., Bravada Garrett-Akinsaya, and Michael Hucles, *Voices of black feminist leaders: making spaces for ourselves*, 42
Hamer, Fanny Lou, 68, 83
Haraway, Donna J., 93, 105
Harlem, 122, 245, 251
Harnois, Catherine E., 198
   race, gender from the black woman's standpoint, 164, 173
Harris, Duchess, 32
   Black Feminist Politics from Kennedy to Clinton, 13, 19
Harris, Trudier, 13, 19
Harrison, Mary, black mothers working outside the home, 36
Hayes, Elizabeth and Flannery Daniel, 216
HBCUs, Historically Black Colleges and Universities, 73
Heidi (Spyri), 88
Height, Dorothy, 13
Heinrich, John and Gil-White, Francisco, 147
Henry, Annette, 236, 246

mothering as a political work among African American women, 284
Higginbotham, Evelyn Brooks, demands for normalcy and conformity regarding black women race, class and gender, 233
Hill, Anita, 104, 105
Hill Collins, Patricia, 9, 13, 18, 24, 73
   black Feminism, black feminist thought, 18, 241
   holding the Black community together, 114
   mothering as political, 9, 13, 18, 24, 124, 236
   motherwork, 109, 236
   othermothers, 155
   standpoint of the oppressed, 155
Hill, Lauren, 51
Hill, Mildred, C., 164, 169
Hill, Shirley, 191
Hill Simona, J., 163–174
Hine, Darlene Clark, 12, 13, 17, 19, 172, 173, 288
   expanding feminism to confront woman to woman racism and classism, 12
   Great Migration, 201
   Hine and Thompson, 167
   Hine Sight, 19, 167, 173, 191
   teaching as activism. *See* Annette Henry
   Hine Sight, *Black Women and Re Construction of American History*, 13
Hollies, Linda A., 77
   Bodacious Womanist Wisdom, 82
Holloway, Karla, ingrained codes of conduct, 204
Honeywood, Varnette, 48
Horne, Lena, 37, 42
Horne, Lena and Richard Schnickel, 37

hooks, bell, 19, 127, 105, 140, 161, 173, 192
  black feminist leaders, 154,
  coming to voice, 99
  connected knowing, 93, 101
  construction and preservation of homespace, 126
  critical consciousness and black women's beauty, 45
  critique of traditional psychology, 28
  differences between black women and white women, 38
  exemplars of contemporary feminism, 39
  hair politics, 50
  home place, 161
  liberatory space, 102
  need for feminism to be inclusive, 39
  politics of mothering, 258
  praxis, 157
  racist, sexist oppression, 164
  special vantage point of black women, 64
  teaching to transgress, 101, 140, 246
  white supremacy, 240
  Womanism, 147
Hopson, Darlene Powell and Derek S. Hopson, team spirited, and cooperative parenting, 192
Horelli, Liisa and Kirsti Vepsa, 147
Hughes, Langston, "Mother to Son," 127
Hull, Gloria T., Smith, Beverly, and Scott, Patricia Bell, 13, 19, 42, 43
Hurston, Zora Neal
  "jump at de sun," 56
  Tell My Horse, 152

"I am a leader," 7
ìdílè, 67, 68, 71–73, 75, 79

identifying and modeling productive ways for daughters to thrive and survive, 172
In a Different Voice, 140, 161. See Gilligan
incongruous values, 219
independence
  collective liberation, 9
  feminine, 73, 75
  financial, 124, 182
  and outspokenness, 176
  self-reliance, 194
  strength, 210, 218
  and sexual choices, 116
  social, 229
individualism, 239, 242
In Search of Our Mothers' Gardens, xvii, 21
internalized Oppression, 11, 17, 127, 188
intestinal fortitude and will, xii
"I Remember Mama," a poem, 143, 144. See also Rhunette Diggs
"It takes a village," 242
Invisibility and voicelessness, 221. See also silence

Jahn, Jaheinz, The Pantheon of Yoruba deities, 141
James, Joy, *Transcending the Talented Tenth*, 161
Jean Marie, Sherman and Williams, 232, 243
Jensen, Arthur, the theory of black intellectual inferiority, 31
Jim Crow racism, 34, 49, 179, 180
Johnson, Debra, *Proud Sisters*, 37, 43
Johnson, Lakesia, D., viii, 177, 217–230, 239
Johnson, Ollie and K.L. Sanford, *Black Political Organizations in the Post Civil Rights Era*, 245
Johnson, Pamela and Harris, J. (Eds.), *Tender Headed*, 54

INDEX

Jones, Charisse and Kumea Gooden, *Shifts: the Double Lives of Black Women in America*, 14
Jones White, Annette, 39
Jordan, Barbara, 13
Jordan, June, 13, 229
Joseph, Peniel E., raising communal consciousness of issues for radical feminist action, 237

Kasl, Elizabeth, and Dean Elias, on consciousness and unconsciousness, 156
Kawahara, Debra M., et al., the outsider status of black women leaders, 171, 173
Kennedy, Florynce, 12
Kennedy, Gregory E., 43
Kidwell, Clara Sue, et al., 171, 174
Kim, Lili, separating out the results of racism and sexism, 172
King, Martin Luther, 231
King, Toni C., xv, xvi, xx, 68
 King, et al., xvi
 Third shift work among black women academics, King et al., xvi
 "Don't Waste your Breath," 68, 97
 The dialectics of Communal Leadership, 87–107
Kingsolver, Barbara, *Animal Dreams*, xv
Kinser, Amber, 121
kitchen table talk, x
Klein, Ralph, W., 208
Knupfer, Karol, 75
Komives, Susan R., Wendy Wagner and associates, privileged notion of leadership, 4
"Know thy self," 211

Lakota Proverb, 1
leadership
 and autonomy, 219
 definitions, 11
 development knowledge, xiii
 generative leader, 103
 for a new generation, 231–247
 identifying and naming leadership strategies, 217
 mentoring, xii, xiii
 transmission process, 13, 238
 learning, development and applying leadership strategies, 217
Lee, Valerie
 Granny Midwives and Black Women Writers, 13, 19, 53, 55, 274
 "Sisterlocking Power Or How is Leadership Supposed to Look?" vii, xvi, 13, 19, 23, 24, 25, 45, 46, 47, 48, 50, 52–55, 161, 238, 252
legacy of teaching and community action, 146
Lennox, Annie, 138
Lewis, Leah C. K., "Like Mother, Like Daughter," viii, xv, xx, 176, 207, 208, 210, 212, 214, 216
Lewis, Mary C., 225
Lewis, Thelma, L.K., 209, 214, 215
liberatory Space, 102. *See also* hooks, bell
"Lift as we climb," 11
Light skinned, 13, 36, 43, 50, 93, 95, 99, 102, 105, 106, 113, 118, 120, 122, 236, 246
 with good hair, 46,
 "High Yella," 28
Linthwaite, Illona, 36, 43
Lorde, Audre
 Age, Race, Class & Sex, 246
 black women's code of ethics, 99
 the Erotic, 140
 "Man child: A Black Lesbian Feminist's Response," 246
 love and Resistance, 236
 "Poetry is not a luxury," 102, 105
 silence, 95

Lorde, Audre (continued)
  Sister Outsider, 246
  struggle for liberation, 236
  transformation of silence into action 99, 106
Lowinsky, Naomi, motherline roots and significance; mother archetype, 1, 2, 19, 23, 26, 33, 34, 39, 43, 175
Lucaites, John Louis and Celeste Michelle Condit, 215, 216. *See also* C. M. Condit
Lugones, Maria, multiplicative identities, 93, 106

Maccoby, Eleanor Emmons and Martin, John A., 147, 161
Madame, C. J. Walker, 10, 18, 53
Mahmoud, Vanessa, M., 39, 43
Malcolm X, 231
Mama Sellers, "strength, love and power," 35
Manning, Marable, 146, 161
Marley, Ziggy, 51
Martin, John A., 147, 161. *See also* Maccoby, Emily Emmons
Mbiti, John S., 82, 106
McCombs, Harriet. G., 106
McCourt, Kathyrn, Thomas Bouchard, David Lykken and Auke Tellegen, 147, 161
McDonald, Kevin B., 76, 82, 240, 246
McDonald, Trevy, 14
McDonald, Trevy, and T. Ford Ahmed, *The Nature of A Sistuh*, 14, 20, 162
McFarland, Beverly, Margarita Donnelly, Micky Reamon, Teri Mae Rutledge, et al., *A Line of Cutting Women*, 18, 20
McIntosh, Peggy, the invisible knapsack of privilege, 140, 251

McKay, Nellie, 13, 20
McKenzie, Vashti
  Not Without A Struggle: Leadership Development for African American Women in the Ministry, 14
  Strength in the Struggle, 20
memoir, xv
Miller, Jean Baker, 94, 244, 246
Million Man and Million Woman March, 146
Mining the Motherlode, 105, 163, 164, 166, 167, 170, 171. *See* Floyd-Thomas
Mom Mom Ione, viii, 111, 163, 164, 166, 167, 170, 171
Moore, Thomas, The Care of the Soul, 93, 106
Moraga Cherrie and Gloria Anzaldua, *This Bridge Called My Back*, 27, 106, 104
Morrison, Toni, playing in the dark, xvii, 13, 50, 51, 53, 55, 246, 48
"Moses" of the Underground Railroad, xi, 10
mother-daughter
  conflict; contrariant strains, viii, 103
  leadership transmission, xiv, 4
  strong mother, strong daughter, 205
mother's medicine, 179–291
  mother's medicine and side effects, 179–191
  mother's medicine and healing, 179–291
  transformative medicine, 239
motherline
  introduced, xv, xix, xx
  defined, 1–2. *See* Naomi Lowinsky
  negotiations, 109, 177, 236
  unlocking motherline leadership wisdom, 68, 240
  value of Epic stories, 9

Mother to Son (Hughes), 127, 140, 154
mothers and othermothers, 138
Moynihan, Daniel Patrick, 78, 82
multiple consciousness, 227, 274
multi-generational transmission process, 184
Murphy, Nancy and George F.R. Ellis, 148, 161
Murphy's Law, 49
Murray, Pauli, 13
Myers, Linda James, 156, 162
Myerson, Debra and Maureen Scully, 228
  "delicate balancing act," 228
Myth and its various contexts, 19, 89, 93, 103, 105, 119, 129, 140, 164–165, 170, 175, 246

Nadasen, Premilla, 140, 127
nappy hair, 50, 222
negative perceptions of leadership, 6
negotiating race, class, gender, 205. *See also* Suzanne Carothers
negotiations between mothers and daughters, 236
neo-slave narrative, 47. *See also* Williams, Sherley Anne
networking, 161, 205
  with teachers, principals, school officials, church members, 186
  at the grass roots level, 190
Nikuradse, Tamara, 42
Nix, Robert, N. C., 165–166
Nkomo, Stella, M. and Ella Louise Bell Edmonson, 14, 18
Nobles, W. Wade, 68, 69, 81, 98, 106, 141. *See also* Dixon, V. J.
Noddings, Nel, 102, 106
Normore, Anthony H., 170, 174
North Carolina Agricultural and Technical College, 151
Nussbaum, Jon F. 148, 162

Nzegwu, Femi, 72, 82

Ogun energy, 84, 80
old folks' sayings, 11. *See also* adages and old folks' sayings
Omolade, Barbara
  black woman griot, 171, 174
  Otherness and Silence, 15. *See also* silence
  the political nature of mothering, 236, 246
  The Rising Song of African Women, xvii
  "the tradition that has no name," xii, xvii
On Becoming a Leader, 111, 140. *See also* Bennis, Warren
oral Tradition, xv
ordinariness, 124, 141
organizational citizenship and full citizenship, 234
O'Reilly, Andrea
  "motherhood's funk and ancient properties" xv, xvii, 242, 246
  A Politics of the Heart, xvi, 246
  Mothers to Mothers: Daughter to Daughters, 26
oppression, 33
  and black women, 11, 80
  classist, 164
  cultural, 23
  gender, 15, 41, 69, 89
  Haiti, 99
  interlocking, 8, 38, 41, 114, 177
  internalized, 11, 15, 17, 53, 69, 127, 188
  institutionalized oppression, 8, 112, 164, 188, 273
  patriarchal oppression, 8
  racist/racial oppression, 40, 80 189
  resistance to oppression, xi, xiv, 11, 15, 48, 64, 80, 89, 95, 109, 125
  sexist oppression, 38

INDEX

oppression (continued)
  social oppression, 10, 95, 272
  writing as resistance to oppression, 11
Ortiz, Victoria, *Sojourner Truth, A Self-Made Woman*, 12, 20
Othermothers, 146, 147, 284. *See also* allomothers
Owens, William A., Black mutiny, 104, 106
Oyeronke, Oyewumi, *The Invention of Women*, 122

Painter, Nell Irvin, *Sojourner Truth: A Life, A Symbol*, 13
Palmer, Parker J., 43, 106
Parham, Thomas A., Joseph L. White, and Adisa Ajamu, internalized oppression, 188, 192
Parker, Patricia, 32
  "border crossing guard, 235
  Race Gender and Leadership, 2, 14, 20, 162, 235, 246, 254
Parks, Rosa and Gregory J. Reed, 36, 43
permitting the construction of possibilities, 93
persistence of dialectics, 94
Perry, William, stages of ethical development, 233, 246
Peterson, Carla L.
  Eccentric Bodies, 45, 52, 54, 55
  Recovering the Black Female Body, 55
"Poetry is not a luxury," 102, 105. *See* Audre Lorde
Porter, Jeanne L., 20, 146, 112
poverty induced stressors, 138
practicing social justice theory, 170
praxis, xii, 82, 129
primacy of the family an African worldview, 80
privileged notions of leadership, 4, 5, 14, 20
professionalism and hair, 45–55
prophets, 209, 212
Psalm 8, 163, 196
Psalm 75:6, 214

Quashie, Kevin E., 205, 206
queen bee dynamics, 22
Queen Latifah, 121, 148

racial inferiority and IQ, 31, 44
radical creativity, 102. *See also* James Cone
Rampersad, Arnold and David Roessel, *The Collected Works of Langston Hughes*, 140
Reading Lolita in Tehran (Azar), 246
Reagon, Bernice Johnson, 67
Recovering the Black Female Body (Peterson), 52
Reed, Gregory J. and Rosa Parks, 36–43
Reese, Della, 117
Reid-Merritt, Patricia, 14–20
Reinharz, Shulamit, methodology, 106
Relational, cultural psychology paradigm. *See Miller, Jean Baker; Jordan, June; Carol Gilligan*
re-segregation, 239
resistance
  building capacities for, 235
  and love, 236
Rich, Wilbur C., 232
Richardson, Laurel
  methodology, 103
  recasting stories, 286
  Writing: A Method of Inquiry, 17, 103, 106, 276
Richardson, Laurel, Verta Taylor and Nancy Whittier, *Ain't I A Woman*, 21
right to self-defense, 198

INDEX

The Rising Song of African Women (Omolade), xvii
Robb, Christina, 94, 102, 106
   This Changes Everything: The Relational Revolution in Psychology, 106
Robbins, Vernon K., 215, 238
Roberts, Dorothy, *Killing the Black Body*, 51
Robinson, Tracy and Ward, Janie Victoria, "A Belief in self Far Greater then anyone's Disbelief," xvi, 64
Robnett, Belinda, 14, 101
Rodgers-Rose, La Frances F., *The Black Woman*, 230
role flexibility and African American women, 182
Rooks, Nowlie, 52–54
Roosevelt, Eleanor, 165, 169
Rose, Syenia, 14, 20
Ross, Diana, 36
Rothman, Barbara K., 60
   Weaving a Family, 82
Rotheram-Borus, Mary Jane, Steve Dopkins, Nuria Sabate and Marguerita Lightfoot, 147
Royster, Jacqueline Jones, 11, 13
Rudolph, Wilma, xi
Ruiz, Donna Smith, 34, 72
Rumpel Stilts-kin, 97

Sabate, Nuria and Marguerita Lightfoot, 147
Safe Place Syndrome (SPS), 203
"Sapphire," 75
sassiness, 77
Scafe, Suzanne, 164
Schacter, Daniel L., memory an encoding, 145
Schaef, Ann Wilson, 141
Schieffelin, Bambi, 150
self advocacy, 129

self reliance, 124
self sufficiency model of feminist leadership, 124–128, 135, 137, 138, 139
Servant Leadership, 77, 102. *See also* Robert Greenleaf
"Service is the rent we pay for living," 11
seamless web, 87, 88, 90, 91, 94, 96, 102
Sevaa/Service, 135, 139
Shaka, Oba, T., 80
Shakur, Assata, 222
Shange, Ntozake
   For Colored Girls who have Considered Suicide When the Rainbow is Enuf, 26
   Nappy Edges, 50
shaping an understanding of black womanhood, 217
Sheilds, Cydney, and Sheilds, Leslie C., *Work Sister Work*, 14
Shostak, Marjorie, *Nisa: The Life and Words of a !Kung Woman*, 119
Shugart, Steve, 73, 82
Sisterlocking, 45
silence, 95, 147, 99. *See also* Belenky, Mary Field, et al.
Smith, Barbara, 13, 27
Smith, Liz, *The Mother Book*, 43
Smooth, Wendy G. and Tamelyn Tucker, A line of separation, 6
socialization to deny one's contributions, 6
social justice consciousness, 234
speaking and holding one's piece, 204
spirituality, 38, 73, 156
Springer, Kimberly, 14
Spyrii, Johanna, *Heidi*, 88
stability, 148, 149
stereotypes and black women, 10, 12
Sterling, Dorothy, and Mary Helen Washington, *We are Your Sisters*, 13

stories of leadership, 4
storytelling, 68, 88–89
"Stupes," 199
Sudarkasa, Niara, on black family structure, 39
surrogate mother, 226
Sweet Honey In the Rock, 134
synesthesia. *See* Bennis, Warren

task of the black mother, 172
Tell My Horse (Hurston), 126
"Tellin' it like it T'is," 77
telling and retelling stories, 129
tensions along the motherline, 175
Thelma's Self Sufficiency Paradigm, 8
Theosophist, 136, 139. *See also* Bailey, Alice
The Soul's of Black Folks (DuBois), 3
"thick skinned leadership," 65
Third Shift Writer's Collective, xv, xvi
"This Bitter Earth," 117
This Bridge Called My Back (Anzaldua), 101
This Bridge We Call Home (Anzaldua and Keating), xvi
Thomas, Stacy Floyd, *Mining the Motherlode*, 161, 216
Thompson, Mary Crutchfield, 44
Tolnay, Stewart Emory, the Great Migration, 174
"to thine own self be true," 211
"tradition that has no name," xii, xvi, 105, 160
trained up to lead, xiii
training the daughter, 67
translating, silence into action. *See under* Lorde, Audre
trickster, 99
Troester, Rosalie Reigle, 44
Trotman, Frances K., "Legacies of Our Mothers," 23
Trotman, Frances K. and Gallagher, 27, 252

Tubman, Harriet, xi, 12, 126
Truth, Sojourner, xi, 12, 13, 17, 20, 21
Turk, Jessica, *Subverting Stagnation*, 106
tactical naming, 93
Turner, Sonya, M., 175
Turner, Tina, xi
twoness/Double consciousness, 3

unveiling the Motherline, 236

Vanzant, Iyanla, xi
Vasquez, Melba and Lillian Comas-Dias, 174
Vaughn, Sarah, 117
"village," 34
visions of the motherline, vii, 14, 109, 111, 112

Wade-Gayles, Gloria, "keep your eyes on the prize," 21, 37, 44, 104, 107
Wagner, privileged notions of leadership, 4
Walker, Alice
  black feminists, 13
  The Color Purple, 120, 120
  definition of a Womanist, 10, 16, 79, 83, 129, 147
  friendship with June Jordan, 229
  hair, 50
  "in charge and serious," 88
  In Search of our Mothers' Gardens, 21, 162
  We are the Ones We have Been Waiting For, 229
Walker, Maggie Lena, 12
Wallace, Michele, The Black Lady and the Amazon, 13, 53, 218
Ward, Janie Victoria and Robinson, Tracy, 66
Ward, Kathryn, B., "Lifting as we climb, how scholarship by

women of color shaped my life as a white feminist," 247
warnings and red flags for the maiden girl. *See under* Estes, Clarissa Pinkola
Washington, Dinah, "This Bitter Earth," 117
Washington, Margaret Murray, 12
Waters, Kristen and Conway, Carol, 35, 43
Wells, Ida B., xi, 12, 126, 223
West, Cornell, dialogue with bell hooks, 192
Wheatley, Phillis, xi
white privilege, 40, 140, 164, 170. *See also* Peggy McIntosh
Whittier, Nancy 17
wild creativity, 205
Wilde, Lyn Webster, 221, 230
Wildman, Stephanie M., *Privilege Revealed*, 40, 44
Williams, B., and Frances Trotman, 33, 44
Williams, Charmane, 170, 174
Williams, Delores, 154, 162
  on movement, 13
Williams, Gary, iv, 253
  Secrets from my Mother, iv
Williams, Jean-Marie and Sherman, V. A., 243, 246
Williams, Lea E., *Servants of the People*, 83
Williams, Patricia, 13
Williams, Sherley Anne, *Dessa Rose*, 47

Wilson, Marie C., Elizabeth Debold, and Idelisse Malave, 245
Winfrey, Oprah, xi
wisdom, xx, 1, 68
Womanism, 9, 147, 79
Womanists, 10, 12. *See also* Walker, Alice
womanish behavior, xvii, 77, 215
women's circuits of power, 76, 80
women's stories, 2
Woodard, Charlayne, 37, 44
Woodson, Carter G., 174
Woolett, Anne and Ann Phoenix, tasks for black mothers, 2007, 172
work ethic cultivation/vocational maturity formation, 234
Works Progress Administration (WPA), 168
World War II, 168
Wounded healer, 179
Wren, J. Thomas, 66, 106, 231, 247
Wright, M., white male imperialism, 38
Wyatt, Nancy, 146, 162

Yahweh, 208
"yellow wasted," 53
Yemaya, 119
Yorùbá cosmology, 50

Zackodnik, Teresa C., 83, 174
Zen
  of everyday life, 124, 133, 136
  of work, 124